FALLING THROUGH THE SAFETY NET

AMERICANS WITHOUT HEALTH INSURANCE

John Geyman, MD

Common Courage Press   Monroe, Maine

Library of Congress Cataloging-in-Publication Data is available
from the publisher on request.

ISBN 1-56751-254-2 paper
ISBN 1-56751-255-0 cloth

Common Courage Press
P.O. Box 702
121 Red Barn Road
Monroe, ME 04951

(207) 525-0900; fax: (207) 525-3068
orders-info@commoncouragepress.com

See our website for other editions of this book.
www.commoncouragepress.com

First Printing

Printed in Canada

Contents

Part III

Acknowledgments

This book has been made possible through the support and encouragement of many. I am indebted to these colleagues, who reviewed selected chapters and offered helpful suggestions: Drs. Robert Crittenden, Rick Deyo, Bruce Gilliland, Thomas Norris, and Roger Rosenblatt at the University of Washington; Larry Green (Robert Graham Center for Policy Studies in Family Practice and Primary Care, Washington, DC); Don McCanne, past President, Physicians for a National Health Care Program; Fitzhugh Mullan, Georgetown University and Contributing Editor of *Health Affairs*; John Saultz, Oregon Health Sciences University; Joseph Scherger, Founding Dean, Florida State University Medical School; and Eric Wall (regional medical director of Lifewise, a Premera Health Plan, Inc., Portland, Oregon).

Extensive resources were required in putting together this book. Sarah Safranek of the University of Washington Health Sciences Library and Yuki Durham of the University of Washington Health Services Library both pointed me in the direction of useful materials. Judie Tucker of *Health Affairs* provided needed back issues of that publication. The Henry J. Kaiser Family Foundation made available many useful reports and monographs. Dr. Ida Hellander, Executive Director of Physicians for a National Health Program, contributed many resources developed by that organization over the years. Thanks are also extended to the journals, organizations and publishers that generously granted permission to reprint or adapt materials originally published elsewhere, as cited throughout the book.

The book came to fruition through the dedicated and meticulous efforts of Virginia Gessner, who prepared the entire manuscript. Graphics were prepared by Pat McGifford at UWired Health Sciences at the University of Washington.

Thanks are also due to Greg Bates, publisher at Common Courage Press, for encouragement and helpful editorial suggestions in skillfully converting manuscript to book.

Finally, the work could not have been envisioned and completed without the ongoing support of my wife, Gene, who tolerated my immersion in the project and graciously steps around stacks in my study without complaint.

Preface

The U.S. health care system is in meltdown. It is a patchwork non-system with decreasing access, escalating costs, variable quality, and poor performance compared to many less affluent countries. For-profit health care corporations now dominate our health care, with an overriding goal to maximize return on investment for their shareholders rather than to serve the public interest. If you are fortunate enough to have employment-based insurance or be in a higher-income group, you may not appreciate the extent of meltdown—until you lose that job, your employer stops offering affordable health insurance, or someone in your family becomes seriously ill. Then the problem will be a real threat within days.

Forty-five million Americans are now without health insurance—one in six of our population, equivalent to the combined populations of Texas, Florida and Connecticut. Many others are underinsured or at risk of losing their insurance coverage. Over one-third of people losing their jobs lose their health insurance and cannot afford to regain coverage in the individual market.

During the 1990s, the longest period of economic expansion and prosperity that this country has ever seen, access to health care did not improve. Now, with economic questions during a "jobless recovery" and in the aftermath of the September 11 tragedy and the Iraq war, our budget surplus has disappeared into a mushrooming deficit, the ranks of the uninsured are increasing, and governmental budgets for health care are falling short of urgent and basic health care. In Texas, for example, legislators passed a bill providing free medical care for uninsured women with breast and cervical cancer using state and federal Medicaid funds, but a year later about 200 women with diagnosed cancers have no such funds available—they could not be found in the state's $114 billion 2002 budget.[1]

Is there a safety net to catch people without health insurance? After all, we have emergency rooms, community hospitals and health centers, local health departments, and other public facilities in many parts of the country. If you are one of many who believe or hope that there is a reliable safety net, by the end of this book, you will find that to be a myth.

The lack of health insurance leads to very serious outcomes for the uninsured and their families, as well as their communities and the larger society. The uninsured have less visits to a physician, less preventive care, more hospitalizations that could have been prevented, worse clinical outcomes and higher mortality than their insured counterparts. By the time they do get care, the uninsured have more advanced disease, and their care creates stresses on an already tattered safety net of public sector facilities.

What is the predicament of the uninsured? What does it look like in human terms? And what does that picture tell us about social justice in U.S. health care? As much as possible, we will take an evidence-based approach to answer these questions and to examine the problems and potential remedies of our failing health care system.

My perspective is that of a family physician with 13 years of practice experience in rural practice and more than 25 years in teaching and research in academic family medicine. My interest in health care policy and systems has grown as our health care system has deteriorated. I have found first hand as well as through colleagues and studies that it has become difficult, at times nearly impossible, to provide good medical care in such a bad system.

This is an issue that concerns every health professional, as well as legislators and policy makers, consumer groups, and lay readers who are aware that the heath care system is sick and in need of structural reform.

The book is organized in three parts: Part 1 presents an overview of the uninsured nationally and describes an increasingly fragile public sector safety net. Part II presents more than 30 family stories and patient vignettes, which collectively illustrate the problems faced by uninsured patients and their families, as outsiders to the system, in dealing with their medical problems. These are real people and situations drawn from press reports and other publications. Part III discusses remedies to the access problem, with particular emphasis on the prospects for national health insurance as the only one of the available policy alternatives to guarantee universal access to health care at affordable cost.

The politics of health care remain highly contentious and continue to be held hostage by powerful stakeholders in the pro-market status quo. A strong national grassroots reform effort will be required to establish universal coverage to health care in the United States. I hope that this book will provide one more push in that direction.

John P. Geyman, MD, October 2004

PART I

CHAPTER ONE

EVERYONE GETS HEALTH CARE ANYHOW, SO WHAT'S THE PROBLEM?

*D*alton Dawes was an apparently healthy five-year-old on his first day of preschool until his shoulder kept bleeding internally after a collision with a classmate on the playground. On that day he and his family learned that he has hemophilia. Since then he has needed weekly injections of Mononine ($2,000 per dose) to prevent serious bleeding from the usual mishaps of childhood. No private insurer would provide coverage. Both of his parents were employed, and they held their income to $22,900, 33 percent over the poverty line, to qualify for Medicaid in their home state of North Carolina. That worked until a year ago, when Dalton's Medicaid eligibility stopped because his parents then exceeded a lower maximum income limit of $15,492 a year. Dalton's mother, a paralegal, tried to place him in the Children's Health Insurance Program (CHIP), but those funds were already exhausted for the year and he went on a waiting list with 23,000 other children. Several months ago, and just three weeks before his Mononine supply ran out, funding was renewed, at least for the moment, through CHIP.[1]

It would be one thing if this case example were a rarity, but endless variations on this theme take place every day in every state. Dalton is just one of 45 million Americans without health insurance, who happen to have landed, at least for the moment, on a safety net of Medicaid and CHIP. As we shall see, however, this net is riddled with holes. Dalton's situation is just another typical example of how far short of universal access to health care is the most affluent country in the world. Yet, there is a continuing and pervasive myth that everyone gets care somehow in this country without much of an access problem.

HOW DID WE COME TO THIS?

The debate concerning universal coverage for health care goes back almost 100 years in the United States. We could have decided on such a system on several occasions. Theodore Roosevelt first brought national health insurance (NHI) into the public debate as a part of the Progressive Party's platform in 1912.[2] Many countries in Europe had established such programs over the preceding 30 years.[3] Some states introduced health insurance bills as Congress held hearings in 1916, and there seemed to be growing momentum toward a national plan.[4] Even the American Medical Association (AMA) was an initial supporter of the idea. Its social insurance committee made this recommendation in 1917:[5]

> The time is present when the profession should study earnestly to solve the questions of medical care that will arise under various forms of social insurance. Blind opposition, indignant repudiation, bitter denunciation of these laws is worse than useless; it leads nowhere and it leaves the profession in a position of helplessness as the rising tide of social development sweeps over it.

Over the next year, however, as state chapters weighed in, the AMA reversed its position to strong opposition to NHI, and was joined by business and organized labor in killing the proposal as the country entered World War I.[6,7]

On at least three other occasions, in later years, the country could have enacted NHI but for changes in the winds of politics. The principle of national health insurance was endorsed in a report by the Committee on Economic Security in 1933 (which was instrumental to the passage of the Social Security Act of 1935), but President Franklin D. Roosevelt decided against confronting the AMA's opposition and withdrew NHI from the package.[8] Later attempts to establish a system of national health insurance, proposed by President Truman in 1946 and President Nixon in the early 1970s, were defeated by strong opposition of the stakeholders in the private system, led by the insurance industry, business and the AMA.[9-12] As Paul Starr observed in his book *The Social Transformation of American Medicine*, we could well have had national health insurance in 1974 "if the name on the Administration's plan had not been Nixon and had the

time not been the year of Watergate."[13] The most
the Clinton Health Plan proposed in 1993, was actu
national plan for mostly private insurance; it was dead on
Congress after bitter debate and the powerful opposition by
holders in the status quo. This opposition is described by Charl
Andrews, author of *Profit Fever: The Drive to Corporatize Health Care
and How to Stop It*, in these graphic terms:[14]

> *Every special interest in the health industry—big insur-
> ance companies and middle-sized ones, the managed care
> industry, employers who provide health benefits and those who
> do not, big corporations and small business, hospitals, and
> physicians—rolled into Washington, DC, with fat bankrolls
> and slick lobbyists.*

The stage was set in the mid-1930s for private health insurance
as the supposed backbone of American health care. Blue Cross was
being promoted by its leaders as an alternative to compulsory health
insurance with this kind of claim—Blue Cross coverage will "eliminate the demand for compulsory health insurance and stop the rein-
troduction of vicious sociological bills into the state legislature year
after year—Blue Cross Plans are a distinctly American institution, a
unique combination of individual initiative and social responsibility. They perform a public service without public compulsion."[15] Blue
Cross was initially not-for-profit, but notice in later pages of this
book how far the private health insurance industry has strayed from
the public interest.

The employer-based insurance system, which today is an erod-
ing core of our non-system of health care, is more an accident of history than a solid, well-planned base for a system. Health insurance
coverage was an urgent need for the millions of workers engaged in
the industrial war effort in World War II. Employer-based insurance
grew rapidly during the 1940s, spurred on by its tax-deductible status for employers and tax exempt for employees. Again, we will soon
see how fragile this system has become today.

The passage of Medicare and Medicaid in 1965 as part of
President Lyndon Johnson's Great Society program provided some
access to care for the disadvantaged and those over 65 years of age.
But these services were not comprehensive, eligibility for Medicaid

varied widely by state, and the overall health care system became only more fragmented. An unanticipated negative result was the steady decline in charity care by health professionals and hospitals.

The costs of health care have grown enormously since 1960. While the U.S. population has grown by 57% since 1960, national health care spending has increased by more than 900%.[16] Many factors feed this relentless inflation of costs, including increasing intensity of health care services, the impact of new technologies, aggressive marketing by suppliers and providers of care, administrative costs of insurers and of providers responding to insurers' requirements, and a considerable amount of inappropriate and even unnecessary care. Each technological advance, for example, starts a new cycle of escalating costs, which may or may not be based upon supporting clinical evidence. Examples at this writing include the rapidly expanded use of cardiac resynchronization devices for congestive heart failure (supported by new practice guidelines) and the marketing hype for full-body CT scans, touted by proponents (without supporting evidence) for early detection of cancer and heart disease.[17,18]

The 1970s and 1980s were halcyon days for physicians and hospitals, with most of their services paid by open-ended cost reimbursement and professional fee schedules. Health care costs were out of control by the 1980s, and both the federal government and larger employers were forced to move to restrain costs. Health maintenance organizations and managed care were touted as ways to build more efficiency into health care. However, an unfettered corporate drive to profit-motivated growth and consolidation took place which soon left more people, especially the sick and disadvantaged, without coverage. Managed care became recognized as managed *costs*, not care, and its opponents would substitute the term "*damaged* care."

That all cost containment efforts by government and business to control health care costs in the 1990s were temporary at best is demonstrated by Figure 1.1. Despite an overall inflation rate of little more than 2 %, average health plan costs for 2003 were soaring at 15 % for active employees and 19 % for retirees over age 65. Much of these increases are due to the rapidly rising costs of prescription drugs.[19] Health care expenditures in the U.S. are expected to total about $1.8 trillion in 2004 ($6,167 per capita and 15.5% of GDP).[20]

Figure 1.1

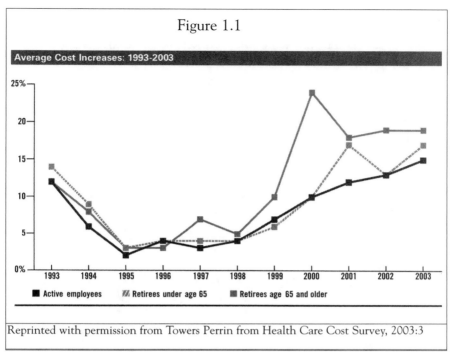

Average Cost Increases: 1993-2003

■ Active employees   ▨ Retirees under age 65   ■ Retirees age 65 and older

Reprinted with permission from Towers Perrin from Health Care Cost Survey, 2003:3

Although both were working, Dalton's parents found themselves, together with many millions of Americans, caught without health insurance and ineligible for Medicaid. A flexible workforce is growing rapidly in this country of self-employed workers, part-time workers in multiple jobs and temporary employees, none of whom will get employer-based health insurance. This only aggravates the already weakened employer-based system with less than two-thirds of the nation's workforce covered by health insurance.[21]

We now have a multi-tiered, fragmented health care non-system which is difficult to navigate for most Americans. In its book *Health and Health Care 2010: The Forecast, the Challenge*, the Institute of the Future divides our population into three distinct groups—a top group of the affluent and securely employed, a middle group of insecurely franchised, and a disenfranchised group at the bottom of over one quarter of the population (Table 1.1).[22] As a result, the population is effectively split into three nearly equal groups—empowered consumers, those excluded, and those that are worried.

This divisive and unfair non-system has led Arnold Relman, former editor of *The New England Journal of Medicine*, to summarize our predicament by commenting upon a recently released report by the

Institute of Medicine on the quality of U.S. health care:[23]

> *As is the case with other markets in the U.S., economy, the part of medical service that is privately insured is distributed primarily according to the ability to pay. The multiple independent private insurers (mostly investor-owned) constantly seek to reduce their payments to providers and their financial obligations to sick patients. Similar economic pressures and*

The Tiers of Coverage		Table 1.1
	Traditional Consumers	**New Consumers**
The Securely Enfranchised (Roughly 38% of total U.S. population) *Total U.S. population 1999 = 273,652,000*	■ age 18 to 64, no college education, high-income workers (and spouses) with no PCs but high job security, with private managed care plans or fee-for-service insurance (paid by employers or self) ■ age 65+, no college education, moderate to high savings/resources, no PCs, Medicare only or Medicare and private insurance ■ children securely insured	■ age 18 to 64, college-educated, high-income workers (and spouses) with high job security, with private managed care plans or fee-for-service insurance (paid by employers or by self) ■ age 55 to 64, early retirees, college-educated, private managed care plans or fee-for-service insurance (paid by generous former employers or by self) ■ age 65+, college-educated, moderate to high savings/resources, with PCs, Medicare + private insurance ■ children securely insured
The Insecurely Enfranchised (Roughly 34% of total U.S. population)	■ age 18 to 64, no college education, low- to moderate-income workers (and spouses) with low job security, in managed care plans (paid by employers or military) ■ age 55 to 64, early retirees, no college education, low to moderate incomes, in managed care plans (paid by former employers who are not reassuring about keeping retiree benefits, or have already tried to reduce them) ■ children securely insured	■ age 18 to 64, college-educated, middle-income workers (and spouses) with PCs and low job security, in managed care plans (paid by employers, by military, or by self) ■ age 55 to 64, early retirees, college-educated, high incomes, in managed care plans (paid by former employers who are not reassuring about keeping retiree benefits, or have already tried to reduce them) ■ age 18 to 54, no college education, high-income but low-job-security workers (and spouses), with PCs, in managed care plans (paid by employers) ■ children securely insured
The Disenfranchised (Roughly 28% of total U.S. population)	■ age 18 to 64, no college education, unemployed and/or very poor, uninsured or on Medicaid ■ children uninsured ■ children on Medicaid or other government assistance	■ age 18 to 34, temporarily uninsured, some college, with PCs, no full-time job yet or between early low-income jobs
Source: IFTF.		

PC indicates ownership of a computer as a marker for some experience with information technology. (Source: Reprinted with permission from Institute for the Future. *Health and Health Care 2010: The Forecast, the Challenges.* San Francisco: Jossey-Bass, 2000: 130) *incentives are at work in the governmental half of the system. In all parts of the system, the providers of care (i.e., hospitals and physicians) see themselves as competing businesses struggling to survive in a hostile economic climate and they act accordingly. The predictable result is a fragmented, inefficient, and expensive system that neglects those who cannot pay, scrimps on the support of public health services and medical education, and has all of the deficiencies in quality that are so well described and analyzed in this report. It is a system that responds more to the financial interests of investors, managers, and employers than to the medical needs of patients.*

WHO ARE THE UNINSURED?

The profile of the population without health insurance is both complex and surprising. Age, ethnicity, and income level certainly are major factors, but there are others as well. If you are now insured and think you will never be at risk for losing your health insurance, look at this current profile of the uninsured to see how comfortable you should feel:

- One in six non-elderly Americans, including more than 9 million children, now have no health insurance over an entire year.[24]
- According to an August 2004 report of the U.S. Census Bureau, the percentage of uninsured increased in 2003 among all groups with household incomes less than $75,000 a year.[25]
- One in five of America's 85 million families have one or more uninsured members.[26]
- Individuals experiencing major family life changes are at particular risk of losing their health insurance (e.g.s, divorce, separation, death of spouse).[27]
- About 20 million American families, representing 43 million people, had trouble paying medical bills in 2003; many had trouble gaining access to health care and paying for other basic necessities—rent, mortgage payments, transportation or food.[28]

- Almost 82 million people lacked coverage at some
  time during the last two years, and most of these were
  uninsured for at least nine months; Texas has the
  highest rate in the country for lack of health insurance, with 43% of non-elderly Texans uninsured.[29]
- One in five workers cannot afford insurance when
  offered by employers.[30]
- More than one-third of workers who lose their jobs
  are unable to regain their health insurance.
- Over one third of applicants in the individual insurance market are turned down, even with a $500
  deductible and $20 co-pay for physicians' visits.[31]
- 2 million people lost their jobs in 2001.
- People who are overweight (more than 10% above
  norms), especially between the ages of 50 and 65, are
  usually denied coverage.[32]
- Nearly one-third of young adults age 18 to 29 are
  uninsured.[33]

It is a myth that most uninsured are unemployed. In fact, 80%
of the uninsured live in working families. Even in families with two
full-time wage earners, 10% are uninsured. Over three-quarters of
the uninsured are U.S. citizens, and about one-half are non-
Hispanic whites.[34] The proportion of uninsured people less than 65
years of age varies considerably by state (highest in Texas at 26%) as
shown in Appendix 2.

Income level is closely correlated with being uninsured, with
the biggest impact on those earning incomes above Medicaid eligibility levels. Appendix 3 lists federal poverty guidelines for 2002 and
2003. The average annual Medicaid income-eligibility threshold for
a two-child family was $9,672 in 2001, with a wide range from the
lowest state ($3,048 in Alabama) to the highest state ($40,224 in
Minnesota).[35] A December 2001 report from the Commonwealth
Fund found that three-quarters of the currently uninsured have
annual incomes less than $35,000.[36]

Women and children are particularly likely to be uninsured. In
1998, 24 million non-elderly women—almost one in three—lived
in a household with a family income below 200% of poverty

($24,240 for a family of two and $36,800 for a family of four in 2003). Those are the levels below which individuals are considered low-income. These women are more likely than non-poor women to be single parents, have less education, be women of color, have more limited coverage, and have poorer health.[37] The 1996 federal welfare reform law did lead many former welfare recipients back to the workforce, but one-third of these women remain uninsured, as are one quarter of the children of working adults.[38]

Ethnicity is also a major risk factor for being without health insurance. Hispanics, for example, are less likely than non-Hispanics to be offered employer-based coverage. Even after 15 years in this country, one-third of immigrant Hispanics are still uninsured, more than twice the level of non-Hispanic immigrants.[39] One in five blacks are uninsured, compared to about one in ten whites.[40]

One might assume that health care personnel themselves would be well covered by health insurance, yet even this group is at risk. Health caregivers are losing coverage faster than other workers. Between 1988 and 1998 the proportion of uninsured health care personnel less than 65 years of age increased from 8 to 12%. Households with a health worker included over a million uninsured children. That's how well the health care sector takes care of its own employees.[41]

DOES HAVING NO HEALTH INSURANCE REALLY MATTER?

Imagine yourself confronting the loss of Medicaid coverage, or the termination of CHIP coverage, as Dalton's parents have been forced to do. As a hemophiliac, Dalton has a lifetime chronic disease requiring very expensive ongoing treatment. His injections cost more than $100,000 per year, year after year. Private insurance coverage will never be available or affordable to them. The health budgets of most states are way below the needs and the politics surrounding their allocation are turbulent and unpredictable at best. This example makes clear why medical bills account for almost one-half of personal bankruptcies each year.[42]

Insurance coverage, either private or public, is the most important single factor required for adequate access to health care. The uninsured are less likely to have a usual source of primary care than any of their insured counterparts. Lacking access to primary care leads to serious outcomes. One study of low-income patients hospitalized for preventable or avoidable conditions, for example, found that three of five patients received no care before admission, while only 3 in 20 had been seen in an emergency room.[43] Uninsured newborns are more likely to have low birthweight or to die than their insured counterparts.[44]

States with higher proportions of uninsured people have been found to have more access problems and lower health status.[45] A recent study of over 7,000 continuously uninsured adults between 51 and 61 years old found that almost three times as many of the uninsured experienced a decline in their health or functional status compared to the insured.[46] Almost one in five American women between ages 18 and 64 are uninsured.[47]

The uninsured, even when employed, are much more likely to forego a visit to their physicians, follow up for tests or treatments, or fill a prescription than workers with insurance. Figure 1.2 shows how dramatic these differences are.[48]

In addition to having inadequate access to health care, less care and poorer outcomes of care than people with insurance, the unin-

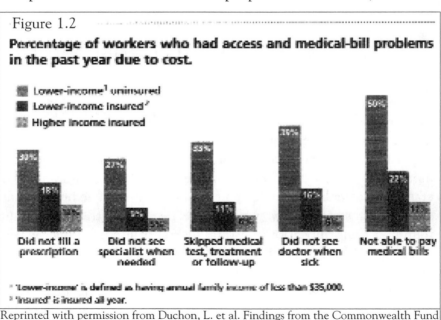

Figure 1.2

Percentage of workers who had access and medical-bill problems in the past year due to cost.

- Lower-income[1] uninsured
- Lower-income insured[2]
- Higher income insured

| Did not fill a prescription | Did not see specialist when needed | Skipped medical test, treatment or follow-up | Did not see doctor when sick | Not able to pay medical bills |

[1] 'Lower-income' is defined as having annual family income of less than $35,000.
[2] 'Insured' is insured all year.

Reprinted with permission from Duchon, L. et al. Findings from the Commonwealth Fund 2001 Health Insurance Survey. New York: Commonwealth Fund.

sured are often treated badly by health providers and hospitals. Two examples make the point. In California, 40% of Latinos have no health insurance. A recent study by Consejo de Latinos Unidos in Los Angeles reviewed the medical bills of 123 Latinos who received emergency care or were hospitalized in southern California. These patients were being overcharged (in one instance, a couple was charged more than 10 times what an HMO would have been paid for equivalent services). Patients who could not pay were harassed by collection agencies, often forced to sign statements that they would repay the full charges, and told that their medical debts would threaten their applications for U.S. citizenship.[49] In the midwest, a university-affiliated teaching hospital has sought 164 arrest warrants since 1995 for debtors who missed court hearings on their hospital bills.[50]

A recent comprehensive study reported by the Kaiser Commission on Medicaid and the Uninsured has estimated that extending health insurance to the nation's uninsured would reduce their mortality rates by 10–15%, comparable to the overall reduction of mortality in the U.S. over the last 40 years. This study also found evidence suggesting that improved health would lead to increases in educational attainment as well as annual income from work.[51] A 2003 report by the Institute of Medicine's Committee on the Consequences of Uninsurance put all this in economic terms. The Committee estimated that the aggregate, annualized cost of the diminished health and shorter lifespan of Americans without health insurance amounts to $65 to $130 billion for each year of health insurance foregone.[52]

WHAT'S BEING DONE ABOUT THE ACCESS PROBLEM?

Inadequate access to health care has been a chronic and unrelenting problem for many years in this country. Medicare and Medicaid, enacted in 1965, improved access for the elderly and many disadvantaged people, but left many millions of people out in the cold. Many incremental attempts have been tried over the last 30-plus years to address the problem of the uninsured, but all are band-aids without effective results.

In the private sector the main emphasis has been to encourage the participation of employers to provide health care coverage to their employees within the voluntary employment-based insurance system. But employers are plagued by the soaring costs of health insurance. Many employers, especially smaller firms, either don't offer insurance coverage or are looking for opportunities to decrease their coverage. Current federal policy initiatives are seeking to help employers by providing tax credits, and/or medical savings accounts to workers by which employers' contributions can be capped and risk shifted to employees. Facing a growing public backlash against harsh billing and collection practices by U.S. hospitals providing care to the uninsured, legislators in some states (e.g., Connecticut) are passing limited consumer protection statutes and the American Hospital Association is calling for more compassionate care of the uninsured.[53] Other efforts in the private sector to increase access include various philanthropic programs, especially those funded by private foundations, but these programs have marginal impact on the overall problem and were never designed or expected to fill the gaps of coverage for the uninsured.

In the public sector, the emphasis has been upon expanding coverage through Medicaid, the state Children's Health Insurance Program (CHIP) and similar programs. Here again, the impact on the uninsured is marginal for many reasons. CHIP was established in 1997 but, by 2000, up to 21 million children were still estimated to have significant access problems.[54] During the second half of 2003, total enrollment in CHIP nationally dropped for the first time since 1997, mostly as a result of economic downturn and decline in state revenues.[55] One third of the country's 13 plus million poor mothers are uninsured, often because they earn more than eligibility limits for Medicaid. There are wide variations from one state to another in eligibility requirements for Medicaid. In Louisiana, for example, a mother with two children cannot qualify for Medicaid coverage if the family income exceeds as little as $3,048 per year.[56] As most states grapple with fiscal deficits, these programs are facing cutbacks and are underfunded. They are subject to the vagaries of politics from year to year, and fail to assure participation by providers of care. We will explore these problems in more depth in later chapters.

WE'VE ALWAYS HAD THE UNINSURED; WHAT'S SO DIFFERENT NOW?

If you feel that the access problem in American health care is just a chronic and inevitable problem without threat to our health care system, consider these interrelated and unavoidable facts in 2004:

- Escalating costs of health care are out of control (e.g.s., health care costs rose by 16% in 2003, are expected to increase by at least that much in 2004, with similar cost increases continuing through 2007).[57]

- The for-profit private insurance industry, with over 1,200 insurers, takes one quarter of the health care dollar while separating the relatively healthy from the sick and fragmenting the risk pool.[58]

- Consolidation and decreasing choice for employer-based insurance.

- Growing inequality and disparities of health care by income, ethnicity, and class, which increasingly threaten the middle class.

- The nation still has economic problems in a jobless recovery, and the war on terrorism is certain to divert funds from critical domestic programs.

- The federal budget surplus has become a deficit projected by the Congressional Budget Office to total $1.9 trillion by 2013 with a record budget deficit of $477 billion in 2004.[59]

- Public facilities, such as specialized burn centers and trauma centers, are increasingly overwhelmed and underfunded—their weakness or closure will affect all U.S. citizens needing that care regardless of income.

- The long tradition of charity care has been eroded as beleaguered hospitals and providers struggle to stay economically viable.

The prevailing approach in both the private and public sectors to problems of the health care system has been one of incrementalism. But tinkering around the edges of a flawed system without universal access can never work, as is demonstrated by our experience over the last 30 years. The "access problem," so often described in impersonal statistics, has become a national disgrace in the most affluent country in the world, which prides itself on its commitment to individual opportunity and civil rights.

In the next chapter, we will consider just how secure our "safety net" is.

CHAPTER TWO

IS THERE A SAFETY NET?

A man in his early twenties without health insurance developed a dental infection. He could not afford to see a dentist and finally saw a physician who prescribed antibiotics. He couldn't pay for the prescription and later went to a walk-in clinic at a large county hospital in San Antonio, Texas which serves a county where about one-third of the county's population of 1.3 million are uninsured. Unfortunately, however, he was septic when seen, with spread of infection to his mediastinum, and died shortly after admission to the hospital.

This is regrettably, a common example of the failure of a health care "safety net" to protect people without health insurance from preventable serious medical outcomes and even death. Dr. Michael Ferrer is a general internist who works in that walk-in clinic. Here's his view of this and other similar tragic stories:[1]

> I wish this was top-ten list of lamentable stories, but it is not. The egregious is commonplace in our setting. My colleagues and I are part of what is widely known as the health care "safety net" for the uninsured, but to work here is to realize that, for many, the safety net does not provide a soft landing, nor are its failures the random "accidents" implied by the image of missing a net. In actuality, events such as these are the product of a system, an increasingly coherent system of exclusion that denies care to the uninsured: the system of no-system. The system of no-system's components are the fragmented resources locally available to the uninsured, embedded within the national nonsystem of health care. It is a netherworld of closed doors and shrinking services. The paradox of the system of no-system is that it is becoming increasingly systematized. Unintended consequences of changes in health care organization and financing, positive feedback loops enabled by the nonsystem, and maladaptations to the health care market are solidifying the barriers to care for the uninsured.

The above example is just one of thousands of preventable bad outcomes that happen every day throughout the country among uninsured people with acute and chronic diseases. One might think that public outrage might have been galvanized by now to provide a real safety net, but this is not the case. Much of the public, including most of our legislators (all of whom are well insured) buy into the prevailing myth that everyone can get care anyhow. Perpetuation of this myth serves the interests of all who profit from the present market-based system of health care, especially the huge for-profit insurance industry which has so many ways to avoid coverage of those who need it most. This myth also serves to absolve our collective guilt and perpetuate denial of serious and unacceptable flaws of our present system.

WHAT IS THE "SAFETY NET"?

There is a loosely woven, patchwork non-system of federal, state and local programs which include hospitals (mostly public, together with their emergency rooms and urgent care clinics), community health centers, and local health departments. Other safety net providers, which may be available in some communities, include teaching hospitals and some community hospitals, as well as facilities serving selected populations, such as school-based centers, family planning clinics, the Veterans Health Administration, the Indian Health Service, and the National Health Service Corps. Collectively, these facilities and providers attempt to serve a wide range of vulnerable populations, as shown in Table 2.1.[2]

Safety net programs may be funded from federal, state or local sources, but in general they are underfunded and precarious in their support. The most important single source of funding is Medicaid, which provides last-resort coverage for about one in six Americans, including one-fifth of all children in the United States.[3] In addition to providing coverage for acute care services for adults and children, Medicaid is the main payer of nursing home costs as well as care of the low-income elderly, blind and disabled.[4] Medicaid eligibility for non-elderly adults is limited to pregnant women, single parents, couples with an unemployed primary earner, and the disabled. Medicaid is intended to address coverage gaps in the states, which vary widely from one state to another. As the bulwark of the country's safety

> ## Table 2.1: The Core Safety Net Serves a Wide Range of Vulnerable Populations
>
> - Uninsured and underinsured
>   - —Working poor whose employers do not offer insurance
>   - —Non-Medicaid-covered unemployed poor
>   - —Children who are not included in parents' coverage
>   - —Adults who carry afford employer-sponsored coverage
> - Medicaid beneficiaries
> - Chronically ill individuals
> - People with disabilites
> - Mentally ill individuals
> - People with communicable diseases
>   (e.g., HIV infection/AIDS or tuberculosis)
> - Legal and undocumented immigrants
> - Minorities
> - Native Americans
> - Veterans
> - Homeless people
> - Substance abusers
> - Prisoners
>
> SOURCE: Adapted from Gage (1998). Reprinted with permission of *The Future of the U.S. Healthcare System: Who Will Care for the Poor and Uninsured?* By S. Altman, U. Reinhardt, and A. Shields (eds.) (Chicago: Health Administration Press, 1998).

net, the program now costs more than $250 billion a year in federal and state expenditures.[5] Federal matching funds to the states vary from about 50 to almost 80 percent.[6]

Established in 1965, Medicaid expansion during the late 1980s and early 1990s helped to alleviate the impact of decreasing employer-based health insurance in those years, but those gains were temporary. Despite the strong economy throughout the 1990s, the numbers of uninsured and underinsured continued to grow, as outlined in the previous chapter.

The most recent federal initiative to improve access to health care targeted children through the Children's Health Insurance Program (CHIP). Established in 1997, CHIP has provided federal matching funds to states for the care of uninsured children in families below 200 percent of poverty level.[7] While the program now covers over three million children, it is still too early to know how successful this program will be. By 2000, it was estimated that as many as 21 million children still had significant access problems.

Recent federal and state budget cutbacks threaten its further development.[8] The Bush Administration has projected that 900,000 children will lose CHIP coverage between 2003 and 2005.[9]

Although most safety net facilities and providers are in the public sector, the private sector does make important contributions to the care of the uninsured. One recent study found, for example, that over one-third of uninsured respondents reported a physician's office as their regular source of care.[10]

HOW POROUS IS THE "SAFETY NET"?

Let's look at four key elements of the "safety net" to assess how much confidence the uninsured should have in relying on it for last-resort care.

Hospitals and their Emergency Departments

With the only federal mandate to provide care on a 24-hour basis, seven days a week, for everyone regardless of insurance status or ability to pay, hospital emergency departments are under stress all over the country. There are many reasons, and the issues are complex. Managed care in recent years has squeezed excess capacity out of the health care system, with the closure of hundreds of emergency departments. Other contributing factors include increasing numbers of uninsured patients and those without access to primary care; the aging population with more complex and chronic medical conditions; severe shortages of nurses and support staff; funding cutbacks by payers; and soaring costs of physician liability insurance. In many communities around the country, overcrowding and long waits in emergency rooms have become normal, while the patients presenting for care are more acutely ill than in the past. For example, a recent study of emergency departments in California found that critically ill visits increased by 59 percent and urgent visits by over one-third over the last ten years.[11] Physicians at the Los Angeles County USC Medical Center have recently testified that some emergency room patients regularly wait as long as four days for a bed and that some die before receiving critical medical treatment.[12]

As a growing part of the population has come to rely on the emergency room for acute care, emergency departments are increasingly overwhelmed, especially at night and on weekends. When they feel that patient care may be compromised by seeing more patients, their only recourse is to go on divert status, directing ambulances to other hospitals in the area. This has become an everyday occurrence in many communities around the country. Examples abound. On a typical day in Los Angeles County, one-third of its hospitals are closed to new emergency patients. As a board member of the L.A. County Medical Association, Dr. Brian Johnson says that "Los Angeles County is the Chernobyl of health care"; one-third of its residents are uninsured, physicians' groups are failing, there is a nursing shortage, and a 13-hospital trauma network teeters on the brink of collapse. In Detroit, Michigan, three of the city's hospitals have closed, as well as over one-half of its primary care clinics, while emergency departments are seeing 30 to 40 percent more patients and deaths are increasing from preventable and treatable conditions.[13]

Today's growing use of divert status among hospital emergency departments exacerbates a long-standing problem of "patient dumping," whereby hospitals and physicians deny treatment of people with acute illness or injuries. In response to a public outcry in the 1980s, the federal Emergency Medical Treatment and Active Labor Act (EMTALA) was enacted in 1986. Almost one-quarter of the nation's hospitals have had violations documented since then, with for-profit hospitals about twice as likely to be cited than not-for-profit hospitals. Here are just two examples of these violations:[14]

- *A kidney failure patient's screening exam at Colquitt Regional Medical Center in Moultrie, GA demonstrated fluid volume overload and probable heart failure (indications that the patient likely needed a dialysis treatment), as well as EKG abnormalities, poor oxygenation and possible pneumonia. A nephrologist (kidney specialist) contacted by the ER physician refused to admit the patient or give a dialysis treatment until the following day. The patient died at home approximately seven hours after she was discharged.*
- *A motor vehicle accident victim was brought to an ER unconscious, with multiple facial fractures and brain injury. Because the hospital lacked the capacity to treat neurological patients, the ER physician sought to transfer the patient to a facility*

where he could receive such specialized care. Memorial Medical Center of East Texas (Lufkin, TX) was contacted. A neurologist there agreed to examine the patient. Transfer arrangements were initiated but apparently curtailed when a hospital administrator at Memorial refused to accept him.

Even when an uninsured or underinsured patient is seen in an emergency room, the downsides of inadequate access to health care continue. Initial treatment of acute or chronic conditions is not helped much when the patient is referred on to the patient's non-existent private physician for followup. The ER system was neither designed nor intended as a substitute for primary care. If the patient without insurance is admitted to the hospital, the resulting bills often lead to huge debt, often put onto credit cards with rising rates, and personal bankruptcy. Ironically, patients least able to pay are charged the most by hospitals. Price discrimination is practiced widely. Because payments from insurers and government programs are discounted, hospitals raise the price of their standard charges to compensate. These "standard charges" are typically three to six times higher than discounted payments from managed care plans and other payers.[15] These are just two of many typical stories:

- *After a fainting spell, college student Soklinda Ein landed in a Norwalk, CA hospital emergency room for six hours. The hospital bills, totaling $4,572 at last count, are now threatening to ruin the 21-year-old's credit. She quit her job, which provided her insurance, just a month before her fainting spell.[16]*
- *A 25-year-old uninsured college graduate from West Texas seeking a career in New York City, Rebekah Nix, had a $19,000 bill after two days in a hospital for an appendectomy. She was ineligible for Medicaid. Her attempts to negotiate with the hospital reduced the bill to $15,000. Only after the Wall Street Journal called was her bill reduced to $5,000, but she was forced to return home to West Texas and work toward paying her bill.[17]*

Community Health Centers (CHCs)

Federally qualified community health centers have played an important role as safety net providers since the 1970s. There are now over 1,000 such centers located in underserved communities across the country. They are staffed by dedicated health professionals providing basic primary care services with funding from the federal CHC program and smaller public and private grants. Upper Cardozo is one such CHC located in the Washington, D.C. area serving an El Salvadorian population with a mix of other Latino-groups, Africans, African Americans and Vietnamese. Since two-thirds of these patients are uninsured, there is no alternative but to beg for services when medications, x-rays, specialty consultations, or hospitalization are needed. Dr. Fitzhugh Mullan, a pediatrician practicing there, puts it this way in describing an everyday situation:[18]

> We needed the tin cup for Shirley, (by which I mean the perpetual, frustrating, quixotic, creative, and demeaning process of begging for services from others for our patients). Upper Cardozo provided her with a pediatrician, some basic blood tests, and the diagnosis of precocious puberty. But then we needed help: special tests and a specialty consultation. A local hospital offers free consultations to a limited number of uninsured patients from health centers such as ours. Our social worker helped the family fill out the many forms required by the hospital; I called the endocrine department myself to make her the appointment. A week later I received a distress call from Shirley's father on a pay phone reporting that the hospital required a down payment of $200 before Shirley could be seen. I then spent 20 minutes talking to voice mail and an occasional person at the hospital clinic, the finance office, and the president's office—which resulted in Shirley's being seen that morning without a deposit. The endocrinologist was good enough to call me with her findings that Shirley's growth was probably a normal variant not caused by a tumor. But the doctor wanted to see her back after more tests, presaging another round of tin-cup challenges.

Despite their proven value over many years, CHCs are chronically underfunded and unstable financially. This is even more true in recent years with the increasing number of uninsured, the proliferation of Medicaid managed care, and erosion of subsidies which could assist in covering the costs of providing charity care. Although the Bush Administration has announced its intent to double the number of CHCs by the year 2006, that goal, even if achieved, may not help much. More than one-half of the country's CHCs had operating deficits in 1997, 1998, and 1999.[19] A 2001 national survey found that CHC physicians find it much more difficult to arrange specialty or nonemergency hospital care for their uninsured patients than for patients with insurance. The authors of this study caution that increasing the number of CHCs without major increases in their funding and its insurance coverage, will fall far short of the needs of CHC patients, especially since other cuts in safety net programs are expected.[20]

Practicing Physicians

Uncompensated charity care has long been a valued tradition among U.S. physicians. Regardless of practice setting, a majority of physicians still provide charity care despite the increasing pressures on their time and decreasing ability to do so. However, there has been a drop in charity care in recent years. Employed physicians and those in predominantly managed care practices offer (or are permitted to offer) the least amount of charity care.[21]

Medicaid

In 2002, the federal-state Medicaid program surpassed the Medicare program for the first time as the country's largest health insurance program. As the single largest funding source of the health care safety net in America ($259 billion in 2002), its finances provide a critical window to assess the stability of the safety net.[22] The story is disturbing, with no real improvement in sight. Federal law requires states to provide basic health services for pregnant women, poor children, and needy disabled adults, with the federal government paying over three-fourths of the costs. In prosperous times during the 1990s, some states expanded their Medicaid programs to include other needy groups, such as low-income working families, AIDS patients, transplant recipients, and hospice patients. For the states, Medicaid costs consume almost as much money as is spent on public schools—more than spent on welfare, roads, and prisons combined. In times of recession, their Medicaid budgets are therefore prime targets for the budget ax. For many states, Medicaid spending accounts for 20 percent of their total budget.[23]

Here are some examples of state Medicaid cutbacks in 2003:

- More than one-quarter of Medicaid beneficiaries nationwide could not afford to get all their prescriptions filled in the last year[24]

- A recent 50-state update of Medicaid for fiscal year 2003 found that 49 states planned to impose new cost controls in fiscal 2003 if not already in place; these include controls on the costs of prescription drugs (45 states), reducing or freezing reimbursement to providers (37 states), restricting eligibility (27 states), reducing benefits (25 states), and increasing copayments of patients (17 states).[25]

- In Utah, some benefits which have been provided to Medicaid beneficiaries will be eliminated, including vision, dental and home health care; co-payments will be charged for other services, even for families earning as little as $7,500 a year.[26]

- In Illinois, reimbursement to Medicaid providers will be cut further, despite the current situation wherein most physicians find their own costs are not covered by Medicaid payments.[27]

The story for CHIP is much the same as for Medicaid, with many states cutting back, freezing enrollments, adding co-pays and/or charging monthly premiums. Even for a child with Medicaid coverage the situation is difficult. Here is the experience of the Horton family in White Hall, Arkansas:[28]

Their oldest child, 11-year-old Caitlyn, has cerebral palsy. No private insurance company will cover the astronomical bills for her care. The Hortons earn too much to qualify for regular Medicaid coverage. But Arkansas is one of 20 states that extends Medicaid to severely disabled children, even in wealthy families. Medicaid has sent Caitlyn to physical therapy twice a week for years. She has learned how to communicate using a special device. "She can say when she's happy, when she's sad, when she's hungry, when she's thirsty," her mother, Tina Horton, reports with delight. "Before it was mama's intuition that told me."

Caitlyn's progress has cost the state $22,000 a year just for the therapy. Add in medical bills for her and the 3,350 other kids on the program, and the state's tab comes to $30 million a year. Now Arkansas is asking families to shoulder some of those costs. The Hortons estimate that they will be billed about $400 a month. Paying that will require sacrifices, of course. Yet Tina Horton does not begrudge them. "We can cut back. For years we haven't had to pay anything for the services, so I can't complain."

She can worry, though. And she does, a good deal. If, in some future fiscal crisis, Arkansas cuts Caitlyn off Medicaid altogether, how would she pay for the therapy that has given her daughter a voice? The question haunts, because she has no answer. "What will the situation be next year? That's what scares me," she said.

The impacts of Medicaid shortfalls are further aggravated by cutbacks in Medicare and the soaring costs of physician malpractice liability insurance, both of which lead to more physicians opting out of the care of Medicare and Medicaid beneficiaries. In 2002, emergency physicians were hit with an 8 percent decrease in reimbursement from the Medicare program, more than the 5.4 percent cut affecting most other physicians caring for Medicare beneficiaries. Malpractice liability insurance premiums have increased by up to 300% for some physicians in the last year, exceeding $200,000 annually for emergency physicians in some parts of the country. Contributing factors to these surging premium increases have been fewer insurers, lack of tort reform, increase in settlement awards, and the losses unrelated to malpractice claims which have been incurred by many insurance companies in the aftermath of September 11, 2001. All of this leads to a vicious cycle where more emergency departments can be expected to close and more physicians will stop accepting Medicare and Medicaid beneficiaries, thereby further exacerbating the crisis in emergency and primary care. By 2002, nearly one-half of California physicians did not treat MediCal (Medicaid) beneficiaries,[29] while a national survey by *Medical Economics* found that one-third of physicians have dropped out of the Medicaid program with another one-third thinking about doing so.[30]

CAN THE SAFETY NET BE SALVAGED?

This has been the recurrent question for many decades in America. There are basically two kinds of answers. The first is to say that the safety net *can* be fixed, if only we patch it up just a bit better. This approach has been favored by politicians, legislators, and pro-market interests, and strongly pushed by the stakeholders in the present system. Many "reforms" have been introduced through Medicaid, for example, in an attempt to patch holes in the safety net. These range from special programs intended to provide coverage for specific conditions, (e.g.s., pregnancy, cervical and breast cancer, tuberculosis, disabilities) to special compensation arrangements for safety net institutions.

None, however, have led to a reliable safety net, as we have already seen. Dr. Gerald Gollin, a pediatric surgeon at Loma Linda University, observes that our health care infrastructure is crumbling and in need of a fundamentally different solution:[31]

> *The cuts in funding to California's "safety net" hospitals will certainly affect the poor. But even if one is cynical enough to ignore the plight of the uninsured and underinsured, the impact upon services that we all take for granted will be devastating. If well-insured individuals are involved in an automobile crash and there is no trauma center, where will they go? If a wealthy couple's newborn needs emergency surgery and there is no children's hospital, what will they do? We can no longer deny the crisis situation in our health care infrastructure. Support of the "safety net" is not in the business interests of the insurance industry. Until a publicly administered system of universal coverage is enacted we will continue to drift closer to health care meltdown.*

At the present time, with the federal budget surplus shifted into deficit, the states facing stark budget deficits, and the nation involved in post 9-11 armed conflicts around the world, health care safety net problems are still below the radar screen of public attention. Federal and state Medicaid spending has increased by almost 60% over the last five years.[32] States look to the federal government for help, while the federal government looks back to the states to solve their own problems. Here are some of the proposals by governors in 2002 concerning the Medicaid crisis:[33]

- The federal government should pick up a larger share of the costs, at least for some elderly and disabled people.
- Allow states to charge higher co-payments for drugs and services provided to Medicaid recipients.
- Expand Medicare coverage of home health care.
- Increase the discounts that drug manufacturers must provide to state Medicaid programs.
- Freeze or increase federal Medicaid payments to hospitals serving large numbers of poor people.
- Eliminate cuts in Medicaid payments to public hospitals.

The Bush Administration has refused to increase its share of Medicaid spending, and instead is proposing to give the states more flexibility to run their own programs without increased matching dollars.[34]

The second kind of answer to the question of how, or if, the safety net can be salvaged is to take a hard look at history. There have been many incremental attempts to provide a safety net, but more than 30 years of incremental changes have led to where we are now. A growing army of realists, including many physicians and health professionals, now see a national system of universal health insurance, *not* administered by the for-profit insurance industry, as the only way to provide a secure safety net for the entire population. In their ongoing monitoring and analysis of the safety net, John Holahan and Brenda Spillman, in a report from the Urban Institute, draw this conclusion:[35]

> *No matter how the uninsured are supported—whether by third-party payers, the presence of community health centers, a high level of disproportionate share payments, or local government subsidies—we find no evidence that these efforts have the ability to eliminate, or even narrow, barriers to access to the extent that insurance can.*

We will address options for health reform and the need for a national system of universal access in Part III of this book. For now, let's shift gears and look more closely at what today's porous "safety net" means to uninsured patients and their families.

PART II

VARIATIONS AND NUANCES: UNIQUE BUT SIMILAR

Most commonly held stereotypes about the uninsured are false. People without health insurance come from all walks of life, and are mostly working hard to avoid that situation. In Part II we will look at what it means to be uninsured as experienced by a cross-section of uninsured people. Each has his or her special story to tell, but similarities sort out into some common themes.

The categories chosen for chapter headings represent the most typical circumstances encountered by people without health insurance. While there is some overlap between these headings, collectively they give us an accurate profile of being uninsured in America. Chapters 3 through 7 will start with family stories abstracted from a recent national interview project conducted by the Kaiser Family Foundation. Other shorter vignettes from published press reports and other sources are added to the mosaic picture in each of these chapters. Chapters 8 and 9 apply not just to the uninsured, but also to the many millions of other Americans who are *underinsured*, including those on Medicare and Medicaid.

CHAPTER THREE

I WORK, BUT MY EMPLOYER DOESN'T PROVIDE INSURANCE

Meet the Pafford family from Elon, Virginia, who have raised four sons over their 28-year marriage. Despite their strong work ethic and continuous employment as a couple, their story illustrates the instability of employment-based health insurance in our system, as well as their own vulnerabilities and insecurities when uninsured.[1]

> Tom, 46, has worked full-time over all of their married life, while Virginia has worked most of these years, often part-time while raising their children. Most of these years neither one had employers that provided health insurance benefits. Tom has done many different jobs, including sheet metal fabricator, machine mechanic, construction supervisor, and assistant minister. Along the way, he has acquired such a variety of expertise and skills that he has built four of his family's homes.
>
> During times when the family had health insurance, everyone in the family had regular medical and dental checkups. During their many times without coverage, the parents delayed or avoided health care while still assuring immunizations and necessary care for their sons. They did their best to pay their medical bills directly. With a family income less than $30,000 per year, they couldn't afford health insurance without employer assistance. Their budget was stressed by the high medical expenses of two of their sons (recurrent leg fracture and Crohn's disease, a chronic inflammatory disease of the gastrointestinal tract). These major expenses occurred when they were faced with sizable college tuition bills for their sons.
>
> When their medical debts were highest, Tom accepted a pay cut to take a job as a painter at a local hospital, but his new

employer pays only for his coverage. Virginia has looked for jobs with health insurance benefits, but has not found one yet. Meanwhile, they keep their medical expenses at a minimum by avoiding care. Several years ago, Virginia had a mammogram by combining a $10.00 newspaper coupon with a cash Christmas gift from Tom to pay for it. She has since found that free Pap smears and mammograms are provided to uninsured women by the local health department.

Both Tom and Virginia have had to deal with the erosion of employer-based insurance over the years. Medical bills at times have wreaked havoc on their family's finances, and they have foregone basic medical care on many occasions. Although Tom now has his own coverage, he feels guilty about using it when others in the family can't. As Virginia says, " I would never tell anyone else to do it like this."

EMPLOYER-BASED COVERAGE: HARDER TO FIND ALL THE TIME

As the Paffords have found out, it is more difficult with each passing year to find an employer offering health insurance benefits. According to a 2003 random survey of U.S. employers, the typical employer now spends over $6,600 per family for health insurance premiums with a typical employee adding over $2,400 to that amount.[2] Two-thirds of small employers with less than 25 employees do not offer coverage. When offered, coverage tends to be more limited each year and with more cost-sharing with employees. Even among large employers with over 1,000 employees, one-third do not provide coverage.[3] Health benefits also vary considerably by industry, as shown in Figure 3.1.[4]

George and his sister, Tina, illustrate the largely preventable problems encountered despite full-time employment without health insurance. Tina worked as a waitress and George worked in factories. Both were diabetics since childhood, but their family rarely had health insurance. They were ineligible for Medicaid and couldn't afford insurance (or often even insulin and glucometer sticks). With blood sugars averaging

200, George became blind at age 20. Unable to see or work, depressed and housebound, he finally qualified for Medicaid, but died a year later of multiple organ failure due to uncontrolled diabetes. Tina's first baby died of complications from gestational diabetes, and a year later Tina had a heart attack. Despite a cardiac bypass, she died at age 25. Both really died from lack of health insurance.[5]

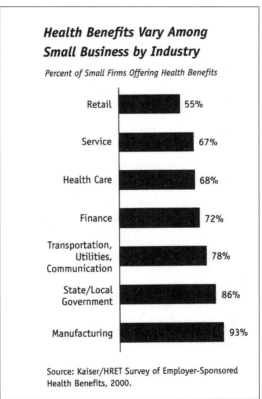

Health Benefits Vary Among Small Business by Industry

Percent of Small Firms Offering Health Benefits

- Retail — 55%
- Service — 67%
- Health Care — 68%
- Finance — 72%
- Transportation, Utilities, Communication — 78%
- State/Local Government — 86%
- Manufacturing — 93%

Source: Kaiser/HRET Survey of Employer-Sponsored Health Benefits, 2000.

Figure 3.1. Source: Reprinted with permission from Kaiser Commission on Medicaid and the Uninsured. In Their Own Words: The uninsured talk about living without health insurance. Kaiser Family Foundation, September 2000, 43.

Another common problem in our increasingly mobile workforce—being in between jobs.

A college professor in Boise, Idaho with a cervical disk needing surgery delayed care to the point of hand numbness and permanent nerve damage. He eventually had surgery, but had to undergo the humiliation of filing for bankruptcy.

The self-employed have their own special problems. Consider this example of a hard-working carpenter who was literally whittled down by the lack of health insurance.

> *George developed adult-onset diabetes. Though self-employed full time, his income varied from job to job, and he couldn't afford health insurance. He had difficulty affording physician visits and medications, and his diabetes was poorly controlled as a result. At age 58, he presented to an emergency room with blood in his urine, and a kidney tumor was found. Unable to afford surgery, he refused it at the time. Six months later, he cut his thumb on the job, was unable to work, and agreed to cancer surgery. After removal of a cancerous kidney and mounting bills, his untreated diabetes progressed to amputations of toes, near-blindness and a stroke. Another cancer was found in his bladder, which was removed. His one remaining kidney was failing, and he was put on dialysis. Six months before becoming eligible for Medicare, he died. Yet this downhill course of complications could have been largely prevented by basic medical care. All he lacked was adequate insurance coverage.*[7]

As we saw in Chapter 1 (page 7), a growing part of our nation's work force works part-time, often at two or even three jobs. Employers not only don't provide health benefits to part-time workers, but they often set their own rules on what constitutes "full-time." Consider this particularly egregious example of unwillingness of even large employers to cover part-time workers in this, the most affluent country in the world.

> *As a 14-year-old paperboy, Nelson Chong Gum was recently delivering The Honolulu Star Bulletin on his motorized scooter when he was hit by a van. After 12 days in the hospital, he was left with a disfigured leg and medical bills over $80,000. Neither of Nelson's parents carries health insurance. His father works as a security guard, his mother as a restaurant worker.*

The newspaper company isn't legally obligated to pay these bills. The industry has contended for many years that newspaper carriers aren't employees, but "little merchants" who buy papers wholesale and sell them at retail prices. They are usually uncovered by any insurance. But the job is quite hazardous—16 teenagers under 18 were killed between 1992 and 2000 while delivering newspapers or collecting subscription money. About 140,000 young people are involved in this work each year in the U.S. Only a few states require workers' compensation coverage for the young carriers.[8]

SPECIAL IMPACT GROUPS

As the employer-based insurance system becomes progressively more incomplete and unreliable, these large population groups are particularly disadvantaged.

Working Women Without Insurance

Working women are especially disadvantaged without employer-based health insurance for a number of reasons. They are usually the principal caregiver, both for their children and their parents, thereby often forcing them into relatively low wage, part-time jobs. Many are single parents struggling to make ends meet with low-income jobs. When in need of medical care, they typically delay care and have worse outcomes. Even when women know they are pregnant, they cut corners on prenatal care, mostly because they can't afford or can't get appointments. In fact, American women have the worst rates for prenatal care of any developed nation in the world. Overall, 17.5% of pregnant women (27.7% for African-American women) do not receive any prenatal care during the first trimester. This compares to rates of less than 10% for other affluent nations.[9]

According to a 2002 national survey by the Kaiser Family Foundation of 4,000 U.S. women aged 10 to 64, about one in four report delaying or skipping care during the last year due to costs. Two in five report not filling a prescription for the same reasons, compared to only 15% of insured women.[10] Figure 3-2 shows the extent to which uninsured women limit their own care compared to those with insurance.

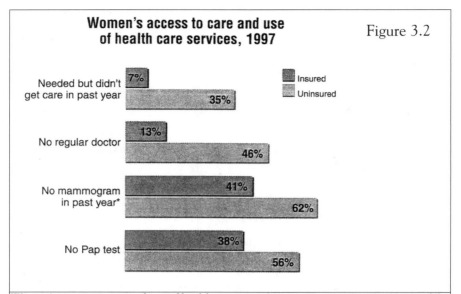

Women's access to care and use of health services, 1997: mammograms were measured for women 50 years of age and over. (Source: Kaiser/Commonwealth 1997 National Study of Health Insurance. Reprinted with permission from Finger AL. Caring for the uninsured. Will the problem ever be solved? *Med Econ* December 20, 1999; 134.)

Here are just two of many examples of these problems which, unfortunately, are all too typical.

- *A 28-year-old mother of two worked in a convenience store and earned too much to qualify for Medicaid. Because she couldn't afford care, she delayed seeking care. When seen by a physician, she had bacterial endocarditis, an infection of a heart valve, and soon died of an embolism to the brain.*[12]
- *A 64-year-old women had vaginal bleeding due to uterine cancer. Without savings and ineligible for Medicaid, she needed $10,000 for surgery. She was turned down for care until, finally, the County loaned her the money to proceed with the surgery.*[13]

Children

Because of Medicaid and the State Children's Health Insurance Program (CHIP), children fare a bit better than adults in terms of coverage. Even at that, however, 22% of low-income American children (i.e., those from families with income less than 200% of poverty levels—$30,040 for a family of three in 2002)[14] were without health insurance of any kind in 2002.[15]

Here is one example of how a minor problem became a serious, life-threatening problem.

> A young boy has a congenital heart defect that makes him vulnerable to infections. His working mother, as a janitor, couldn't afford dental care when he developed an infected tooth. Some weeks later, he was seen in an emergency room with fatigue, chest pain and spiking fevers. After a preventable hospitalization of six weeks for subacute bacterial endocarditis, he was left with irreversible heart damage.[16]

Minorities

Overall, minorities are much more likely to be uninsured than white Americans. About one-third of both Hispanic and Native

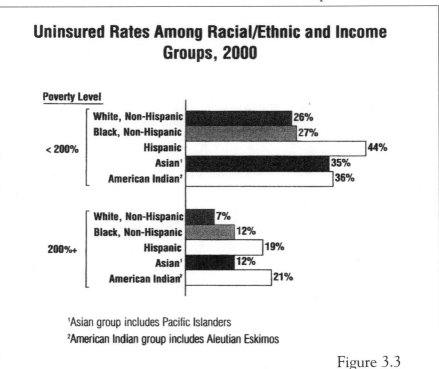

Uninsured Rates Among Racial/Ethnic and Income Groups, 2000

Poverty Level

< 200%
- White, Non-Hispanic — 26%
- Black, Non-Hispanic — 27%
- Hispanic — 44%
- Asian[1] — 35%
- American Indian[2] — 36%

200%+
- White, Non-Hispanic — 7%
- Black, Non-Hispanic — 12%
- Hispanic — 19%
- Asian[1] — 12%
- American Indian[2] — 21%

[1]Asian group includes Pacific Islanders
[2]American Indian group includes Aleutian Eskimos

Figure 3.3

Source: Reprinted with permission from Kaiser Commission on Medicaid and the Uninsured. Health Insurance in America: 2000 Data Update. February 2000:12.

Americans are uninsured, as well as about 20% of African Americans and Asian Americans. The comparable figure for whites is 11%.[17]

Minorities now account for 32% of the general population under age 65 in the U.S. Because they are disproportionately represented among the uninsured, however, they make up one half of uninsured Americans. Figure 3.3 compares uninsured rates by racial/ethnic and income groups.

Just one example from the practice of Dr. Bob LeBow, for many years a family physician in Boise, Idaho and author of an excellent recent book *Health Care Meltdown: Confronting the Myths and Fixing Our Failing System.* This shows what often happens when you have too little income to cope with even minor medical bills.

> *A Hispanic mother brought her 17-year-old son to the community health center. He needed antibiotics for his septal defect and an inhaler for his asthma. The clinic's pharmacy charge was just $8.00, yet the mother started crying and left with her son without the medication.*

As Dr. LeBow said:

> *We went after her. She didn't have any money and felt ashamed. The system skims off the healthy and leaves the poor and sick to fend for themselves. It humiliates people and makes them beg. It's shameful. I see it every day and it makes me very angry.*[19]

These stories are not unusual, but everyday and more typical than not. They cannot be idly dismissed as anecdotal since they cast light on an archaic system of employment-based insurance which no longer serves as a solid base for our system. Created during the war effort of World War II, it no longer meets the needs of our disintegrating system 60 years later. For more on how it is becoming unaffordable for those who are offered this insurance, we turn to the next chapter.

CHAPTER FOUR

MY EMPLOYER OFFERS INSURANCE, BUT I CAN'T AFFORD IT

Let's now meet the Taylor family, who had to give up their health insurance due to rising premium costs.[1]

Charlynne, 27, and Monty, 29, are both working full-time in the fast-food industry. They have been married five years, with one child, Kenyon. Charlynne manages a Taco Bell restaurant in Edmond, Oklahoma, about 15 miles north of Oklahoma City, while Monty is a shift manager for a Taco Bell restaurant in Oklahoma City. When the couple first married, they lived in an apartment in Oklahoma City. After Charlynne became pregnant, they moved to Guthrie, a small town 30 miles north of Oklahoma City, in order to find better housing and be closer to her parents. Instead of a one-bedroom apartment at $300 per month, they found a four-bedroom, two-story house in Guthrie for $250 a month. Despite having a family income of $35,000 a year, together with health insurance, they soon found that the insurance wasn't as good as they'd hoped. Charlynne needed a cesarean section, and the family ended up with thousands of dollars in bills, which were later turned over to collection agencies. It turned out that their move to Guthrie, with its zip code falling outside of their insurer's preferred provider network, triggered an increase of their deductible to $4,000, as well as co-pays for physician visits of 50 to 60%. This was an unexpected blow to the couple, who both continued with their same jobs, the same physicians, the same hospital, and the same insurance. In fact, the hospital in Guthrie didn't provide obstetric care. Nobody at the insurance company advised them of this coverage feature. Instead, they kept receiving unpaid bills from the insurer saying, "apply to

deductible." When Charlynne called to protest the cut in bene-
fits, for which they were still paying the full premium, the cus-
tomer service representative told her how she could have out-
witted the insurer by taking a post office box in Oklahoma City.
As Charlynne says "Isn't it ridiculous that everything would be
fine if I had just lied." Faced with $4,000 in medical and hos-
pital bills, the couple decided to cancel their insurance and use
what had been previously deducted from her paycheck and put
towards health insurance to help pay off their bills over time.
Since then they have gone without regular medical care, and
they wonder if they can ever afford to have a second child.
Charlynne gets her annual Pap smears and prescriptions for
birth control pills at the local Health Department. The couple
explored the possibility of CHIP coverage for Kenyon, but that
program, in Oklahoma, has set the maximum annual income
for a family of three at $26,178. (Across the line in Missouri,
the comparable eligibility figure is $42,450.) Under growing
financial pressure from their medical bills, Monty is exploring a
job change to one with better health benefits. As Charlynne
says, "I worry a lot. We have a plan for the future, but I don't
know what we would do if something major happened."

The Taylor's story illustrates the problems faced by a small family with both parents working full-time and an annual income of
$35,000. Unfair and counter-intuitive as it is, employees in low-
wage firms pay more for insurance coverage (average monthly family coverage employee contributions of $174 versus $139 for other
firms).[2]

INCREASING CO-PAYS AND DEDUCTIBLES

A survey by Hewitt Associates found that HMOs have asked
employers for premium increases of 22% for 2003, on top of increases of 15% in 2002 and 10% in 2001. A recent survey of nearly 3,000
U.S. employers projects premium increases of 9.6% for 2005, plus an
additional 3% increase in cost sharing with employees.[3] These costs
are being passed on to employees as increases in premiums, co-pays
and deductibles. Here is what this means to some Americans working full-time.

- *Liz Carvin was attracted to government work in 1984, when she joined the General Services Department in Sacramento, California, in large part due to the generous health benefits that were provided. This is no longer the case, as a result of soaring costs of health care for the 1.2 million workers covered by CalPERS (California Public Employees' Retirement System). Liz works full-time as a janitor, taking home about $1,600 a month. In response to rising costs, CalPERS has been forced to increase its premiums for 2003 by 25%, and its employees are anticipating out-of-pocket increases of up to 66%. Even with the state government paying at least 85% of total premium costs, Liz can expect her contributions to increase from about $70 a month in 2002 to over $100 a month in 2003. Even at that, she will fare better than most other employees in public sector jobs, whose average share for family health coverage has gone up to 29%.[4]*

- *Ed Bonsignore, 58, had a heart attack four years ago. He and his wife, Marie, are retired restaurateurs in Palm Beach Gardens, Florida. His insurance company, American Medical Security, notified Ed of a 60% rate increase at his last renewal date. Ed couldn't afford that, and avoided the increase by accepting a deductible of $9,000 each for himself and Marie. American Medical Security reported a 56% earnings increase in 2001, which its CEO attributed in part to "aggressive rate action." Meanwhile, Ed takes nitroglycerine, tries to relax and hopes to avoid the hospital when he gets his anginal chest pains. As he says "I try to ignore the pains. Either I drop dead or it blows over."[5]*

- *Regina Hagerman, 29, is a full-time health aide helping elderly and disabled patients. At her minimum wage income, she can't afford the $75 a month needed to purchase insurance through her employer. She has had surgery for breast cancer, but hasn't been able to see a physician in months.[6]*

- *Christine Zamora, 62, lives in Corpus Christie, Texas, with her husband, Porfirio. She worked as a private-duty licensed practical nurse until two years ago when she had to stop due to several medical conditions, including hypertension, migraine headaches, and rotator cuff problems of one shoulder. With an* *annual income of just under $20,000, the couple had to drop her health insurance through Porfirio's employer when its cost went up from $72 to $85 a week. Coverage for both would have cost 21% of their total income. Although Christine now receives $544 a month in disability income through Social Security, it is well short of what her income was when she was able to work. As she says, "I find myself in a very bad situation, and it's scary. I can't afford several of my medications. I take two types of hormones, and they cost $48, and my blood pressure medicine costs $8 a bottle. So, I have to make a choice. I just don't take the hormones."[7]*

AFFORDABILITY OF HEALTH INSURANCE: A "MEDICAL DIVIDE"

Health insurance has become unaffordable for a growing number of full-time employees of employers which "provide" health benefits. A June 2002 national survey by the Kaiser Family Foundation revealed these interesting findings:[8]

- Problems paying medical bills reported by:
    - 38% of families earning less than $25,000 a year.
    - 23% of families earning $25,000 to $50,000 a year.
    - 9% of families earning over $50,000 a year.
- One half of families reported:
    - Concern about not being able to afford health coverage.
    - Concern about benefits being reduced.

When these findings are put in perspective of the population affected, the numbers become striking. Figure 4.1 gives a breakdown of the non-elderly population in the U.S. by poverty level. If $50,000 is taken as the critical point along the "medical divide," then those earning less than about 300% of the federal poverty level represent about one-half of the non-elderly population.[9]

While annual costs of health care continue to increase at three or more times the cost of living, the ranks of the poor and uninsured are increasing and income has stagnated for many millions of

Figure 4.1

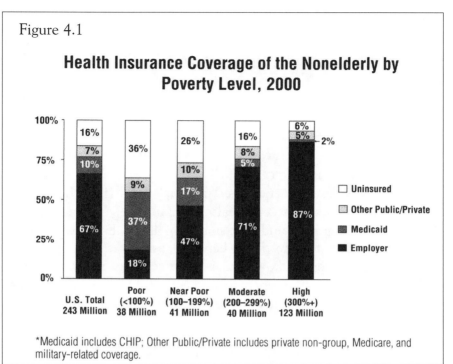

Health Insurance Coverage of the Nonelderly by Poverty Level, 2000

*Medicaid includes CHIP; Other Public/Private includes private non-group, Medicare, and military-related coverage.

Source: Reprinted with permission from Kaiser Commission on Medicaid and the Uninsured. Health Insurance Coverage in America: 2000 Data Update. February 2002:9.

Americans. Between 2001 and 2003, the number of people living in poverty ($18,660 for a family of four in 2003) rose to 35.9 million, or 12.5% of the U.S. population. The number of children living in poor families increased by 11% over that period, while the number of children receiving welfare payments declined by 10%. Meanwhile, median family income dropped from $44,853 in 2000 to $43,318 in 2003. 1.6 million American households filed for personal bankruptcy in 2003, up 33% from 2000. The middle-class in the United States continues to shrink as reflected by a decline in the percentage of families with annual incomes between $25,000 and $75,000 (adjusted for inflation in 2003 dollars), from 51.9% in 1980 to 44.9% in 2003.[10]

The U.S. maintains wide income disparities between rich and poor, leading the industrialized world in income inequality.[11] These income disparities are increasing in recent years.[12] Household incomes for poor families (lowest 20% of the population) averaged $14,232 during the late 1990s, while the top 20% averaged

$155,527, a difference of more than ten-fold.[13] Families with annual incomes less than $10,000 spend 17% of their income on health care, compared to 6% for those earning $45,000 and only 3% for those making over $100,000.[14] Since workers' earnings have been relatively flat in recent years as health insurance rates escalated, the "medical divide" gets more divisive all the time.[15] As Edward Wolff, economist at New York University documents in a recent book, the gap between haves and have nots is greater at the start of the 21st century than any time since 1929.[16]

Employers can influence the "take up" rates (i.e., the rates at which their employees accept health insurance coverage as offered) through their eligibility and cost-sharing policies. Employers setting high limits for part-time work (no benefits), as well as delayed onset of benefits after starting work, will have lower coverage rates. Employers with large numbers of low-income workers will have the lowest take-up rates, as already illustrated by the story of the Taylor family.[17]

IMPACT ON THE UNINSURED: PREVENTABLE DEATH, ILLNESS AND DISABILITY

In its 2002 report, *Care Without Coverage: Too Little Too Late,* the Committee on the Consequences of Uninsurance of the Institute of Medicine (IOM) explored the differences in outcomes of people with and without health insurance. They confirmed striking differences for the uninsured in terms of less preventive care; greater likelihood of premature death from heart disease, cancer and other chronic diseases; less care for mental health conditions; and higher risk for disability. The IOM has also estimated that over 18,000 Americans between the ages of 25 and 64 died in 2000 as a result of not having health insurance.[18] That figure would be very much higher if estimates were to include uninsured children, many millions of underinsured people, and those over 65 without prescription drug coverage.

A recent study based on the 1997 National Health Interview Survey, as analyzed by the Urban Institute, sheds further light on how employees who can't afford their employers' health coverage fare compared to those who "take up" coverage. This study involved

Table 4.1: Health Status of Uninsured Decliners and Insurance Takers, 1997

	Uninsured decliners	Employer coverage takers
Physical Health		
Ulcer, ever	8.3%	7.4%
If yes, in past year?	40.5	27.5
Mental Health		
Sad (past 30 days, no cheering up)	13.7%	7.6%*
Hopeless	7.5	3.6*
Worthless	5.7	2.6*
Effort for everything	17.4	10.7*
If one MH condition, it interferes with life	34.1	24.3*
Health behavior and general access		
Health status, compared with 1 year ago		
Better	18.7%	18.4%
Worse	7.0	4.9*
If ever smoked, smokes now?	79.7	52.8*
Have usual source of care	61.6	87.2*
Can't afford drugs (in past year)	16.9	2.8*
Can't afford mental health care (in past year)	4.5	1.1*
Can't afford dental care (in past year)	22.8	6.1*
Seen an MD in past 12 months	46.7	66.7*
Had at least one ER visit in past year	21.9	16.2*
Flu shot in past 12 months	13.3	21.1*

Source: Urban Institute analysis of 1997 National Health Interview Survey.

Notes: Asterisks denote statistical difference from the decliner group at the .05 level or better. Individual mental health conditions represent answers of "all," "most," or "some" of the time. Mental health condition interference with life represents answers of "a lot" or "some." Smoke now, given smoked ever, represents an answer of "every day" or "some days." Questions were asked only of sampled adults. Sample sizes: 1,020 uninsured decliners, 11,255 employer coverage takers. Sample excludes the self employed and active-duty military. ER is emergency room.

Adapted with permission from Blumberg, LJ, Nichols, LM. The health status of workers who decline employer-sponsored insurance. *Health Aff* (Millwood) 2001; 20 (6): 180-7.

almost 40,000 U.S. households, and included a number of measures of health status. Results on most physical measures were mixed, but important differences were found in the areas of mental health and access to care. Table 4.1 shows some of the major differences found.[19]

The above stories and reports reveal how unstable and inequitable the employer-based insurance "system" has become. Many millions of hard-working Americans are now being excluded from health insurance coverage. About two-thirds of the uninsured have no regular physician and have cost-related barriers to physician visits, prescription drugs and necessary care.[20] People are dying unnecessarily, dealing with more advanced disease and disability, and falling into bankruptcy when medical bills become overwhelming. Having insurance greatly reduces these calamities. Reflecting on our loss of more than 18,000 young Americans annually, in May 2002, Dr. Don McCanne, past president of Physicians for a National Health Program, drew this stark comparison:[21]

> *Since 9/11, our government is turning the world upside down because of the tragic loss of life that day. Yet just since 9/11, FOUR TIMES AS MANY YOUNG ADULTS HAVE DIED because of the lack of insurance. Each two months of inaction duplicates the loss of that tragic day. And our government remains silent. Our leaders won't even discuss real solutions because, "We don't want 'the government' involved in our health insurance." Why does America tolerate this rhetoric? It's sick! Our health care system is sick! And our political leaders are doing nothing to cure the problems!*

CHAPTER FIVE

ONCE YOU LOSE YOUR INSURANCE, JUST TRY TO GET IT BACK

The Nelson family of Louisville, Tennessee knows the volatility of employer-based health insurance all too well. Here is their story:[1]

> Patricia, 44, and her 12-year-old son, Sam, are now uninsured, through a difficult personal choice, since she left a job with health benefits to help her sister and brother-in-law with their convenience store and bakery. The business cannot afford health insurance for their five employees. Nor can Patricia afford to continue her last insurance coverage through COBRA, which would cost her $4,260 a year (16% of her $27,000 annual income).[2]

> Unfortunately, Patricia has been without health insurance on many occasions over the years since most of the small firms she has worked for did not provide health benefits. She has often had to take two jobs in order to pay on her medical debts. Her husband, William, a former college football player and pre-medical student, suffered from bipolar disorder, requiring hospitalization once or twice a year. He later developed Lou Gehrig's disease (amyotrophic lateral sclerosis), could no longer talk or feed himself, and died at home after a prolonged downhill course of progressive disability. Patricia became the principal caregiver, quitting her job and losing the family's health insurance, but that allowed William to die at home of his terminal disease. When William became fully disabled, Medicare paid most of his bills, but the rest of the family had no coverage for ongoing medical bills.

> Sam had a severe episode of asthma at age five, requiring hospitalization in the intensive care unit, and leaving Patricia with a $6,000 hospital bill. She explored the possibility of

Medicaid coverage for Sam, but missed the eligibility cut off by earning just $4 more than the maximum allowed. Since then, she has been paying off the bill at $25 a month, and the balance is now less than $1,800. During some years, when she wasn't needed as a caregiver at home, she has worked 60 to 70 hours a week.

Patricia's brother-in-law has offered to cover (without insurance) any of Patricia's major medical bills. Knowing the high cost of medical care, however, she can't avoid saying, "If Sam ended up in intensive care again, one of us would end up in bankruptcy court. There'd really be no choice."

The Nelson family's experience typifies that of many families in not being able to afford coverage once lost, as well as the difficult circumstances faced by caregivers as they place highest priority on care of their families. Even with an annual income of $27,000 from her full-time job, including Social Security survivor's benefits, Patricia once again joined the ranks of the uninsured. Without employer-based coverage, the only remaining option to get private health insurance lies in the individual insurance market, which is fraught with high costs, and sometimes devious practices.

PERILS OF THE INDIVIDUAL MARKET

According to Families USA, a national, non-profit, non-partisan organization working to achieve affordable health care for all Americans, about 2.2 million people lost their health insurance in 2001. This is the largest one-year increase in almost 10 years. About one-half of this number are newly unemployed workers, with the remainder their spouses and dependents.[3] If they turn to the individual market, here is what they are likely to find.

A study by Georgetown University's Institute for Health Care Research and Policy for the Kaiser Family Foundation constructed seven hypothetical applicants. These included persons with hay fever, asthma, a repaired knee injury, and HIV. Nineteen insurance companies and HMOs in eight markets around the country were then asked how they would respond to these applicants. In 90% of the cases, the applicants were unable to obtain coverage at a standard rate. More than one-third of applicants were rejected. All plans rejected the HIV applicant. Of the 63% accepted, over one-half imposed restrictions of benefits, premium surcharges ("rate-ups") or both. The average "rate-up" was 38%.[4]

According to a former Blue Cross vice president, overweight is the most obvious and pervasive reason for rejection in the individual insurance market. Coverage is often denied automatically to applicants more than 10% above weight norms. A former marketing director of a health insurance company was even denied coverage because her 14-year-old son has acne.[5]

The following vignettes show just how hard it is to get health insurance in the individual market if you already have medical problems.[6]

- *Arlene Shallan, a diabetic and a widow in Boca Raton, Florida, purchased health insurance six years ago since her clothing store employer didn't provide coverage. Six years later, she was notified of a 60% rate increase to $1,318 a month, more than her mortgage payment. Upon calling the company's underwriting chief, she was asked, "Do you realize how terrible diabetes is?" None of the other insurers that Arlene called would offer coverage due to the diabetes. She had to wait until age 65 to get coverage through Medicare.*

- *Mary Rogers was paying $429 a month for her coverage, but the rate more than tripled, to $1,448 a month, after she had a stroke. As a former food-service worker, this was more than twice her Social Security disability checks. Although her children helped out, she took out a second mortgage on her home in Hollywood, Florida. She complained to state regulators and became involved in a class-action suit against the insurer. She dropped her policy as soon as she became eligible for Medicare.*

- *Premiums for a 64 year-old woman with diabetes and a cardiac pacemaker went up 60% on the last renewal date to $4,861 a month, or $58,332 a year. Nine years previously, her monthly premiums were $252 a month. George Bernstein, Miami insurance agent with 48 years of experience in this industry, was so outraged that he quit selling policies for that company (American Medical Security). In his words "It's highway robbery."*

Almost all insurance companies are for-profit. Most aggressively try to sort out the relatively healthy and avoid insuring the sick, whose medical expenses eat into those profits. If they offer coverage, they charge individuals much more than they charge employers on a group policy for their employees. Health insurance has simply become too expensive for most uninsured, even if they can find an insurer willing to quote them an offer (Figure 5.1).[7] Family health insurance costs over $9,000 in annual premiums in 2003.[8] Re-underwriting is the procedure by which insurers reassess and increase premiums after a subscriber has a change of health status. In Chapter 11, we will describe other practices pursued by many insurers which are geared more to their self-interest than the needs of the public.

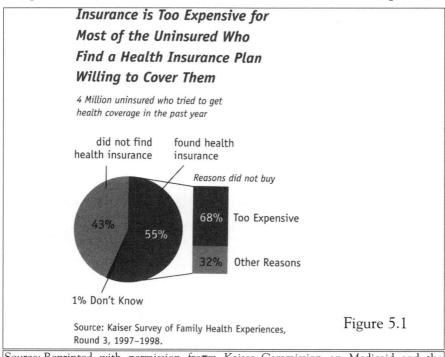

Insurance is Too Expensive for Most of the Uninsured Who Find a Health Insurance Plan Willing to Cover Them

4 Million uninsured who tried to get health coverage in the past year

did not find health insurance

found health insurance

Reasons did not buy

43%

55%

68% Too Expensive

32% Other Reasons

1% Don't Know

Source: Kaiser Survey of Family Health Experiences, Round 3, 1997–1998.

Figure 5.1

Source: Reprinted with permission from Kaiser Commission on Medicaid and the Uninsured. In Their Own Words: The uninsured talk about living without health insurance. Kaiser Family Foundation, September 2000: 28.

THE FAILURES OF ATTEMPTED FIXES

There have been a number of well-intended efforts on the part of government, at both state and federal levels, to rein in abuses of the insurance industry. Unfortunately, they have not been very effective.

COBRA

The Consolidated Omnibus Budget Reconciliation Act of 1985 (COBRA) was enacted to require that insurers and health plans provide health coverage for at least 18 months to people after they leave a job with health benefits. The problem, however, is that most newly unemployed people cannot afford such coverage, as Patricia Nelson, whose situation was discussed above, found out. Only 7% of unemployed workers or their families used COBRA in 1999.[9] A national survey reported by the Commonwealth Fund in late 2002 showed that only one in four working Americans could afford to continue their health insurance through COBRA if they became unemployed.[10] In addition to the cost barrier, COBRA does not apply to employers with less than 20 employees, and of course, not to employers who are not already providing health benefits.[11]

HIPAA

The Health Insurance Portability and Accountability Act of 1996 (HIPAA) was passed by Congress with broad bipartisan support with these laudable provisions.[12]

- Preexisting conditions. Group health insurers (including HMOs and self-insured employers) may not limit or deny coverage for preexisting conditions for more than 12 months; after that waiting period, full coverage is "portable" if the employee changes jobs or the employer changes health plans.
- Availability of coverage for small employers. Insurance carriers and health plans cannot refuse to offer small-group products to employers with 2 to 50 employees.
- Availability of coverage for individuals. Insurers and health plans must offer coverage to persons who had had group health insurance for at least 18 months, who have exhausted coverage under the Consolidated Omnibus Budget Reconciliation Act of 1985 (COBRA), and who are ineligible for coverage under any other employment-based health plan.
- Renewability. As long as premiums are paid, insurers may not drop coverage to employers, except in instances of fraud or misrepresentation by an employer.

In the individual insurance market, however, HIPAA has been relatively ineffective since Congress (intentionally) avoided any regulation of premiums to be charged for coverage. After a change of health status, a rate increase of 2,000% was documented in one state, and Congress did not appropriate funds for oversight, enforcement, and public education.[13]

High-Risk Insurance Pools

Another approach which theoretically could help uninsured people gain health coverage is the development of high-risk insurance pools. Twenty-nine states have established these pools in an effort to broaden the risk pool and help those who have already been denied coverage in the individual market. In practice, however, this concept has been ineffective. Because of high costs, restrictions on benefits and waiting periods, state high-risk pools insured only about 1% of all those insured by individual insurance. The average annual premium of about $3,000 was 8% of median family income in 1999. Premiums ranged up to almost $5,000 in some states, while deductibles paid for by the patient were $10,000 in three states (Alaska, Arkansas and Florida).[14] Extended waiting periods were often imposed for applicants with preexisting conditions, and restrictions were frequently placed on maternity, mental health, and lifetime benefits.[15] Another problem with state high-risk insurance pools, of course, is the budget crunch in states operating them. In California, as an example, the program is facing cutbacks and has insured only 18,000 of the estimated 125,000 people eligible for coverage.[16]

In short, COBRA, HIPAA and high-risk insurance pools have had a very limited effect on the problem of providing everyone with quality care.

SPECIAL IMPACT GROUPS

Three groups—women who are not elderly, young adults, and those with mental health problems—are especially hard hit by the difficulties of re-establishing health insurance coverage once coverage has been lost.

Non-Elderly Women

As Patricia Nelson, Arlene Shallan, and Mary Rogers each discovered painfully, costs for individual health insurance become prohibitive for many women in their middle years. This is especially difficult when they are providing care for family members, often their own parents. Uninsured women with any health problems are at high risk of remaining uninsured, especially since they are also likely to earn less than twice the federal poverty level. As a result, those who need help the most are least likely to get it.

Two large national studies show just how steep the costs are for individual insurance coverage, particularly beyond age 50. In a 1996 national survey of almost 23,000 individuals, almost one in four women between ages 55 and 64 who reported themselves in good, fair or poor health, were uninsured.[17] In a later randomized national study of over 1,500 adults from 50 to 70, costs of insurance were unaffordable for most uninsured, even with large tax credits or in those few states with community rating requirements.* In Boston, regardless of age (a community rating market), one could expect to pay over $8,300 for individual coverage, with a deductible of $1,000 and a co-pay of 30% after the deductible was met. In Miami, coverage would cost over $11,000 a year with a deductible of $250 and a co-pay of $10 per office visit. In most of the markets studied, insurers reserved the right to increase rates based on the applicant's health history or change of health status. In the 12 markets studied, an annual income of $50,000 would be necessary in order to keep the costs of individual health insurance to no more than 10% of income at age 60 at prevailing rates.[18] In view of double-digit premium increases throughout the insurance industry in recent years, all of these numbers would be considerably higher if the study was carried out today.

Young Adults

About one-third of young adults between 19 and 29 years of age are uninsured. Although many are healthy, those with disabilities or chronic illnesses are severely affected without health insurance. Figure 5.2 shows the rates of uninsurance by age and level of disability in

*By community rating, the same coverage and premiums are offered to enrollees throughout the covered community regardless of individual risk.

1996, with the highest rate of uninsurance in the 19 to 29 age group. Two-thirds of uninsured adults who work earn less than 200% of poverty level, and adults earning more than $700 a month are ineligible for Supplemental Security Income (SSI) benefits. Young adults with chronic illness such as cancer, severe asthma, and HIV infection fare no better.[19]

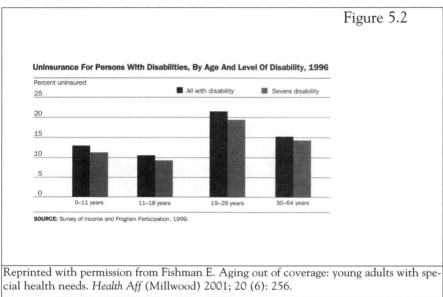

Figure 5.2

Uninsurance For Persons With Disabilities, By Age And Level Of Disability, 1996

SOURCE: Survey of Income and Program Participation, 1999.

Reprinted with permission from Fishman E. Aging out of coverage: young adults with special health needs. *Health Aff* (Millwood) 2001; 20 (6): 256.

As children with disabilities or chronic illnesses age out of whatever coverage they may have had as children, they face a formidable obstacle course in continuing health coverage beyond age 18. Most, if not eligible for SSI or Medicare, won't qualify for Medicaid and availability or affordability of individual insurance are out of the question.[20]

Mental Health

Almost 40 million people older than age 18 are estimated to have a mental disorder of any severity in a given year. They include depression and anxiety disorders, as well as schizophrenia and affective disorders, such as bipolar illness. Unfortunately, however, insurance coverage for mental health care has been difficult to obtain for many years. When available, it has often been prohibitively expensive and restricted in benefits.[21] Even if insured, many people lose coverage within a year after diagnosis of a mental disorder.[22] The insurance industry remains wary of offering coverage for mental health problems, fearing escalating demand and adverse selection, while shifting the burden for coverage to the public sector. There is still some societal stigma concerning mental illness which insurers use to avoid extending coverage on an equal basis with physical disorders.[23]

Although most mental health disorders can be effectively managed in the general medical care sector, mostly on an outpatient basis, many people so affected are without insurance coverage and delay or avoid primary care. Whereas 60 to 80% of people with heart disease obtain diagnosis and treatment from the health care system, only 25% of people with a mental disorder do so.[24]

There are pervasive inequities in the care received by people with mental health problems. Two examples make the point. According to the Inspector General of the U.S. Department of Health and Human Services, about 70,000 people with mental illness are improperly housed in nursing homes nationwide. State governments place them there in order to gain federal subsidies for their care through Medicaid, instead of covering their costs in apartments or psychiatric hospitals at state expense.[25] Many people with severe mental illness are "criminalized" in jails without receiving treatment; the Los Angeles County jail has been called the largest de facto mental health facility in the country.[26]

The lack of care for many children with mental health problems has become a national disgrace. Congressional investigators have recently found that 15,000 children with psychiatric disorders were improperly incarcerated in 2003 because no mental health services were available. Over 70 juvenile detention centers in 33 states were holding mentally ill children without charges. Many were depressed and some were suicidal. As Dr. Steven Sharfstein, president-elect of the American Psychiatric Association, recently observed: "We are in a much better position to diagnose and treat mental illness in children than we were just 15 years ago. Many kids who get in trouble should be in treatment. But because of the lack of money and the lack of services, they end up in the criminal justice system.[27]

There have been efforts at both the national and state level to establish parity of mental health coverage and care with physical, biomedical disorders. The Mental Health Parity Act of 1996 was passed by Congress in an attempt to establish some degree of parity, but there were many loopholes and the law sunsetted in September 2001 without extension. The insurance industry has successfully lobbied Congress since then to block attempts to re-establish parity of mental health coverage.[28] State laws vary widely, but the Employee Retirement Income Security Act (ERISA) of 1974 still exempts self-insured plans from state regulation.[29]

The last three chapters have dealt with various ways by which employer-based health insurance is neither available nor affordable to many millions of people. The next three chapters will assess to what extent Medicaid, as the main fabric of the "safety net," can make up for the lack of health insurance. In the meantime, based on what we have just seen, this observation by Professor Uwe Reinhardt, well-known health economist at Princeton University, is precisely on target:[30]

> *Ours is the most dishonest health system in the world—To pretend that this is a market that even vaguely resembles the model trotted out in economics textbooks is, in my view, inherently dishonest. It is also cruel... The dishonesty lies (a) in not being forthright in the advocacy of rationing health care by income class and (b) in the pretense that the retail "market" for health care is a properly functioning market that will allow individuals to shop around for cost-effective health care.*

CHAPTER SIX

I HAD MEDICAID, BUT I LOST IT

The Combs family from Hemet, California are hard at work with two or more jobs at any one time. Yet they must still rely on Medicaid coverage which is both intermittent and insecure. The trajectory of coverage for the Combs family over the last five years is complex, but it illuminates underlying system problems.

Shannon, 30, is now 7 months along with her second pregnancy. She has Medi-Cal coverage for pregnancy care, as well as high-deductible ($980 a month) coverage for care unrelated to pregnancy. Her husband, Derek, 31, has been in good general health, while their five-year-old daughter, Kelsey, has chronic asthma and allergies. Although both have worked since their marriage, none of their employers have provided health benefits. They now have an annual income of $20,400 in their joint position as resident managers of a storage unit facility. Most of the time the family has been without health insurance as their income was too high for Medi-Cal and too low to afford other coverage. In her early twenties, Shannon had multiple medical problems, including the need for surgery for bleeding ulcers and an ovarian cyst. By the age of 25, she had accumulated $9,000 in unpaid medical bills, forcing her to declare bankruptcy. That mars her credit record for 10 years, and the only credit cards she can qualify for carry a 22% interest rate. When Shannon became pregnant for the first time, she was working as a personal assistant and running her own small airplane detailing business, while Derek had a minimum-wage job with a golf ball retrieval company. Shannon couldn't find a physician willing to provide obstetric care without payment in advance. In desperation, she quit her job, closed down her business, and applied for welfare as a route to Medi-Cal. Her first prenatal visit was in her sixth month of pregnancy, and she went into premature labor two weeks after receiving her Medi-

Cal card. Kelsey was born 10 weeks premature at 4$^{1/2}$ pounds. After a 10-day stay for Kelsey in the neonatal ICU, the family was left with a $25,000 bill, which fortunately was covered by Medi-Cal in its entirety.

Over the next year, Derek worked at two part-time jobs, but his income was still low enough to qualify for Medi-Cal for all three of them as well as a partial cash welfare payment. When, however, the couple accepted their present job managing a storage unit facility, their income went up sufficiently to lose the welfare payment. Their Medi-Cal benefits continued on a transitional basis for 12 months, and then stopped. Soon thereafter, again without any health insurance, Shannon became pregnant again, and restarted the challenging process of renewing eligibility for Medi-Cal, at least for pregnancy care. This was even more urgent this time in view of her complicated first pregnancy. She checked again on private insurance, but pregnancy would be excluded as a preexisting condition. The doctor who delivered her told her that his charge would be $3,200, assuming a normal delivery, with half of that to be paid before delivery. Shannon then found out about Medi-Cal's "share of cost" program. This program is available to pregnant women at any income level, and also provides coverage for non-pregnancy-related medical costs at a deductible ($980 a month at Shannon's income level). Her pregnancy coverage doesn't cover routine ultrasound or circumcision for a male child. She has to re-qualify each month for continued coverage. In fact, at one point her coverage was canceled through a bureaucratic lapse, and was re-instated only after another form was filled out. Her pregnancy coverage ends two months after delivery.

Well into the third trimester, Shannon is hopeful of an uncomplicated delivery. They still have trouble paying for prescription drugs, and can't afford much needed dental work. The family will qualify for California's Healthy Families program, covering both children as long as the family income stays below 250% of the poverty line ($43,750 for a family of four in 2000). For themselves, Shannon and Derek are hoping that their employer will decide to pay 75% of a health insurance pol-

*icy. Even then, they would have a co-pay of $30 for each physi-
cian visit and a $4,000 annual deductible. If the employer
decides against coverage, they will look for another job. As
Shannon says, "We don't like to think of that, because loyalty
is one of the things we believe in. But we don't want to wait
until one of us is sick, because we'd never be able to get coverage then."*[1]

The saga of the Combs family raises major questions about system problems. For one, what kind of a health care system, in a country as affluent as ours, forces patients into quitting their job and
applying for welfare in order to gain access to basic obstetric care?
For another, since Medicaid is the main bulwark of what safety net
this nation has for health care, how can it be made more stable and
reliable? As it was, Shannon had to declare bankruptcy at an early
age due to overwhelming medical bills, joining over 325,000 families each year in the U.S. who do so as a direct result of illness or
injury. Health insurance is supposed to provide some safeguards
against catastrophic medical costs, yet about 80% of those families
filing for bankruptcy had at least some kind of insurance.[2]

This chapter will look at three trends—welfare reform, fiscal
deficits, and employee cost-sharing—which have weakened
Medicaid in recent years, either through restricting eligibility, benefits, or utilization of services.

WELFARE REFORM
AND LOSS OF COVERAGE

Federal and state welfare reform policies since 1996 have result-
ed in rising employment rates for low-income people but, unfortunately, many have lost any health insurance coverage at the same
time. Although most of the increased employment has been in full-
time jobs, these have largely been in low-wage jobs with small firms
without any insurance coverage by employers. Working parents,
especially single mothers, have been especially hard hit. From 1994
to 2000, the proportion of poor parents without any health care coverage increased from 34% to 41%. By 1999, more than 4 of 10 working women were uninsured, as shown in Figure 6.1.[3]

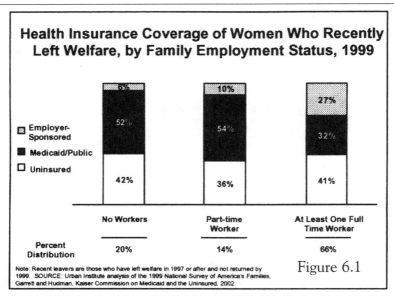

Health Insurance Coverage of Women Who Recently Left Welfare, by Family Employment Status, 1999

Figure 6.1

Note: Recent leavers are those who have left welfare in 1997 or after and not returned by 1999. SOURCE: Urban Institute analysis of the 1999 National Survey of America's Families, Garrett and Hudman, Kaiser Commission on Medicaid and the Uninsured, 2002.

Source: Reprinted with permission from Kaiser Commission on Medicaid and the Uninsured. Women who left welfare: health care coverage access, and use of health services. June 2002: 1.

Federal welfare reform legislation in 1996 was intended to protect those leaving welfare from losing their Medicaid coverage, but this has not held true for many. Most states have not complied with that intent, and there has been no federal enforcement of that provision. Instead, over the first five years after welfare reform, the number of low-income parents enrolled in Medicaid dropped by 27% in 15 of the most populous states.[4] Most states put strict limits on how much a parent can earn and remain qualified for Medicaid. In Louisiana, a mother with two children is ineligible for Medicaid if the family earns more than $3,048 a year![5] In 32 states, a parent working full-time at the minimum wage ($5.15 per hour) also earns too much to qualify for Medicaid.[6]

FISCAL DEFICITS AND FURTHER LOSS OF COVERAGE

The states have been encountering serious budget deficits as the economic downturn continues across the country and as their tax revenues have fallen.[7] State governments already spend almost as much on health care for the poor as they do on public schools. The average state expenditure on Medicaid is now up to 21% of total state expenditures (over 34% in New York State), and the costs are growing steadily. Medicaid spending by the states exceeds their combined spending on welfare, roads and prisons.[8]

In response to a fiscal crisis in the states and their need by law to balance their budgets each year, Medicaid is an obvious target for deep budget cuts and rethinking the goals of the program. At the annual Governors' meeting in the spring of 2002, there was unanimous agreement that the increasing cost of Medicaid is the most urgent crisis that they face. Governors in both parties have appealed to the Bush Administration for more help from the federal government, which already pays for an average of 57% of Medicaid costs. Facing its own growing budget deficit ($455 billion in fiscal 2003, the largest in our history and estimated to rise to $475 billion in fiscal 2004),[9] the federal government rejects these appeals and provides states with additional flexibility through waivers to meet their own needs; almost 2,000 such waivers have been approved over the last two years.[10]

The core mission of Medicaid, as required by federal law, is to provide basic health coverage for pregnant women, poor children, and the most needy disabled adults. Many states have expanded beyond these groups to include many low-income working families and those encumbered by very large medical bills. However, a massive retrenchment is now in progress, and a meat cleaver is being used. Consider these examples of draconian budget cuts around the country:[11]

- 45 states reduced their Medicaid spending in fiscal 2002, mostly by cost controls on prescription drugs, restricting eligibility, cutting benefits, and/or freezing or reducing reimbursement to providers.[12]
- In Florida, the Governor's plan requires adults to pay their own catastrophic medical bills until a single adult spends down to less than $180 a month for food, rent and other living expenses.
- In Tennessee, as many as 420,000 people are expected to lose their coverage in 2003; Medicaid enrollments and benefits will be cut, and new co-pays will be added for prescription drugs.[13]
- In Illinois, the Governor has proposed cutting reim-

bursement to hospitals providing care to Medicaid patients by 13%, which follows a previous 13% cut the year before, as well as sharp reductions in physician reimbursement.

- In Utah, co-pays for physician visits will be added (up to $500 a year) for families with annual incomes as low as $7,500 and coverage of vision, dental and home health care services will be eliminated.

- In California, co-pays up to $5 for visit will be added and physician reimbursement will be cut (by 40% for pediatric specialists);[14] eligibility for Medi-Cal will be restricted to families earning less than 67% of the federal poverty level.[15]

IMPACTS OF COST-SHARING ON LOW-INCOME PEOPLE

As we have seen, cost sharing is now being widely used throughout the health care system, including within the Medicaid program. There have been many studies, however, that show that cost-sharing applied to low-income patients has a deleterious effect on both access and outcomes of care.[16-22] It has been shown that even small co-pays ("small" as viewed by insured or more affluent people) can have a major impact. Because of this burden, people avoid and delay of care, skimp on needed medications, require more visits to emergency rooms, have more hospitalizations that could have been prevented, and have worse clinical outcomes. A 2001 report makes these points, once again. A large study of more than 55,000 adult welfare medication recipients was conducted in the province of Quebec, Canada before and after introduction of a prescription co-insurance and deductible cost-sharing policy. Before the change in drug policy, welfare recipients received their medications free; in 1996, they were required to pay a 25% co-insurance fee up to an annual maximum of $200. Although the use of non-essential drugs was reduced by 22% (one of the cost containment goals of the policy), these unintended and counterproductive results were also documented.[23]

- Use of essential drugs dropped by 15%.

- The rates of adverse events, as measured by hospitalizations, nursing home admissions, and mortality, doubled.
- Emergency room visits nearly doubled.

More recent studies in the U.S. add further evidence of the negative effects of co-payments on access and outcomes of care. A national study by the Washington-based Center for Studying Health System Change found that 26% of Medicaid enrollees reported not being able to afford needed drugs in the last year, while 29% of uninsured people said the same thing.[24] A 2002 RAND study found that increased co-payments for prescription drugs led to reductions in annual spending by patients by up to one-third, but since fewer prescriptions were filled, almost all of the cost savings accrued to the health plans themselves.[25] A 2004 RAND study found that when co-payments were doubled, the use of prescription drugs by patients with asthma and diabetes fell by more than 20%, while emergency room visits increased by 17% and hospital stays rose by 10%.[26]

There is now ample evidence to say that consumer cost-sharing, especially with low-income individuals, sets up additional barriers in accessing needed care and affording essential drugs, with the unintended consequence of increasing the rates of preventable complications, hospitalizations, and even deaths. Dr. Donald Light, Professor of Comparative Health Care Systems at the University of Medicine and Dentistry of New Jersey, notes that the U.S. has for many years had by far the greatest amount of cost sharing and by far the most costly health care system with the least effective controls on escalating costs. As he further observes:[27]

> No other advanced system considers co-pays as a serious tool for cost containment or income, and most consider them clinically perverse as well as unethical. Several have used them and then dropped them because of their administrative costs, nuisance and perverse effects on patients and staff. No evidence exists that co-pays lower the rate of increasing costs— they just make the sick pay some of them.

Medicaid, the single most important part of the nation's supposed "safety net," has been seriously underfunded for many years. It is now even worse off, and in crisis. State budget shortfalls across the country are projected to total $49 billion in fiscal 2003.[28] The states are now in their third straight year of fiscal deficits, and the outlook for fiscal 2004 is still bleak. According to a new report by the National Conference on State Legislatures, 27 of the states have plans to cut Medicaid further in 2004.[29]

The three major trends discussed here are firmly in place, to the detriment of many people losing Medicaid coverage every day. As further Medicaid cuts occur in enrollees, benefits, and reimbursement to providers, stories like that of the Combs family will become commonplace. As we shall see in later chapters, this crisis can be managed, but only through major structural reform of the entire health care system, not by the ineffective incremental changes we have seen for these many years. Meanwhile, in the next chapter we will see how much of the population has little hope of qualifying for Medicaid, but still has serious problems in affording health care.

CHAPTER SEVEN

I'M NOT POOR ENOUGH FOR MEDICAID, BUT I CAN'T AFFORD CARE

T he story of Yolanda Smith and her family demonstrates the travails of a single mother raising two children, fully employed in the workforce, and mostly ineligible for Medicaid.

> Yolanda Smith, 29, lives in Paterson, New Jersey, with her two daughters, Dominique, 8, and Destiny, 6. She works full-time as a customer service representative for a cigar-distribution company. The children's father lives in another town and rarely sends child support payments. Yolanda rents her duplex from an aunt, and expects that the thousands of dollars in back child support will never be paid. Yolanda had some Medicaid coverage until six years ago, when she started her current full-time job. Her annual income is about $20,000 a year, placing her in the large near-poor group of working families with incomes 100 to 200% of federal poverty levels. Her employer offers health insurance but she can't afford it. The premiums for a family policy would be almost $4,000 (almost 15% of her annual household budget), plus deductibles of $200 for each family member and co-pays. Even though her mother helps out with the costs of childcare and the girls' clothing, there is no income left after basic costs of living for insurance payments (Figure 7.1).
>
> Since Yolanda's budget barely covers the most basic necessities, she has had to confront many difficult choices over the years. Without any health insurance, she had to rely on emergency room care for her children's acute illnesses, and soon accumulated high medical bills and letters from collection agencies. There have been times when she couldn't afford a telephone. She couldn't afford Albuterol for her daughter's nebuliz-

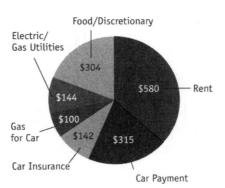

**Smith Family Budget Leaves
Little Room for Insurance Premiums**

Figure 7.1

Family Income of $1,585/month

Food/Discretionary

Electric/
Gas Utilities

$304

$144

$580 — Rent

Gas
for Car

$100

$142 $315

Car Insurance

Car Payment

*Ms. Smith's mother helps out with the cost of child
care and the girls' clothing. Income is the amount
after a $29.91 monthly retirement contribution.

Reprinted with permission from Kaiser Commission on Medicaid and the Uninsured. In Their Own Words: The uninsured talk about living without health insurance. Kaiser Family Foundation, September 2000: 23.

ers for asthma, and had to substitute saline for it. As she says: "Sometimes I have to hold off paying a bill to keep the gas and electricity on. My most important priorities are getting the girls fed and paying for the car so I can get to work, so health care falls low on the list. I wish it didn't have to be that way, but that's the way it is."

After several very difficult years, Yolanda successfully qualified her daughters in 1999 for coverage by New Jersey's CHIP program, which then covered children in families making up to 350% of the federal poverty level. Even then, however, it took five calls to find a physician participating in the plan, and she still didn't have coverage for herself. She hasn't been able to afford any dental care, and she can barely get together $50 if she has to see a physician.[1]

RESTRICTIVE AND VARIABLE MEDICAID ELIGIBILITY

As we saw in the last chapter, Medicaid eligibility is now beyond the reach of many needy people, even for those with incomes well below the federal poverty level. The median U.S. income threshold for unemployed parents is just 45% of the poverty line for a family of three (about $6,500) and 69% of poverty for employed parents (about $10,000). Despite the relatively higher costs of living in Alaska, its income eligibility threshold for unemployed parents in a family of three is less than $2,000 a year, only 13% of federal poverty levels! The degree of variability in income thresholds is surprising and difficult to account for. Alaska's level is on the low end, with Minnesota's threshold 20 times higher at over $40,000 for a family of three.[2]

Children fare better than adults in terms of eligibility for Medicaid. Unless disabled, single adults and childless couples are excluded from Medicaid in most states no matter how poor they are.[3] On the other hand, 40 states have set their eligibility thresholds for children under Medicaid or CHIP at 200% of the poverty line or higher. Figure 7.2 shows the differences as of mid-2001.[4]

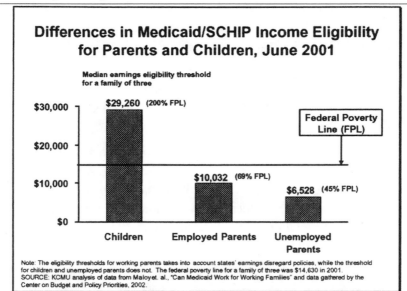

Figure 7.2. Adapted with permission from Kaiser Commission on Medicaid and the Uninsured. Low-income parents' access to Medicaid five years after welfare reform. June 2002: 5.

ALONG THE "MEDICAL DIVIDE"— DIFFICULT CHOICES

Almost one half of the U.S. population is on the low-income side of the "medical divide." In terms of health coverage, the hardest hit are working Americans earning less than $50,000 a year (about 300% of federal poverty levels). Here is just one example of an uninsured family without a safety net.[5]

> *Kim Godboldt, 25, is a single mother of two living in the Chicago area. She brings home about $40,000 a year as an office manager in a pediatrician's office. She is not eligible for Medicaid, and can't afford the $2,300 deductible for coverage of her children by CHIP. She explored the private insurance market, but found that also unaffordable at about $4,800 a year. While her pediatrician employer provides free care to both of her children, she found a bill of $1,450 for recent x-rays and blood tests for her 6-year-old daughter to be difficult to manage. She is completely vulnerable to the high costs of any major illness.*

As Kim discovered, subsidized coverage through CHIP is also out of reach for many. CHIP has become as unstable and unreliable a part of the safety net as Medicaid. In New York, for example, one-half of New York children enrolled in Medicaid and CHIP lose coverage at re-enrollment time as a result of cumbersome bureaucratic requirements.[6] In Washington State, premiums are going up by 35% for its Basic Health Plan, the state's subsidized health insurance program for near-poor working families. This will be a blow to the Boro family.[7]

> *Keith Boro is a Seattle portrait photographer, while his wife, Patricia, has studied occupational therapy. With their 9 year-old daughter, they live on an annual income of about $30,000. After paying their mortgage and other fixed expenses, they find premiums for the Basic Health Plan already difficult to afford (over $1,400 a year before the increase).*

Lower income families pay much more in out-of-pocket expenses for health care, as a proportion of total income, than do those with incomes above 400% of the federal poverty level. In view of the ongoing costs of basic necessities of living, more than 5% is generally considered a large amount to spend on health care. The three largest cost-of-living expenses for U.S. households are housing, transportation (especially car ownership and operation), and food eaten at home; these account for 64% of the total income of families without health insurance. After paying for these three major outlays, uninsured families spend both a smaller percentage of income and fewer dollars on other items than do insured families.[8] Figure 7.3 compares out-of-pocket spending for health care across income groups.[9] When one recalls from Chapter 1 (page 12) that low-income people face the highest charges from health care providers, this challenge becomes even more onerous.

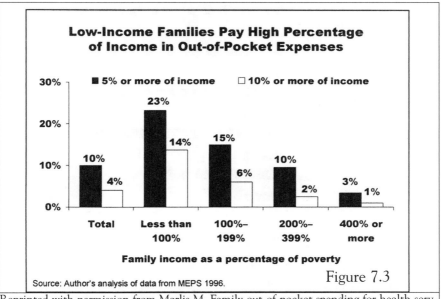

Low-Income Families Pay High Percentage of Income in Out-of-Pocket Expenses

Source: Author's analysis of data from MEPS 1996.

Figure 7.3

Reprinted with permission from Marlis M. Family out-of-pocket spending for health services: a continuing source of financial insecurity. Commonwealth Fund. June 2002: 5.

Despite the economic boom through the 1990s, the U.S. Census Bureau has found that many Americans cannot afford the basics, such as food, utilities and rental/mortgage payments. About 15% of the uninsured report unmet needs for a doctor. These findings belie perceptions that medically uninsured adults may choose to spend their money on less important things.[10]

IMPACTS ON LOWER-INCOME UNINSURED

As we have seen in earlier chapters, the uninsured face many more barriers to health care than those with health insurance. Compared to the insured, they have less preventive care, they delay or avoid primary care, present with more advanced disease to emergency rooms, have more preventable hospitalizations, and have higher rates of mortality and complications. The differences are marked and bear a linear relationship to income, as shown in Figure 7.4.[11]

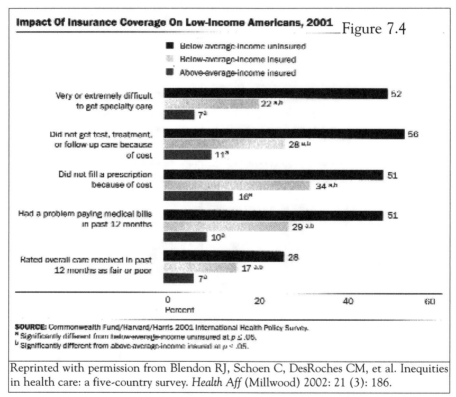

Impact Of Insurance Coverage On Low-Income Americans, 2001 Figure 7.4

SOURCE: Commonwealth Fund/Harvard/Harris 2001 International Health Policy Survey.
[a] Significantly different from below-average-income uninsured at p ≤ .05.
[b] Significantly different from above-average-income insured at p < .05.

Reprinted with permission from Blendon RJ, Schoen C, DesRoches CM, et al. Inequities in health care: a five-country survey. *Health Aff* (Millwood) 2002: 21 (3): 186.

Women of childbearing age are especially disadvantaged by lack of health insurance. About one in five American women between the ages of 15 and 44 were uninsured in 1999. Almost 14% of all pregnant women in 1997 had no health coverage, and about one in three young women in New Mexico are uninsured.[12]

Since minorities are much more likely than whites to be uninsured, they experience increased barriers and worse outcomes of care. According to a recent report by the American College of

Physicians and the American Society of Internal Medicine, Hispanics are the most likely of any racial group to be uninsured, and they have the worst outcomes as well. Hispanics are six times more likely than whites to develop end-stage kidney disease as a complication of diabetes. Hispanic women are more than three times less likely than the general population to seek care for hypertension, and are more than twice as likely than Caucasian women for breast cancer to progress to a later stage before diagnosis.[13]

Other impacts of being uninsured are also important, but more difficult to measure. Just two examples make the point:

- How can you assess the impact of lifestyle decisions such as this one, made on the basis of insecurity about health care, especially as these are so common?[14]

   Joseph Mosqueda of San Diego kept his two sons, 7 and 8, off of the local soccer team in order to avoid the risk of a fracture that could break the family budget.

- Between 1999 and 2001, during a time of decreasing welfare benefits and recession, a Boston University study found a 45% increase in the ranks of hungry children treated at that hospital as well as at a medical clinic in Minneapolis. The percentage of underweight children also increased. One social worker, who has worked at Boston Medical Center for the last seven years, has observed a marked change over the last two years, with more families filling their children's cups with Kool-Aid instead of milk or juices.[15]

These stories and the statistics they illustrate demonstrate that it is not just the poor (most of whom are in the work force) who have trouble getting health care. It is also many millions of hardworking Americans earning up to $50,000 a year, often working at two or more jobs. Health care has become increasingly unaffordable and inaccessible to a growing part of the U.S. population. So far, we have dealt mainly with the uninsured. In the next two chapters, we will expand our view to also include all those covered by Medicare and Medicaid, since the difficulty in affording medications and finding a physician willing to take care of them applies to all three groups.

CHAPTER EIGHT

I CAN'T AFFORD MY PRESCRIPTIONS

The costs of prescription drugs are soaring at a faster clip than almost any other segment of the health care industry. They are now unaffordable for many large population groups, including the uninsured, those on Medicare and Medicaid, and many others who are underinsured with private insurance. Since drug therapy of one kind or another has become such a large part of medical treatment today, as it becomes less affordable, it contributes to decreased access to care for many millions of people.

This chapter provides an overview of inflationary trends in prescription drugs, their impact on the uninsured and those on Medicare and Medicaid, adverse health consequences to those lacking prescription drug coverage, and what's being done to alleviate this serious access problem.

INFLATION OF PRESCRIPTION DRUG COSTS

The volume of prescription drug sales, especially of more expensive drugs, has been going up at rapid rates in recent years. Americans spent $208 billion in 2001 alone for prescription drugs, almost double that spent just five years before. Sales of prescription drugs went up by 18%, and the over 3 billion total prescriptions were the equivalent of almost one prescription every month for every American.[1] The average retail prescription prices for brand-name drugs have more than doubled from $27 to $65 over the last 10 years.[2] IMS Health, a pharmaceutical information and consulting company, projects an average annual growth rate of prescription drug sales of 12% in the U.S. from 2002 to 2006.[3]

Many factors combine to cause these price increases, including surging demand driven by aggressively effective direct-to-consumer advertising; development of new, more expensive (but often not better) drugs; the needs of an aging population, and the shift from sur-gery to drug therapy for many conditions. However, as we shall see in Chapter 11, the pharmaceutical industry is the most profitable of any industry in the U.S., and much of surging drug prices ends up in profits to drug companies and their shareholders. Drug prices in the U.S. are by far the highest in the world, since Congress has so far rejected all price controls of the industry.[4]

The marketplace for prescription drugs does not serve the public well, especially sick, elderly people who pay cash for their prescriptions. Cash payers at pharmacies, by far the most common purchasers, pay the highest, undiscounted prices. This has been true since the 1950s. The Veterans Administration (VA) and Defense Department have the lowest prices in the country (58% of the cash/drugstore price). Institutional buyers of drugs get dis-counts of 5 to 30% from drug manufacturers. Differential drug pric-ing has become a "hot button" political issue, with more calls for price regulation, as well as for both buying pools and permitting the importation of less expensive drugs from Canada.[5] Price increases of some drugs are impossible to explain except as price gouging. The price of Lanoxin, for example, an old drug and the most commonly used by the elderly, rose about seven times the inflation rate in 1998.[6]

IMPACTS ON THREE LARGE POPULATION GROUPS

The Elderly (Medicare Beneficiaries)

According to the U.S. Census for 2000, people 65 and older represent 12.4% of the population. Beyond their numbers, however, they account for 34% of all prescriptions filled and 42% of spending on prescriptions.[7] Until 2004, traditional Medicare has not provid-ed any coverage for outpatient medications, and that coverage is still very limited. Elderly people in Medicare HMOs are facing cutbacks in drug coverage as their costs escalate. Premiums in the Medigap market (insurance supplementing Medicare) are becoming less affordable. By the fall of 1999, only about 4 in 10 of people over 65 years of age had any drug coverage at all.[8] Even retirees from large companies who used to have generous benefits for prescription drugs are also facing future cutbacks as employers view with alarm the surging costs of these benefits. The prospects for retirees of medium-size companies are fading, and small companies rarely pay for any retiree health care.

The stories of those actually experiencing these problems are revealing.[9]

- *Margaret Cleary, now 80, retired from the Morgan Guaranty Trust Company, a unit of J. P. Morgan & Company, in 1986. The monthly deduction for her Medicare HMO from her $550 pension check almost tripled in 2002 from $50 to $129. She was forced to drop the HMO and take a less expensive plan without any coverage for the drugs she needs for hypertension, diabetes, and high cholesterol.*

- *Lorraine Sablan, 70, is a retired aerospace worker with Allegheny Teledyne in San Diego. The plant where she worked was shut down in 1994. In January 2002, her health care premiums went up 80% to $90 a month. Her monthly pension, however, is just $669. As she says, "If it keeps going up, we won't have a pension."*

Non-elderly who are permanently disabled, as well as those requiring renal dialysis or a kidney transplant, also qualify for Medicare. However, they become vulnerable to unaffordable co-payments charged by Medicare HMOs for chemotherapy, dialysis, radiation therapy and hospitalization. Here are just two examples.[10]

- *Marge Hoopingarner, 62, lives in Fort Worth, Texas, where she receives treatment for leukemia. In January 2002, her monthly costs under PacifiCare, a Medicare HMO, rose to over $1,000. Chemotherapy drugs can cost up to $500. She had to stop taking some medications. As she says: "The co-payments are killing us, literally. People will die because we're not able to get the treatments we need."*

- *Karen Guerrero, 58, also in Fort Worth and with PacifiCare, was hit by co-payments of $150 for each chemotherapy drug, raising her monthly costs of cancer treatment to almost $3,200 in 2002. She qualified for Medicare because of vision impairment. Even after switching back to traditional Medicare, her cancer treatment will cost over $1,300 a month.*

A 2003 national survey by Harris Interactive of more than 1,100 disabled people over 50 years old found that one third have postponed needed health care because they can't afford it.[11]

Medicaid Enrollees

Despite Medicaid's coverage for prescription drugs, that coverage is becoming less and less accessible as states cut their budgets to match reduced state revenue in a time of economic slowdown. As states confront painful cutbacks, the Medicaid budget is the most vulnerable target because of its size, and within that, prescription drugs account for the largest portion. Many states are therefore putting a variety of cost containment measures in place, including limits on the number of prescriptions and increasingly steep co-payments. More than one in four Medicaid enrollees across the country now report being unable to afford prescription drugs over the last year. Medicaid recipients are at much increased risk if they have two or more chronic illnesses, and still higher risk if below the federal poverty line.[12]

The Uninsured

In earlier chapters, we have already seen examples of serious impacts on uninsured people because of the lack of any coverage for necessary prescription drugs. Here is one more example, which would be understandable in a third-world country, but not in our nation of abundance.

> *Imelda, 36, develops thrombophlebitis in her leg after a Caesarean section for placenta praevia. As she leaves the hospital with her third child, she is given a prescription for Coumadin to guard against pulmonary embolism, a potentially lethal complication. She can't afford it, and goes home without it.*[13]

This is far from an unusual event. The uninsured are much more likely to go without prescribed medications than any other group because of cost. (Figure 8.1)[14]

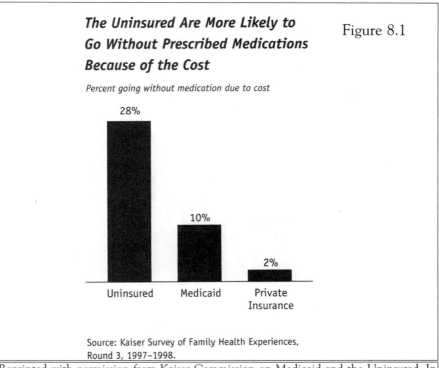

The Uninsured Are More Likely to Go Without Prescribed Medications Because of the Cost

Figure 8.1

Percent going without medication due to cost

28% — Uninsured
10% — Medicaid
2% — Private Insurance

Source: Kaiser Survey of Family Health Experiences, Round 3, 1997–1998.

Reprinted with permission from Kaiser Commission on Medicaid and the Uninsured. In Their Own Words: The uninsured talk about living without health insurance. Kaiser Family Foundation, September 2000: 31.

ADVERSE HEALTH CONSEQUENCES

Although the growing unaffordability of prescription drugs is not a new problem, it is getting steadily worse and there is no end in sight if left to the workings of the marketplace. It already poses a major threat to many millions of Americans. Its adverse consequences long-term cannot yet be known, but they will not be good. One cannot skip doses or stop essential medications for such common chronic diseases as diabetes, hypertension, or coronary heart disease, without serious complications.

It is no surprise that the uninsured are the most vulnerable to bad health outcomes, especially those with serious illnesses. It is not to our health care system's credit that the sickest and most vulnerable among us have the biggest problem in getting necessary prescription drugs. Figure 8.2 presents graphic evidence of this point.[15]

"Non-compliance" is a commonly used technical term in medicine in reference to patients who don't fill, or take, their prescrip-

Figure 8.2   ***Medications Are the Hardest to Obtain for the Uninsured with Serious Health Problems***

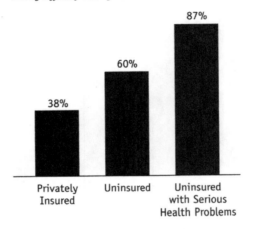

Percent Not Getting or
Having Difficulty Getting Medications

Source: Kaiser Survey of Family Health Experiences,
Round 3, 1997–1998.

Reprinted with permission from Kaiser Commission on Medicaid and the Uninsured. In Theor Own Words: The uninsured talk about living without health insurance. Kaiser Family Foundation, September 2000: 46.

tions as advised by their physicians. It is sometimes used in a pejorative way by physicians, but it should not be. There are many reasons for patients not filling their prescriptions, especially cost reasons, as well as reasons beyond the patient's control for not taking medications as prescribed.

A 2001 national survey of over 1,000 adults sheds some light on the extent of this problem. More than one in five adults in the U.S. had not filled a prescription at least once over the past year. Table 8.1 breaks down the respondents' reports both by income level and by type of "non-compliance." Especially disturbing are the findings for people with disabilities—more than one-third didn't fill a prescription in the last year.[16]

Noncompliance Because Out-of-Pocket Costs or Prescriptions   Table 8.1

In the past 12 months, was there ever a time when you (READ BELOW) because of the cost?

	All Adults %	INCOME						People with Disabili- ties %
		Less Than $15,000 %	$15,000 to $24,999 %	$25,000 to $34,999 %	$35,000 to $49,999 %	$50,000 to $74,999 %	$75,000 and Over %	
Did not fill a prescription for medicine	22	39	40	25	18	17	12	35
Took medicine in smaller doses than prescribed	14	31	24	16	12	10	4	27
Took medicine less frequently than prescribed	16	21	30	20	12	14	5	28

Reprinted with permission from Taylor H, Leitman R, (eds). Out-of-pocket costs are a substantial barrier to prescription drug compliance. Harris Interactive, Health Care News, November 20, 2001: 1 (32).

WHAT'S BEING DONE ABOUT THE GROW-ING UNAFFORDABILITY OF DRUGS?

In one sentence, much activity, but most of it ineffective so far, and no real fix yet on the horizon for a very big problem. In November 2003, after a long and bitter ideologically driven debate, Congress passed, by a slim margin, legislation providing a limited prescription drug benefit for Medicare beneficiaries. While being touted by the Administration and supporters in Congress as a major advance and step toward "modernizing" Medicare, the bill has many flaws and ends up serving the interests of the drug and insurance industries far more than seniors. Consider these examples:[17,18]

- The drug benefit does not start until 2006, but even then the $400 billion earmarked for the benefit over 10 years is expected to cover only 22% of projected drug costs over that period, according to an analysis by Consumers Union.
- Private pharmacy benefit managers will pick the drugs to be covered under the plan, with no transparency or public accountability.
- The government is expressly prohibited from using its purchasing power to gain discounted drug prices for Medicare beneficiaries.
- Without price controls built into the system, big profits are assured for the drug and insurance industries.

- Large subsidies will be allocated to employers with the hope that they will not discontinue prescription drug benefits for their retirees, but the Congressional Budget Office estimates that 3.8 million retirees will have their private coverage reduced.[19]

- More than 6 million elderly people now receiving drug coverage from Medicaid will lose that coverage.

- A drug discount card, offered to seniors in May 2004, provides only limited assistance to eligible seniors; at most, it is expected to reduce costs of their drugs by 10 to 15%; seniors with annual incomes less than about $12,000 will be given only $600 on their cards to cover costs of their medications.[20, 21]

- Of even more concern, $46 billion (more than three times the initial estimate) is provided to the insurance and HMO industries as incentives to provide prescription drug coverage for seniors;[22] under the guise of subsidized "competition," privatization of Medicare is being promoted to encourage seniors to enroll in private Medicare PPOs, despite the failure of Medicare HMOs in recent years to offer comparable coverage as reliably and efficiently as the traditional Medicare program.[23]

- The more Medicare is privatized, with healthier and more afluent seniors enrolling in private plans, the more the Medicare program itself is threatened by adverse selection, with higher costs being shifted to lower income and sicker seniors who are least able to afford higher levels of cost sharing.

- New budget projections put the cost of the 2003 Medicare bill at $534 billion over 10 years (about one-third more than legislators were led to believe at the time of its passage[24]) while the deductible and coverage gap for seniors will have grown by 78% by the eighth year of the program in 2013.[25]

At the state level, some states have started demonstration projects through Medicaid to provide some Medicare beneficiaries with assistance with the costs of prescription drugs. An example is the "Pharmacy Plus" program established in Illinois to offer drug coverage for Medicare beneficiaries with annual incomes up to 200% of

the federal poverty level.[26] The State of Maine enact
which is intended to get about a 20% discount off of re
its Medicaid program.[27] The drug industry fought back
Supreme Court set aside their injunction in May 2003.~~ ~~
states are mobilizing to negotiate discounted rates for their Medicaid
enrollees and introducing bills to create preferred-drug lists.[29] Many
states have recognized that they could save almost 50% of their
Medicaid drug budgets if they could switch patients to generics for
the 17 drugs scheduled to lose patent protection over the next three
years (e.g. Claritin, Prilosec, Augmentin, Zoloft). In New
Hampshire, these cost savings could fund checkups for 43,000 children, a week of meals-on-wheels for 57,000 seniors, and dental care
for 8,000 children.[30]

The pharmaceutical industry has lobbied legislators heavily,
both in Congress and in state legislatures, to resist such price controls. It has fought state efforts to contain prices at every turn.
Realizing that a public backlash has occurred against them because
of their high prices and profits, drug manufacturers have mounted
new efforts to improve their image, such as offering free trials for prescription drugs and discount cards for low-income seniors.[31,32] None
of these approaches offer any real solutions.

Meanwhile, the marketplace for prescription drugs has become
splintered and difficult to understand for many patients, especially
the sick and frail elderly. Although retail pharmacies are still the
main access point, mail-order pharmacies, which often offer dis-
counts, are growing fast. Online pharmacies have also been marketing themselves aggressively. Many Americans are now seeking out
Canadian-based Web sites, since Canada has some price controls
and the currency exchange rate is favorable to the U.S.[33] Some
insurers are beginning to cover prescription drugs purchased in
Canada, a development causing great consternation within the
pharmaceutical industry.[34]

Adequate access to essential drug treatment is but one, albeit
extremely important, part of our larger access to care problem. Major
structural reform of the whole system is required, not patchwork
changes around the edges of the overall access problem. Prices of
prescription drugs in the U.S. are much higher than in the rest of the
world, and the pharmaceutical industry fights fiercely to keep them

nere. Its defenses of these prices are disingenuous and self-serving, as we will see in more detail in Chapter 11. But a more critical question awaits our examination of the safety net: How are physicians, who are key to the critical yet underfunded programs of Medicaid and Medicare, faring?

CHAPTER NINE

MY DOCTOR
WON'T SEE ME NOW

Quite aside from facilities and funding mechanisms, physicians are crucial to the ability of any safety net to provide care to the uninsured and underinsured. Unfortunately, however, current trends within the physician workforce run counter to the urgent public need to reinforce a tattered patchwork of safety net programs.

CHANGING TRENDS AMONG PHYSICIANS

Physicians are a beleaguered and increasingly unhappy group as they try to cope with practicing in a deteriorating system. They are besieged by growing administrative burdens, an increasing hassle factor in relating to our 1,200 private insurers as well as government payers (each with a different set of rules), and soaring costs of malpractice liability insurance. They are finding it more difficult to spend time with patients and to have sufficient latitude to use their own clinical judgment. During the managed care era, invisible bureaucrats progressively intruded into the clinical encounter, upsetting physicians and patients alike. Figure 9.1 shows physicians' views of the impact of managed care based on a national survey by the Kaiser Family Foundation in 2001.[1]

As part of a Community Tracking Study, the Center for Studying Health System Change carried out a large national survey of over 12,000 physicians during 1996-1997. Overall, about 18% of U.S. physicians were dissatisfied or very dissatisfied with their careers. Physicians older than age 55 were more dissatisfied than younger physicians. The most commonly reported causes of dissatisfaction included difficulties in caring for patients, need for more clinical freedom, inadequate time with patients, and compromised ability to provide quality care.[2]

More recent studies have found alarming increases over the last five years in physician dissatisfaction. The Massachusetts Medical Society has monitored physician satisfaction across the U.S. since

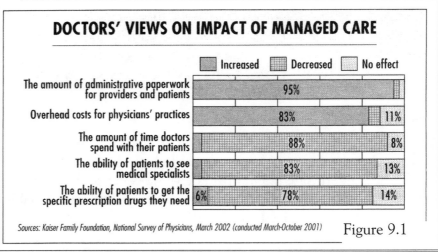

DOCTORS' VIEWS ON IMPACT OF MANAGED CARE

Legend: Increased | Decreased | No effect

The amount of administrative paperwork for providers and patients	Increased 95%
Overhead costs for physicians' practices	Increased 83%, No effect 11%
The amount of time doctors spend with their patients	Decreased 88%, No effect 8%
The ability of patients to see medical specialists	Decreased 83%, No effect 13%
The ability of patients to get the specific prescription drugs they need	Increased 6%, Decreased 78%, No effect 14%

Sources: Kaiser Family Foundation, National Survey of Physicians, March 2002 (conducted March-October 2001)

Figure 9.1

1992. It uses a nine-point index including such factors as physician supply, practice finances, and work environment. It has recently reported that physician satisfaction has declined by 15% since 1992, with most of the drop occurring in the last five years.[3] Almost three-fifths of the decline in 2001 was attributed to the high cost of professional liability insurance. In California, three-fourths of physicians in the California Medical Association reported the practice of medicine as less satisfying in the last five years.[4]

Malpractice liability insurance premiums are skyrocketing in many states across the country. In Florida, for example, insurance rates for a family physician managing an emergency room increased from $54,000 in 2001 to $179,000 in 2002. Many family physicians in Florida had their rates more than double even though they had been in practice for more than 10 years without any claims filed against them.[5] Some insurers are abandoning the market, citing as a main reason the increase in the average jury award from $500,000 in 1995 to $1 million in 2000.[6]

As a result of all of these pressures, physicians have made major shifts in their practice styles. Increased mobility is becoming more common. Spending one's entire practice career in one location is becoming less common. Less than one-half of American adults have had the same physician for more than five years, according to a recent study by the Commonwealth Fund.[7] Locum tenens physicians (temporary, itinerant) used to be mostly older physicia[...] sitioning into retirement. Today a growing number of y[...] physicians take up this style of practice, at least for a time, without commitment to a community. Another response of some physicians is to withdraw from the managed care fray through the development of "concierge" practice, whereby they assure their availability 24 hours a day, 7 days a week to provide care for a smaller number of more affluent patients. In return for an annual fee, these patients can expect ready access to their physician through cell phones or paging devices.[8] They can also expect to have up to hour-long physician visits if needed. Still another effect of managed care has been the decline of charity care by physicians struggling with restricted time with patients and increasing financial pressures. In regions with high HMO penetration, charity care has declined precipitously.[9]

All of these trends threaten already compromised access to care in many parts of the country. Concierge practices may serve upper-income patients well, but decrease the number of physicians providing care to minorities and lower-income patients, typically with more serious clinical problems. As more physicians become so dissatisfied that they take early retirement and leave practice altogether, the physician workforce will have even less capacity to provide safety net care. At the other end of the pipeline, the trends are no more promising. The pool of applicants to U.S. medical schools has dropped from two applicants for every position to 1.5 in recent years. Fewer graduating medical students are opting for residency training and careers in the primary care specialties, thus further weakening the nation's capability to provide comprehensive care for a growing and aging population.[10]

CUTBACKS IN ALREADY UNDERFUNDED PROGRAMS

The federal budget has shifted from surplus to a soaring deficit as the nation confronts terrorism abroad, addresses homeland security, and deals with an economic slowdown. Recent cuts in Medicare have impacted both facilities and providers. Hospitals, nursing homes and physicians now commonly lose money on service provided to Medicare patients. Some facilities will be forced to close,

and many physicians are closing their practices to Medicare patients.
Medicare payments to physicians were reduced by about 5% in
January 2002. Although Congress agreed to change the Medicare
reimbursement formula in March 2003, amounting to a 1.6%
increase in 2003,[11] and a 1.5% increase in 2004,[12] it remains uncer-
tain whether serious access problems exacerbated by physicians
refusing to see Medicare patients, can be avoided for Medicare beneficiaries.[13]

The situation for Medicaid patients is even more worrisome.
The states have to balance their budgets, and are struggling with
major deficits. They tend to base their physician payment schedules
on Medicare levels. Reimbursement in some states is lower than
Medicare levels—in Mississippi, payments were reduced in early
2002 from 90% to 85% of Medicare levels.[14] In Washington State,
legislators are facing up to a $700 million deficit for its Medicaid and
Basic Health Plan programs over the next two years, with the state's
economy in a major downturn and an unemployment rate of over
6.5%. Sharp cuts in enrollment and benefits are inevitable.[15]

PHYSICIAN RETREAT FROM MEDICARE AND MEDICAID

The Community Tracking Study mentioned earlier found that
about 18% of the 12,000 plus U.S. physicians surveyed in 1996-1997
were no longer willing to take new Medicare patients. A recent
analysis of the general/family practice group found that dissatisfaction with practice was closely correlated with refusal to see both
Medicare and Medicaid patients.[16] Obviously, the more Medicare
patients in a given practice, the greater the impact on the practice
and the more likely that it may withdraw from the program.

More recent surveys give more disturbing findings concerning
declining access for Medicare and Medicaid patients, but even they
underestimate the impact of budget cuts on access since they pre-
cede the latest round of federal and state cuts in 2002. The latest survey of the Community Tracking Study found that the proportion of
physicians accepting new Medicare patients had dropped from 72%
in 1997 to 68% in 2001.[17] Here are more specific examples of the
extent to which physicians are less available to Medicare and

Medicaid patients. Current figures are necessarily anecdotal, but these examples are alarming.

- 22% of family physicians nationally now refuse to take new Medicare patients according to a 2002 report by the American Academy of Family Physicians.[18]
- A recent survey of 30 states by the Medicare Rights Center found that residents in New Hampshire, Rhode Island, Virginia, Tennessee, Missouri, Texas, New Mexico and Arizona are having difficulties in finding a physician who will accept new Medicare patients.[19]
- The percentage of physicians accepting new Medicare patients in Seattle dropped from 71% in 1997 to only 54% in 2001.[20]
- The Marshfield Clinic in Wisconsin, with over 600 physicians in the largest multispecialty group practice in the state, may have to cancel plans for a new statewide Medicare Choice HMO. Medicare reimbursement, even before the 5% cut in 2002, covered only 70% of the cost of providing care to Medicare patients.[21]
- In a large group practice in Chattanooga, Tennessee, 60 of 70 physicians who care for adults no longer will accept new Medicare patients.[22]
- A multispecialty group of 50 physicians in Bellingham, Washington, recently closed its doors to new Medicare and Medicaid patients, leaving the immediate community of 70,000 without any practices accepting new Medicare patients.[23]
- In California, back in 1998, 45% of primary care physicians and 43% of specialists reported no Medi-Cal patients in their practices; in view of the trends, those numbers would surely be higher today; below-cost reimbursement and burdensome paperwork were found to underlie physician dissatisfaction with the program.[24]

What these reimbursement cuts mean to physicians with many patients on Medicare or Medicaid is well reflected by this family physician's experience in rural Pikeville, Kentucky. Dr. Baretta Casey, 48 , established practice in an underserved Appalachian community, where Medicare patients make up 60% of her practice. Overhead expenses are typically about 65% of practice revenues in family practice, even before the latest surge in costs of professional liability insurance. Dr. Casey stopped taking new Medicare patients when reimbursement was cut in January 2002. Because many private insurers also link their reimbursement to Medicare rates, the impact on her practice was severe. As Dr. Casey said, "For the last five years, I've watched my income go down and my expenses go up."[25]

IMPACTS OF CUTBACKS ON ACCESS TO CARE

The growing elderly population in the U.S. is of course at risk for one and usually more chronic diseases, which require ongoing primary care with continuity for the best outcomes. Medicaid enrollees likewise need continuity with a primary care provider to manage and coordinate care for the kinds of medical problems at the core of Medicaid's mission—pregnancy, blindness, and total disability from injury or advanced chronic disease. We have already seen that the uninsured, especially those with relatively low incomes, are also at risk for worse outcomes of care due to less access to the system.

The Kaiser Family Foundation has found that the uninsured have more than a three-fold more difficult time in getting an appointment with their usual provider on short notice (Figure 9.2). More than three-quarters of the uninsured with serious health problems are also likely to go without care or have difficulty in seeing a specialist.[26] The problem of access for patients with mental health disorders is even more difficult, as shown by the findings of a survey of over 5,000 primary care physicians by the Center for Studying Health System Change. It found that high quality mental health services, whether outpatient or inpatient, could be obtained less than half of the time.[27]

Access to care through emergency rooms has also become more difficult, even when the presenting problem is of serious and urgent nature. Although one emergency room patient in four needs specialist care, specialists are less available to many emergency rooms around the country. A survey by the California Medical Association found that 80% of specialists report reimbursement problems for

Figure 9.2

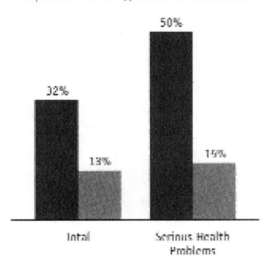

It Is Harder for the Uninsured to Get an Appointment with their Usual Provider on Short Notice

■ Uninsured   ■ Privately Insured

Percent Reporting It Is Somewhat, Very Difficult, or Impossible to Get an Appointment on Short Notice

Source: Kaiser Survey of Family Health Experiences, Round 3, 1997–1998.

Reprinted with permission from Kaiser Commission on Medicaid and the Uninsured. In Their Own Words: The uninsured talk about living without health insurance. Kaiser Family Foundation, September 2000: 41.

emergency department work, while 40% have reduced their frequency of call and 20% have stopped taking any call at all.[28] A 2001 study of California orthopedic surgeons found that 47 of 50 offices contacted refused to treat callers for a broken arm.[29]

It is becoming clear that the concept of a "safety net" in health care is more an illusion than a reality. Many patients with serious and urgent medical problems fall right through it every day in the U.S. Unfortunately, this growing problem is still below the radar screen of public awareness. We have an enormous public education challenge before effective political action can effectively reform this flawed system. As we shift gears with Part III, where we will examine alternatives and approaches to reform, this observation from a September 2000 *Consumer Reports* article correctly identifies the political problem:[30]

> *Few would say the current system works well. But the status quo benefits powerful stakeholders—insurance companies that want to protect their right to insure only people who will make money for them; doctors, hospitals, and drug companies that fear a different system might lower their incomes and profits; large employers that want to protect their exemptions from state requirements that help patients; small employers that want to avoid buying coverage for their workers; state governments that want to avoid ongoing financial commitments; and many people with insurance who fear they will lose their generous benefits.*

PART III

CHAPTER TEN

IS BASIC HEALTH CARE
A RIGHT?

Now that South Africa has legislated universal access to medical services, the United States remains the only industrialized or second-tier country in the world that fails to guarantee its citizens access to medical services. This is a curious omission for a country based on rights and liberty. It is equally strange from an economic and business point of view. For while foreign competitors get full medical benefits at one-third the cost, American employers are weighed down by ever-growing expense for health care.

—Donald W. Light, Professor, Social and Behavioral Sciences, University of Medicine and Dentistry of New Jersey[1]

Although the right to health care has been a hotly debated topic in the United States for more than 50 years, it remains an abstraction that gives no comfort to the many millions of people without access. As Professor Light observes above, this country remains the "odd man out" in the Western world as pro-market forces hold sway in perpetuating the status quo. Whenever a proposal for universal access is raised that would assure a basic right to health care, the political debate becomes mired in the polarized positions of the opposing factions. No holds are barred as well heeled stakeholders in the market-based system lobby legislators and public opinion with disinformation and scare tactics. The debate over the right to health care has become further confused as it has shifted to various kinds of patients' rights unrelated to access to basic health care, such as the right to sue your HMO. As a result, there is now widespread confusion about patient rights and health care. The issues are both simple and complex. This chapter will attempt to make some sense of the subject.

WHAT DO WE MEAN BY
A RIGHT TO HEALTH CARE?

Several kinds of rights to health care can be distinguished, each with very different meanings. The strongest right to health care is of a general, even constitutional type, as is seen in most industrialized Western countries, whereby all citizens are assured the right to be a patient, to have access to basic health care services. A second type of right to health care is established by contract as an employee of a company which provides an insurance plan or as a member of a health maintenance organization. Another kind of right is created by legislation as an entitlement, such as the right of veterans to care by the Veterans Health Administration or the right of people over 65 years of age to care under the Medicare program. Still another type of right is a moral one. As the director of the "Right to Health Care" project of the American Association for the Advancement of Science said ten years ago.[2]

> *The right to health care is fundamentally an ethical issue that raises major questions about the relationship and sense of obligation of members of society to each other, and the role of the government in terms of the expectations of the social covenant.*

The U.S. has so far kept well clear of enacting any general right to health care, instead focusing on various legislative attempts to provide care for specific groups. Examples include provisions for general medical care for convicted and confined prison inmates,[3] uninsured children (CHIP program);[4] right to emergency care,[5] and the right to psychiatric treatment for involuntarily committed patients with mental disorders.[6]

The last 30 years in the U.S. have seen a strong movement to establish many kinds of individual and group rights in health care, which have obscured the more basic need for a general right to health care. The list of such rights is a long one, and bears on such matters as informed consent, privacy and confidentiality, access to medical records, refusal of medical treatment, abortion, and emergency care.[7] The latest example is the ongoing debate in Congress over a Patients' Bill of Rights, intended particularly to address abuses of insurers and managed care organizations. Larry Churchill, an ethicist at the University of Notre Dame, points out the downside our national obsession with rights language in fostering the individual and private notion of self without regard for other views or the needs of other groups. Thus, we see the diametrically opposed constituencies of those demanding "reproductive rights" versus those pushing "right-to-life" for the unborn.[8] As Molly Ivins, well known Texas-based syndicated columnist, succinctly sums up: "A Patients' Bill of Rights is not the answer. It won't provide health insurance for a single additional individual."[9]

HOW REAL ARE RIGHTS TO HEALTH CARE?

Many so-called rights to health care vanish in their lack of structure, resources, or commitment for implementation. This can be seen on many levels. At the global level, for example, the General Assembly of the United Nations adopted this resolution in 1948 as part of its Universal Declaration of Human Rights:[10]

> *Everyone has the right to a standard of living adequate for the health and well-being of himself and his family, including food, clothing, housing and medical care and necessary social services, and the right to security in the event of unemployment, sickness, disability, widowhood, old age or other lack of livelihood in circumstances beyond his control.*

In its Declaration on the Rights of Patients, the World Health Organization (WHO) later adopted a similar universal right to health care,[11] and even added such a broad definition of health that it became at once impractical and unattainable. How could this abstract definition of health, laudable as its intent is, possibly be attained in the real world?

> *Health is a state of complete physical, mental and social well-being and not merely the absence of disease or infirmity.[12] The WHO set a goal for "attainment by all people of the highest possible level of health"[13]*

These lofty international goals for rights to health care can best be described as aspirational, not actual.

ome, legislative attempts to provide rights to health
taged groups also frequently fall short of their goals.
any examples in earlier chapters where potential
beneficiaries failed to qualify for coverage in states which
income levels for eligibility too low. Even if eligible for Medicaid,
the patient so covered may encounter "entitlement without availability" if physicians in the area refuse Medicaid patients.[14] A classic example whereby a state can effectively veto the intent of federal legislation is seen in Alabama, where the state legislature failed to
provide funding for the state's hospitals providing treatment for the
mentally ill, thus forcing closure of a federal court monitor's office
established by the federal government to enforce minimal constitutional standards for their care.[15]

In order to be real, the right to health care is a two-way street
requiring obligations on the part of the patient as well as the guar-
antor of such a right. For both parties, these include "the duty to
respect and be sensitive to the health care needs of others, responsibility for meeting the needs of the most vulnerable and disadvantaged members of society, and individual limits on claims to a reasonable and affordable level of health care."[16]

THE DEBATE OVER
UNIVERSAL ACCESS AS A RIGHT

A brief outline of some common objections to universal coverage to health care, whether national or by state, gives us the flavor
of strongly held views on both sides of the issue. They can be rough-
ly divided into three areas—political, economic and moral.[17]

Political Objections

1. "Everyone gets care anyway, so what's the problem?"

Although this is a widely held misperception among many people fortunate enough to have health insurance, we have already seen
abundant evidence that the "safety net" is in tatters. Each month
brings more reports of how inaccessible the present system is to

many millions of people. A recent study by the Kaiser Family Foundation, for example, found that three of five uninsured women, and two in five women in fair or poor health, delayed or went without care they felt they needed because of costs.[18]

2. "A general right to health care would lead to rationing"

This is another common misperception, again held by a large number of people with health insurance who are used to getting any health care service they desire. What they don't realize is that health care is already rationed in this country, mostly by class and income level. The most common mechanisms of rationing today include the unaffordability of health insurance for many, as well as decisions about coverage of specific services by public and private insurers and managed care organizations. Just one example—managed mental health programs often have overly restrictive policies for hospitalization and detoxification for alcoholism, such as requiring delirium tremens ("DTs," which carries significant mortality) before approval of hospital admission.[19] Stakeholders in our private, mostly for-profit health care system perpetuate the myth that rationing is neither common, necessary, nor moral, even by raising the specter of the "R-word" when proposals for universal health insurance are raised.

3. "Universal access would enslave physicians and other providers"

Some opponents of a general right to health care worry that the rights of physicians and other providers will be infringed upon if they are expected to provide care for all comers.[20] The counter-argument, of course, is that medicine traditionally claims a "social contract" to render care to patients regardless of their circumstances, that the Hippocratic oath lends centuries of moral standing to this claim, and that physicians and other health professionals are usually beneficiaries of public funding in their own training, as well as from reimbursement for care of patients in public sector programs.

4. "A general right to health care would bring a government takeover and socialized medicine"

This is another common scare tactic used by stakeholders, especially the American Medical Association, on many occasions over the years. "Socialized medicine" is a hot button term used by pro-market interests to denigrate the public sector in health care. As we will see in later chapters, however, universal coverage either by states or by national health insurance would be socialized *insurance*, not socialized delivery of care. Physicians could remain in private practice, with reimbursement through a negotiated fee schedule. Hospitals could still be privately owned and operated under a negotiated global annual budget. The difference would be that health care would be redefined as an essential social good, not primarily a commodity for sale on the private market. Thus access to health care would be assured for the whole population, not just certain groups, such as the Veterans Health Administration for veterans. Health care would join other essential services, including public education, police and fire protection.

Economic Objections

1. "Health care is not a right; it is best distributed in the open marketplace"

This classic position of laissez-faire economics, as put forward by Robert Sade and others, holds that the free market is the least restrictive and most supportive of individual rights, while preserving the rights of physicians and other health professionals to dispense their services as they please.[21] The concept of "market justice,"[22] however, breaks down on at least three counts: (1) sick or injured individuals, because they usually cannot earn what they could if healthy, are already compromised as free agents in the marketplace; (2) the usual laws of supply and demand do not work in health care; and (3) "to each according to ability to pay" implies that only those who can afford to pay are deserving of care.[23,24] Edmund Pellegrino, physician, ethicist, and medical philosopher, has argued for years that the profit motive of the marketplace subverts the fiduciary nature of the healing professions and the goal of social justice in health care.[25]

2. "The free market in health care is the most fair and efficient"

This argument is central to the thinking of for-profit interests in the marketplace which claim fairness (only if you can pay) and efficiency through competition. Yet health care economists have recognized for many years that there is no free market in health care, which differs from other markets in important ways. For example, employees with health insurance are largely protected from the full costs of insurance coverage, private insurers compete to cover low-risk subscribers by experience rating (thereby avoiding higher risk sick subscribers), and patients usually don't have the same amount of information available about price and quality of health care services as they would if buying a car.[26,27] In addition, as we shall see in the next chapter, for-profit care has repeatedly been found to have higher costs and lower quality than not-for-profit care, making it less, not more efficient in delivering care.

3. "How can we afford the increased costs if health care becomes a general right?"

Behind this question is a widespread misperception based on the assumption that providing universal coverage to the entire population will necessarily increase health care costs. All the evidence, however, is to the contrary. It is now well documented that cost *savings*, not increases, would result if the risk pool of those covered by government insurance were enlarged to the entire population. The main reason, of course, would result from elimination of the enormous overhead and profits (totalling about 25% of the health care dollar) generated by the mostly for-profit insurance industry. Recent studies show that $280 billion would be saved each year through administrative simplification under a national health insurance program.[28,29] Recent studies of single-payer insurance proposals in several states also show projected annual cost savings (e.g., $8 billion in California[30] and $118 million in Vermont[31]). Moreover, if solid clinical science were the basis for deciding what medical services to provide, (i.e., those shown to be effective), the population could achieve better clinical outcomes through less care. That this would be likely is strongly suggested by the results of a 1998 study by investigators at RAND and the University of California, Los Angeles. After analyzing all available studies in the U.S. of the quality of preventive, acute, and chronic health care, they found that 30% of people receive contraindicated (i.e., not medically indicated) acute care and 20% receive contraindicated chronic care.[32] In other words, if all of the contraindicated care could be eliminated, costs would be saved while improving quality of care at the same time.

Moral Objections

1. "Moral individualism trumps distributive justice"

This is the premise of libertarians as illustrated by Robert Nozick's book *Anarchy, State and Utopia*. As a libertarian theorist, he was not willing to acknowledge that any person or group should have the responsibility or authority to make decisions which allocate resources for the common good. Thus, any attempt to distribute physicians on the basis of public need violates physicians' autonomy and individual rights, whose rights should trump the collective good.[33] This, of course, is a classic confrontation between the individual and societal perspective, and this book already is full of evidence that more, not less, of the societal perspective will be required if we are ever to address the inequities and lack of fairness in today's non-system.

2. "A right to health care is undeserved by individuals practicing high-risk behaviors"

This has been called the "merit argument" against a general right to health care, which questions whether individuals who of their own volition put themselves at high risk for disease and injury, deserve unfettered access to health care. Why should people who ride motorcycles without helmets, smoke, or drink excessively merit the same right to care as those individuals who take more responsibility for their own health? [34] Robert Veach has proposed that individuals who practice high-risk lifestyles should somehow be taxed for putting the public purse at higher risk.[35] The merit argument, however breaks down in the details. For example, how could a fair and accurate merit system be developed and applied for all of the risks that are assumed every day by individuals? To what extent do their individual behaviors contribute to their own costs of care? The merit argument readily leads to a "blame the victim" attitude toward the sick and injured, which tends to define their health problems as problems caused by individual behavioral failures.[36]

WHAT ARE THE LIMITS TO A RIGHT TO HEALTH CARE?

A recent movie, *John Q*, has been a smashing box office success in dramatizing problems of access to health care. Although it is an overdrawn caricature of the issues, it strikes a sensitive public nerve, with audiences often shouting back at the screen. Denzel Washington plays a Chicago machinist who demands a heart transplant for his son who has collapsed on the ballfield. When told that his insurance won't cover a $250,000 transplant, Washington locks a cardiac surgeon and other patients in the emergency room and threatens their lives if his son doesn't get his transplant.[37] The movie exposes widely held public anger about access to health care, as well as frequently inflated expectations of care. Larry Churchill sharpens up the issues in these helpful terms:[38]

> ... A right to health care based on need means a right to equitable access based on need alone to all effective care society can reasonably afford.
>
> ...Effective care means that there is no obligation to provide useless or marginally useful treatments.
>
> ...A right to health care is not a license to demand care. It is not a right to the very best available or even to all one may need. Some very pressing health needs may have to be neglected because meeting them would be unreasonable in the light of other health needs or social priorities. Health care is unique among needs and should enjoy a high place among our basic requirements for life. This does not mean that it should displace all else. My right to a kidney transplant, say, is circumscribed by a wide variety of factors, which are ultimately decisions for society to make about the importance of this procedure: the number of qualified surgeons it trains, the network for histolog-

ical matching it supports, the decision to have optional or assumptive kidney donor policies, and on and on.

It is an ongoing challenge to define the limits of effective care as it can be afforded for the population. Defining *medical necessity* has become a contentious process as insurers and other payers increasingly make these decisions on the basis of cost without regard to clinical effectiveness. Some have called for national legislation to assure close linkage between definitions of medical necessity for individual patients and currently accepted professional standards of clinical practice.[39]

SO WHERE DOES THIS LEAVE US?

A general right to health care would go a long way to improve the present egregious barriers which exclude many millions of Americans from basic health care. This affluent country could well afford to enact a system of universal access. Opponents to such a system raise objections reflecting their own self-interest in the current pro-market system. These objections can readily be countered.

The debate over a general right to health care remains entirely unsettled in this country. The most basic ethical questions are nowhere close to being resolved, such as the relative importance of the individual versus societal perspective or whether or not the care of sick, injured and disabled people should be a for-profit industry. As William Ruddick, a philosopher at New York University, observes: "If a general right to health care turns, as it seems, on our conceptions of money, power, illness, chance, and inequality, then consensus is unlikely."[40]

The status quo in U.S. health care is unfair for millions, and there is an urgent need for a broader reaction of outrage calling for real reform. Former Senator Patrick Moynihan has said, "a society that loses its sense of outrage is doomed to extinction."[41] Churchill adds this observation:[42]

> *A health care system which neglects the poor and disenfranchized impoverishes the social order of which we are constituted. In a real (and not just hortatory) sense, a health care system is no better than the least well-served of its members.*

CHAPTER ELEVEN

CORPORATE HEALTH CARE AND THE PUBLIC INTEREST

As we saw in the last chapter, stakeholders in the present health care marketplace make a strong claim to fairness of the free market (not if you can't afford it!), as well as increased efficiency through competition. Since there continues to be a widespread belief in the market-based system, fueled by stakeholders and their lobbyists, it is time to examine just how well an unfettered market approach to health care serves the public interest. We will look at four major industries within health care—HMOs, hospitals, the pharmaceutical industry, and the insurance industry—as examples of corporatization, which has transformed U.S. health care in recent years (for the worse). Our focus will be upon for-profit, investor-owned corporations, which increasingly dominate the health care marketplace.

CASE PROFILES OF INVESTOR-OWNED, FOR-PROFIT INDUSTRIES

Health Maintenance Organizations (HMOs)

Stephen Parrino, a 34-year-old deputy district attorney, was diagnosed with a brain tumor. Lacking the required specialty services in the area, his HMO authorized referral to Loma Linda University Medical Center in Southern California. Surgical removal of the tumor was successful, and the treating physicians ordered proton-beam therapy no later than 7 to 10 days after surgery. Although proton radiation was being reimbursed by Medicare, Medicaid, and 52 insurance companies at the time, Stephen's HMO denied treatment on the basis of it being an "experimental, unapproved and not medically necessary treatment not within managed care guide-lines." Despite many calls to the HMO and a threatened law-suit, the HMO continued to deny the treatment. Seven weeks after surgery, the HMO finally sought a second opinion, which confirmed the need for proton radiation. Repeat studies revealed metastatic disease beyond treatment. Stephen died soon there-after, and the denial was brought to a state court by his estate.

The HMO claimed ERISA (Employee Retirement Income Security Act) preemption. (ERISA was enacted in 1974 with the intent to regulate employer-sponsored pension plans, to set uniform national standards for health benefits and to protect employees from loss or abuse of their benefits. Ironically, ERISA also pre-empted state regulation of managed care organizations. As a result, physicians, patients, and state regulators are hamstrung in challenging coverage decisions of many HMOs.[1-2]) In Stephen's case, the case was moved to a U.S. District Court, where a remand motion was denied. Later appeals confirmed the ERISA preemption, which protected the HMO from suit.[3]

The above vignette illustrates many of the abuses of HMOs as they pursue profits by avoiding needed care. This kind of case has become so commonplace over the last 15 years that a nationwide backlash to these abuses has been mounted by the public and joined by politicians and legislators at state and federal levels. A 1999 book by Jamie Court and Francis Smith, *Making a Killing: HMOs and the Threat to Your Health*, provides a scathing and well-documented exposé of the abuses of many for-profit HMOs.[3]

HMOs can be categorized along a spectrum of clearcut differences of motivation and values. Some not-for-profit HMOs such as Group Health Cooperative of Puget Sound, tend to be more socially oriented, with an emphasis on prevention, patient education, evidence-based practice, and cost effective care. For-profit HMOs (about two-thirds of all HMOs) fall toward the other end of the spectrum, driven by the market and the interests of their investors with a strong focus on managing costs rather than care. Typical practices of for-profit HMOs have included financial risk sharing with physicians, avoidance of sick enrollees, barriers to specialist referral and hospitalization, and firing of high-utilizing physicians (i.e., those who order too many tests or spend too much time with patients.)[4] These practices have led Robert Kuttner, a well-known health care analyst, to this observation:[5]

> For more than a decade, "market-driven health care" has been advertised as the salvation of the American health care system. In the 1990s, entrepreneurs succeeded in obtaining the easily available cost savings, at great profit to themselves and their investors. By the late 1990s, however, pressure to protect profit margins had led to such dubious business strategies as the avoidance of sick patients, the excessive micromanagement of physicians, the worsening of staff-to-patient ratios, and the outright denial of care. In an industry driven by investor-owned companies, the original promise of managed care—greater efficiency in the use of available resources and greater integration of preventive and treatment services—has degenerated into mere avoidance of cost.

If you still believe in the integrity of for-profit HMOs as servants of the public interest, consider these examples of self-serving behavior of large organizations.

- As the incoming medical director of Humana, one of the nation's largest, for-profit HMOs, Dr. Linda Peeno was oriented to her job as "medical consultant" by an accountant in these words: "We take in a premium; we use about 10–15% to run the business, and we try to keep as much as possible of the rest. Your job is to help us do that."[6]
- Humana subcontracts medical necessity decisions for hysterectomies to a separate for-profit company motivated to deny as many requests as possible.[7]
- Medicare HMOs have been found to "routinely" mislead seniors about benefits, to grossly inflate their administrative charges to Medicare, and to make widespread fraudulent claims to Medicare; in one instance, the Department of Health and Human Services had to expel 80 private for-profit mental health centers from the program.[8]
- Poor quality HMOs are more than three times as likely as higher quality HMOs to stop reporting their quality data to the National Committee for Quality Assurance.[9]
- Faced with the exodus of large numbers of Medicare

HMOs from the market, the new head of Medicare, Thomas Scully (former president of the American Federation of Hospitals and Health Systems, a for-profit health industry trade group) announced in 2002 new Medicare HMO regulations allowing them to drop out of certain communities without leaving the entire county and to develop special benefit packages whereby they can better cherry-pick profitable markets.[10]

- Some state governments turn their Medicaid funds over to private corporations to manage their Medicaid programs. Managed Healthcare Systems (MHS) was a for-profit HMO operating in New York and New Jersey which was found by government regulators to be conducting clinics largely staffed by unsupervised physician assistants and nurse practitioners, while placing barriers to physician visits; now a billion-dollar company under a new name, AmeriChoice Corp, a settlement of more than $2 million was recently repaid to the Medicaid program for services never provided.[11]

- A common but little-known practice called a "carve out" allows insurers to deliver the least amount of care for the maximal financial return while skirting around mental health parity laws; through such a "carve out," an HMO contracts to insure the employees of a large corporation, then turns around and sub-contracts with a for-profit behavioral health company (often for as little as 25 cents per enrollee per month) to provide mental health services. However, as Dr. Rodrigo Munoz, a psychiatrist and president of the San Diego County Medical Society, notes "The only way these firms can make money is by making it virtually impossible for those in need to get treatment; visits to psychiatrists are limited in number and time (typically just 20 minutes) and patients are often prematurely discharged from hospitals without arrangements for adequate follow-up."[12]

After a decade of turmoil, mergers, bankruptcies and consolidation among HMOs as they struggle against public reaction to their practices, for-profit HMOs are re-emerging as a profitable oligopoly with more clout in the marketplace. By eliminating unprofitable subsidiaries, withdrawing from unprofitable markets, and raising their premiums and administrative fees by double-digit increases, they have won plaudits from Wall Street and their investors. Over the first four months of 2002 the Standard and Poor's managed care index climbed 21% as compared to a drop of 4.8% for the S&P 500 index in that period. One large for-profit HMO, WellPoint Health Networks, Inc. of Thousand Oaks, California (the parent of Blue Cross of California) posted a 46% increase in its first-quarter profit in 2002 compared to 2001. All of these HMOs track their "medical loss ratio" (the cost of providing health care services divided by premiums collected) as a key performance indicator. WellPoint is among the leaders on this index at just under 81%.[13] Quite a different performance indicator concerns the behavior of Medicare Plus Choice HMOs that sought increased reimbursement from Medicare to stabilize their programs. After an estimated $1 billion increase in payment for 2001, only a few such programs increased benefits or re-entered the market while more than 80% did not apply the money to benefits at all.[14] Almost 2.4 million seniors were abandoned by their Medicare HMOs as they withdrew from the market, forcing many to find another primary care physician.[15] Medicare HMOs that continued into 2003 were expected to increase premiums or reduce benefits, or both.[16]

As for-profit HMOs aggressively "cherrypick" the market for the healthiest, lowest risk enrollees, they find support from employers (who want to minimize premium increases while trading off comprehensive benefits) and younger, healthier individuals (who seek the lowest premiums on the assumption that they will not need a broader range of benefits). This progressive segmentation of the risk pool threatens the long-term viability of even the most successful, value-driven not-for-profit HMOs. As the nation's largest non-profit HMO and hospital system, Kaiser Permanente is now facing adverse selection within its aging population. As noted by George Halvorson, Kaiser's new CEO: "These shifts in the marketplace will cause many of our healthiest members to leave us for lower-cost, lower-benefit plans. At the same time, employers will save money if their sicker patients voluntarily migrate to us."[17]

Hospitals

Mergers and acquisitions have been the major trend in recent years throughout the hospital industry as hospitals struggled against declining reimbursement from payers, together with declining daily census in many cases.[18] According to an analyst at Bank of America Securities, many hospitals are doing better with higher reimbursements and have become attractive to large corporate purchasers. Not-for-profit hospitals typically sell at a price six times cash flow, while many for-profit chains are selling at 12 times cash flow, before takeover bonuses.[19] Since many hospital chains also own and manage facilities other than acute care hospitals (e.g., laboratories, rehabilitation, long-term care, and psychiatric services), the trend has a broader impact beyond acute care hospitals.[20]

Along with mergers, many U.S. hospitals have changed ownership, especially over the last 15 years. Almost one-third of all hospital conversions between 1990 and 1993 were from non-profit to for-profit ownership.[21] This trend led Molly Coye, former senior vice president of Good Samaritan Health System in San Jose, California, to this concern after her organization was sold to Columbia/HCA, the largest for-profit hospital chain, in 1996:[22]

> *Ultimately the advantages of a more industrialized model of hospital operations—concentrated capital, enormous purchasing leverage, national and regional market strength in contracting, rapid diffusion of technology and best practices in management, and the standardization of processes for quality improvement—have made formidable competitors of Columbia/HCA, Tenet, and other large for-profit systems. These advantages may lead to the demise of independently operated hospitals, whether for-profit or not-for-profit.*

Big insurance companies held the upper hand in controlling hospital charges during the early 1990s. Since then, the power to set hospital rates has shifted to the large for-profit hospital chains, which as an oligopoly, are helping to drive corporate healthcare costs upward, now rising at a rate four times as fast as that of overall inflation. These hospital chains seek to control market share in profitable communities, then assert their clout in rate setting against insurers as well as managed care organizations. As examples of this level of market control, two systems control more than 80% of hospital beds on Long Island, New York, while HCA and Tenet control almost 80% of beds in El Paso, Texas.[23]

In their pursuit of bottom line-profits, these large for-profit hospital corporations shed themselves of rural hospitals and other relatively non-profitable hospitals in communities where they elect not to dominate the local market. They defend their aggressive marketing strategy while claiming to increase efficiency, improve care, and eventually lower costs. These claims ring hollow, however, in the face of huge profits taken by the two largest for-profit hospital chains—HCA and Tenet—during the slowed economy of the last two years. The Nashville-based HCA (formerly Columbia/HCA), which was fined $840 million last year for Medicare fraud, reported a 47% increase in profits for the third quarter of 2001.[24] The Santa Barbara-based Tenet Healthcare (formerly National Medical Enterprises) reported a 41% increase in net income for the third quarter of fiscal 2002.[25] Both Tenet and its predecessor have paid fines and large settlements of almost $1 billion to resolve state/federal fraud investigations.[26] Meanwhile, CEO compensation reflects a robber baron mentality. The CEO of Tenet, for example, received a $3.4 million bonus in 2001 plus a salary of $1.2 million and stock options worth $10 million[27] while boasting at an investor conference that "We truly have leverage, and we're learning how to use it effectively."[28]

A quick look at Tenet's operational strategies sheds light on their values. As the nation's second largest for-profit hospital chain, Tenet owns and runs 116 hospitals in 17 states, including 33 in Southern California, where its more than 7,000 beds and 26,000 employees make it the largest private hospital operator in the region. It has severed relationships with low-paying HMOs and refuses capitation payments. It gets rid of underperforming hospitals and focuses especially on highly reimbursed services in the areas of cardiology, orthopedics, and neurology. It has a national marketing plan in large communities across Southern California, Texas, Louisiana, and South Florida where a growing population of aging baby boomers need these services.[29] After a series of crises over allegations of fraud and other misconduct made by various government agencies, Tenet in 2004 is in the process of selling more than one-quarter of its hospitals.[30]

Curiously, despite the obvious excesses of the corporate hospital industry, the federal courts have endorsed the industry's contention that consolidation is beneficial to the public. Federal and state antitrust enforcers have lost all seven cases tried since 1995 that challenged the benefits of hospital mergers. Ironically, judges have appeared to be sympathetic to hospitals doing battle against the evils of managed care, quite a turnaround since the inflated claims and expectations of HMOs 15 years ago.[31]

Unfortunately, the profit-driven value system that drives the for-profit side of the hospital industry permeates many other parts of the overall hospital industry. One invisible example is illustrated by for-profit hospital-owned purchasing groups. Two such groups are Premier, Inc. and Novation, each with the avowed mission to help almost 1,500 non-profit hospitals hold down costs by finding the best products at the lowest prices. However, these groups are mostly financed by companies that sell the medical products being purchased. Premier, Inc. has increased its spending by 84% over the last three years. Some hospital executives have questioned their accounts, especially concerning salaries, bonuses, and staffing. It appears that Premier and some of its executives received stock or options from medical supply companies in return for business. Premier's "executive team" each earn over $750,000 per year, including bonuses, but financial accounts remain murky.[32]

Pharmaceutical Industry

Spending for prescription drugs in the U.S. has been rising rapidly in recent years. In 2000, for example, expenditures for prescription drugs rose by 14.5% and accounted for almost one-third of the increase in medical costs, nearly equaling the costs of inpatient care.[33] In 2001, the pharmaceutical industry continued to lead all other industries in profitability as measured in the annual Fortune 500 report. During a year of recession, the overall profits of Fortune 500 companies declined by 53% in 2001, while the top 10 U.S. drug companies increased their profits by 33%. The drug industry's profits in 2000 soared to over eight times the median for all other industries in the country. As director of Public Citizen's Congress Watch, Frank Clemente has this to say:[34]

During a year in which there was much talk of sacrifice in the national interest, drug companies increased their astounding profits by hiking prescription prices, advertising some medicines more than Nike shoes, and successfully lobbying for lucrative monopoly patent extensions. Sometimes what's best for shareholders and CEOs isn't what's best for all Americans—particularly senior citizens who lack prescription drug insurance.

Some historical perspective on drug company profits is revealing. Over 40 years ago, Estes Kefauver (D-Tenn) led an investigation of the pharmaceutical industry by the Senate Judiciary Committee's subcommittee on antitrust and monopoly. The investigation found the same problems that exist today, as well as the same arguments used by the drug companies in attempting to justify their profits. The investigation documented pricing of drugs far higher than warranted by research and production costs, as well as prices much higher in the U.S. than abroad. Various reforms were proposed, including shortening of patents to three years and compulsory licensing, but were quickly killed in Congress as the drug industry lobbied hard against them.[35]

The pharmaceutical industry has repeatedly claimed that the high costs of research and development justify their prices, but their estimates of R&D costs are always grossly inflated. The Kefauver report found that drug companies spent about four times as much on promotion than on research in 1960. Today, the drug companies maintain that they spend an average of $800 million to develop a new product. Opportunity costs account for about one-half of that amount, and a majority of "new" drugs are excluded from that estimate.[36] An analysis by Public Citizen sets that figure closer to $110 million. Public Citizen has found, for example, that over 55% of the studies leading to the discovery and development of the top five selling drugs in 1995 were done by taxpayer-supported scientists funded through the National Institutes of Health.[37] Our best current estimates of drug industry expenditures and profit expressed as percentage of revenues, are profits (17%), marketing (15%), and research (6%), so that profits and marketing together are almost five times the amount devoted to research.[38]

Let's look briefly at some everyday practices of the drug companies to see if they can answer our question whether the industry serves itself or the public interest.

Gaming the Patent Laws

U.S. drug companies are protected by patents which provide a 17-year monopoly to manufacturers of new drugs. This monopoly ends up transferring money from consumers to the drug companies. The free market for prescription drugs around the world, including most nations with minimal or no drug patent laws, averages about one-quarter of the U.S. monopoly price. Since the U.S. spent about $106 billion on prescription drugs in 2000, consumers could have saved about $79 billion if this patent protection was eliminated.[39]

Drug companies have developed elaborate strategies to extend their patents and monopolies beyond the 17 years, including setting up diversionary patents on non-essential details of a drug's main patent to serve as a legal minefield and delay generics; filing of new patents for old drugs for "new" uses (which triggers a 30-month delay in generic completion); and filing a "citizen petition" to oppose generic competition.[40, 41] Regardless of how frivolous a drug company's lawsuit is against potential competitors, a loophole in federal law automatically delays the entry of a generic for 30 more months.[42]

Promotion of "Me Too" Drugs

Although the pharmaceutical industry keeps warning us that innovation will suffer if their revenues are cut, very few drugs out of the many brought to market each year are innovative. Most are variants of drugs already on the market without significant differences except their price. These "new drugs" can be developed at much lower cost than breakthrough drugs, then are heavily and disingenuously promoted as superior to their predecessor.[43] A good example is the heartburn drug Nexium, which Astra Merck is trying to market as a replacement (at over $4 per dose) for its blockbuster drug Prilosec, whose patent protection expired in late 2002. But there is no evidence that Nexium is better than Prilosec or its generic equivalent, omeprazole.

Battling Against Generic Drugs

Generic drugs are generally just as effective as their brand name counterparts, but much less expensive. For example, a 30-day supply of ibuprofen, a generic, cost just $7.99 in 2002 compared to $71.73 for the brand name Celebrex, while a 30-day supply of the generic Pepcid was $9.99 compared to $115.51 for the new prescription drug Nexium.[44]

The Drug Price Competition Act was passed by Congress in 1984 with the intent to foster competition between brand and generic drugs and promote the use of generic drugs. However, here's an example of what actually happens. In 2000, Abbott Laboratories contracted to pay a potential generic rival, Geneva Pharmaceuticals, $4.5 million a month (up to $101 million over the term of the contract) *not* to bring a generic to market.[45]

Suppress Negative Research Findings

Drug companies often go to extraordinary means to suppress or denigrate the reporting of research results that are unfavorable to their products. Here are just two of many examples that occur frequently. In 1999, Knoll Pharmaceuticals was fined $42 million by the federal government for making false claims that Synthroid was superior to generic thyroid hormone and for blocking information of negative research findings for seven years.[46] The company also settled a class action lawsuit for $135 million for that abuse.[47] A 1995 study found that short-acting calcium-channel blockers were associated with a 60% increase in risk of myocardial infarction compared to diuretics and beta-blockers.[48] In the following weeks and months, manufacturers of calcium-channel blockers tried to find out which journal was reviewing a followup manuscript and applied pressure through the principal investigator's dean to block its publication.[49]

Misleading and Devious Marketing

Restrictions on prescription drug advertising were loosened by the Food and Drug Administration (FDA) in 1997. Since then there has been a surge of drug advertising, which has played a major role in rising costs of prescription drugs.[50] Direct-to-consumer advertising has been expanding rapidly especially through television and print. Much of this marketing, however, has been misleading, even inaccurate. More than 500 prescription drug advertisements have been found by the FDA to violate federal laws and regulations since 1997. Unfortunately, however, the FDA lacks the authority to impose civil penalties for such violations, and the drug companies just stop the violative ad while launching a widely disseminated new one.[51]

Another little-known but widespread practice in the past several years involves marketing to patients through the back door of their pharmacies. Here's how this works. Drug companies pay drugstores to send letters to patients promoting their drugs. Pharmacies use their prescription drug records to develop letters that focus on drugs appropriate to these patients. As an example, a drug store chain in Florida contracted to contact 150,000 patients with such promotional letters over a six-month period (typical payments to drug stores range from $.85 to $1.50 for each letter and from $2.00 to $3.50 for each telephone call). This practice is being challenged in the courts as an intrusion of privacy, and represents an obvious conflict of interest between drug companies and pharmacies.[52] A subtle variant of this marketing ploy is the "health newsletter," point-of-purchase ads, paid for by drug companies, which are wrapped into warning labels which patients receive when picking up their prescriptions at the drugstore. This practice now blankets more than one-half of all chain drug store prescriptions filled in the U.S.[53]

Above and beyond these kinds of practices, the pharmaceutical industry is frequently found culpable of outright fraud. Two examples make the point. Manipulation of wholesale prices cost taxpayers almost $2 billion in 2001 due to fraudulent charges for drugs on government programs.[54] Two pharmaceutical giants incurred $725 million criminal fines in 2000, while six companies received civil fines of $335 million the same year to settle charges of vitamin price-fixing.[55]

Insurance Industry

The enormous private health insurance industry in the U.S., mostly for-profit, is bloated with administrative overhead, inefficiencies and inequities as it creams profits from enrollees. With more than 1,200 insurers in the country, the risk pool is widely fragmented, leaving sick people either with increasingly unaffordable insurance premiums, public coverage, or without insurance at all. In terms of market "efficiency," a recent study of more than 2,000 patients in greater Seattle found that they were covered by 189 different plans with 755 different policies.[56]

The costs of health insurance are soaring, and these are being passed on from insurers to employers, then on to consumers themselves with less coverage, higher deductibles, copayments and out-of-pocket expenditures. In 2001, the cost of employer-based insurance premiums increased by 11%, and a 2003 projection by Goldman Sachs projected similar premium increases for at least another two years.[57] In 2004, the average annual premium for a family of four is over $9,000 a year, about 21% of the national median household income of $42,409.[58] The Federal Employees Health Benefits Plan (FEHBP) covering federal employees as the largest employer-sponsored health plan in the country, saw a premium hike of over 13% in 2002. Some employers have been forced to deal with even higher insurance costs, such as the University of Miami, which was hit with a 45% increase from its carrier, United Healthcare.[59]

Profit-taking, without added value, by executives in for-profit health plans is obscene and socially irresponsible. According to a survey by Families USA of the top 10 publicly traded parent companies of for-profit health plans, the average compensation of top executives of United Health Group was over $14 million in 2000, plus $119 million in unexercised stock options.[60]

It was not always so. Before the 1970s, following the early traditions established by Blue Cross in the 1930s, "community rating" was the industry norm, by which risk was spread by charging the same premium to everyone within a geographical area. "Medical underwriting," whereby higher premiums are charged to individuals or groups at higher risk of being sick, was considered unethical.[61] Today, medical underwriting is the norm as for-profit insurers seek out the healthy and avoid the sick. The concept of insurance as a social enterprise has broken down to the self-interest of a huge for-profit industry. Two giant investor-owned Blue Cross companies, Anthem, Inc. and WellPoint Health Networks, together cover more than 30% of 84 million Blue Cross enrollees nationwide.[62]

Here are some of the practices of the health insurance industry today which add to the industry's coffers at the expense of patient care.

Re-Underwriting

Shaneen and her husband were paying $417 a month for

*health insurance when she was diagnosed with breast cancer in
1996. Their premiums were increased each year, up to $1,881
per month by fall, 2000, even though her disease was in remis-
sion. The insurer, American Medical Security Group Inc. told
her these rate increases were necessary "because of your dread
disease."*[63]

This is a classic example of "re-underwriting," whereby premiums are increased each year if the enrollee becomes sick, files more
claims, or develops a higher risk of future claims. The overriding
goal of this practice is to maximize profits by minimizing financial
risk and the "loss ratio," the percentage of each premium dollar paid
out in claims. By means of this strategy, American Medical Security
was able to drop its medical loss ratio from over 80% in 1999 to less
than 73% in 2001 while insuring fewer people at higher profit.[64]

Cancellation of Policies

When an insurer incurs an unprofitable loss ratio for a group of
patients, it may elect to drop coverage for the entire group. This is
what happened to 100,000 people in the Southeast, insured by the
Mid-South Health Plan, with six months given to find other coverage (which sick individuals often find unavailable or unaffordable).[65]

Out-of-State Sales

Another marketing ploy used by some insurers is to avoid state
insurance regulations by setting up an administrative base in a state
with lax regulations. Thus 13 of 21 individual insurance companies
that sell policies in Florida, which on occasion disallows premium
rate increases, do so through out-of-state groups.[66]

Short-Term Coverage

With the unemployment rate at its highest level over the last
eight years, a new and highly profitable niche has quietly opened in
the health insurance market—short-term policies aimed at healthy
people. These plans don't cover pre-existing conditions and offer no
continuing protection.[67]

Tiering of Benefits

Another increasingly common practice by insurers is to charge extra co-payments for selected groups of hospitals or physicians. Insurers may have several tiers of hospitals and physicians, and changes in these "preferred" lists may occur frequently and without warning. Thus a patient may be charged as much as $400 per day more for hospitalization in the "best" hospital, which may have been in the policy's small print or a new change in the policy.[68]

There is massive waste throughout the health insurance industry which we, as consumers, get to pay for through higher premiums. This overview speaks volumes, from a recent review by Peter Frishauf of a new book by J.D. Kleinke *Oxymorons: The Myth of a U.S. Health Care System:*[69, 70]

> *Parasitic middlemen, pointless regulation, and waste suck billions of dollars from premiums that could be redeployed to pay for care. Kleinke identifies 2 intertwined constituencies as prime culprits: the 5,000 state insurance bureaucrats who preside over a "mess of state-based benefit mandate laws," and 50,000 health insurance brokers "in bed with them." The brokers, I was astounded to learn; collect commissions ranging from 3% to as much as 20% of the total cost of plans—a "shadow tax" of some $300 billion per year on premiums, more than twice what the nation spends on all prescription drugs! Insurance companies, it seems, have been unable to break the stranglehold of brokers, and those that attempt to offer plans without brokers face massive retaliation.*

And, as we have seen with the other for-profit health care industries profiled earlier, fraud is an ever-present part of the picture. Since 1993, the federal government has recovered more than $400 million in settlements from insurance companies making false Medicare claims.[71] The U.S. Department of Labor now has 102 civil and 17 criminal investigations pending involving fraudulent practices of multiple health plans sold to employers in a number of states.[72]

Although some of these abuses have become more recognized in recent years, incremental attempts by Congress to enact safeguards continue to prove ineffective. A good example is a law passed by Congress in 1996 forbidding charging higher rates for the sick than the healthy. The loophole is that the law expressly allows insurers to raise the rates of a group as a whole, thereby providing no protection against unaffordability of continued insurance.[73]

QUALITY OF CARE PROVIDED BY FOR-PROFIT VS NOT-FOR-PROFIT CORPORATIONS

We now see that for-profit health care is expensive, inefficient, and wasteful, but how about quality of care compared to the not-for-profit sector of health care? Table 11.1 displays a summary of the evidence confirming worse quality and higher costs in the for-profit sector.[74]

Table 11-1 INVESTOR-OWNED CARE Comparative Examples vs. Not-for-Profit Care	
Hospitals	Costs 3-13% higher, with higher overhead, fewer nurses and death rates 6 to 7 % higher[75-80]
HMOs	Higher overhead (25% to 33% for some of the largest HMOs), worse scores on 14 of 14 quality indicators reported to National Committee for Quality Assurance[81, 82]
Nursing homes	Lower staffing levels and worse quality of care (30% committed violations which caused death or life-threatening harm to patients)[83]
Dialysis centers	Death rates 30% higher, with 26% less use of transplants[84, 85]
Mental health centers	For-profit behavioral health companies impose restrictive barriers and limits to care (e.g., premature discharge from hospitals without adequate outpatient care)[86]

Source: Adapted with permission from American Board of Family Practice, Lexington, KY: In: Geyman JP. The corporate transformation of medicine and its impact on costs and access to care. *J Am Board Fam Pract* 16(5):449, 2003.

Beyond comparisons of mortality rates, recent studies of other quality measures confirm worse quality in for-profit plans, facilities and providers. One national study showed that investor-owned HMOs scored worse on all 14 indicators reported to the National Committee for Quality Assurance.[87] Another 2002 report compared enrollees' assessments of their care in for-profit and not-for-profit HMOs across the country. Within a study sample of over 13,000 people, enrollees in for-profit HMOs were more likely to report unmet needs or delayed care, organizational and administrative barriers to care, and higher out-of-pocket spending.[88]

THE HIDDEN WEB PERPETUATING CORPORATE SELF INTEREST

There is a veil of control over the health care system, riddled with conflicts of interest between for-profit corporations, regulators, and legislators. When one lifts this veil, it is no longer surprising that incremental legislative "reforms" are so ineffectual. Consider these examples to see if they pass your filter for conflict of interest:[89]

- Eli Lilly's corporate vice-president, who in 1999 testified against a Medicare prescription drug benefit (concern over price controls), was appointed Director of OMB in 2000.
- Two former top administrators of HCFA (now CMS, the Centers for Medicare and Medicaid Services) have joined the board of the for-profit dialysis company DaVita, which receives 60% of its revenue from Medicare and Medicaid.
- The chair until recently of HCFA resigned from DaVita's board to take the job and was the former president of the American Federation of Hospitals and Health Systems (a for-profit health industry trade group).
- The large accounting firm KMPG was involved with Columbia/HCA in defrauding Medicare from 1990 to 1992, then received government contracts to perform audits for Medicare and other federal health programs from 1997 to 2000.
- In a recent study of the development process for 44 practice guidelines, 90% of participating physicians were found to have financial ties to the pharmaceutical industry, with 60%

having financial ties to the companies whose drugs were considered or recommended by the guidelines.[90]
- More than one-half of the experts hired to advise the FDA
  on drug safety have ties to the pharmaceutical industry, such
  as helping a drug company develop a drug, serving on an
  FDA committee, evaluating it, or holding stock in the company.[91]
- One-half of the FDA's budget for the evaluation of new drugs
  is paid by drug companies' user fees, so that the FDA is
  dependent on the industry it regulates.[92] This co-dependen-
  cy has led to increased political pressure from industry for
  faster FDA approval of new drugs. As an example of this conflict of interest, a 2002 report from the General Accounting
  Office, an investigative branch of Congress, revealed occasions when physicians were precluded from presenting
  adverse drug information at FDA Advisory Committee meet-
  ings and even received harassing phone calls from industry.[93]

Lobbying and campaign contributions represent another big
part of the hidden web perpetuating corporate self-interest. Here are
more, well-documented examples of high-pressure lobbying, often
with obvious conflicts of interest:[94]

- During the campaign for the 2000 elections, the four co-
  sponsors of a bill in Congress, which would permit Medicare
  to negotiate drug prices for all 40 million beneficiaries, each
  faced $1 million advertising campaigns against them funded
  by the drug industry.
- Since 2001, the drug industry has an army of 623 lobbyists,
  typically on salaries of at least $12,000 per month, promoting
  bills to maintain or extend patent rights, shape a Medicare
  prescription drug benefit without price restrictions, and others in the industry's self-interest, while opposing those that
  threaten its profits (e.g., increased use of generics, reimport-
  ing of drugs from Canada at lower prices).
- Of the 623 drug industry lobbyists, more than one-half have
  "revolving door" connections; many previously worked in
  Congress or elsewhere in the federal government, while 32
  were former staffers of the House Ways and Means or Energy
  and Commerce committees, which was involved in marking

up the Medicare legislation of 2003.

- "Astroturf" lobbying is a covert false advertising practice whereby the drug industry manufactures the "grass" in a fake "grassroots" lobbying effort; in a typical operation, a contracted lobbying firm will contact community groups asking for signatures on a petition, with misleading information on the issue without mention of the funding source.
- Successful lobbying by the drug industry in 2001 led to passage of legislation by Congress for six-month patent extensions if a company's drugs are tested for safety in children; there are already about 100 drugs which have received such an extension (safety tests in children will cost an estimated $727 million while the patent extensions are valued at 40 times more at nearly $30 billion; three of the four sponsors of that bill ranked in the top 10 in campaign donations from the drug industry.[95]

CONCLUSIONS

Where does all of this leave us after this long but necessary chapter? From this and preceding chapters, these conclusions are inescapable.

- For-profit health care in America is overly expensive, inefficient, wasteful, and offers less value and inferior quality of care compared to the not-for profit sector.
- The health care of people has become a commodity for sale, opening the door to socially irresponsible profit taking.
- The self-interest of for-profit health care corporations has abused and trumped the public interest, and powerful corporate lobby groups have been effective in maintaining the status quo under the false guise of a free market.
- Broad public awareness of these problems, together with real (not "astro") grassroots advocacy, will be required to counter the self-interest of the stakeholders in the pro-market system.

The pressing need for reform is eloquently stated by Drs. Steffie Woolhandler and David Himmelstein in these words:[96]

The most serious problem with (investor-owned) care is that it embodies a new value system that severs the communal roots and samaritan traditions of hospitals, makes doctors and nurses the instruments of investors, and views patients as commodities. In nonprofit settings, avarice vies with beneficence for the soul of medicine; investor ownership marks the triumph of greed. In our society some aspects of life are off-limits to commerce. We prohibit the selling of children and the buying of wives, juries, and kidneys. Tainted blood is an inevitable consequence of paying blood donors; even sophisticated laboratory tests cannot compensate for blood that is sold rather than given as a gift. Like blood, health care is too precious, intimate, and corruptible to entrust to the market.

CHAPTER TWELVE

HOW, AND CAN, OUR FAILING SYSTEM BE FIXED?

It is clear why economics is called the "dismal science."

In a time when untold billions of additional dollars are being allocated to the US military and to "bioterrorism preparedness" while the DoD makes plans to use nuclear weapons (or threaten to use them), policy arguments about the exact percentage of GDP devoted to medical care (or the false predictions that were made about its rise) are dilatory or worse. Let's devote our time and energy to discussion of the political action needed for the achievement in our lifetimes of an equitable high-quality universal cost-effective medical care system for the United States.[1]

> —Victor Sidel, MD, Co-Founder and Past President, Physicians for Social Responsibility/USA and Co-Founder and Past Co-President, International Physicians For the Prevention of Nuclear War

The above comment by Dr. Victor Sidel, one of the recipients of the Nobel Peace Prize in 1985, was made just before leaving for Moscow in March 2002 in his continuing efforts to decrease the threat of the use of nuclear weapons. It captures the central goal of reform, which tends to get lost in a maze of details, further clouded by the claims and counter-claims of contending interests.

In order to think about reform options, it is first useful to start with a broad perspective and ask the main questions. Our present market-based system is paradoxical in at least two important ways. In his excellent book *Everything for Sale: The Virtues and Limits of Markets*, Robert Kuttner notes these two basic paradoxes:[2]

> *Health care is perhaps the quintessential case of an econ-*

omy of the Second Best, a necessary blend of market and non-market. But the peculiarly American version of this blend is dysfunctional. It yields what Alain Enthoven termed "a paradox of excess and deprivation." Well-insured people receive care that has become ever more technology-intensive and costly with the costs driven by the entrepreneurial part of the system. Others, without insurance, get little or no care at all—a public-health catastrophe with both burden and overt economic costs.

In the 1980s, a second paradox appeared. As private market forces battled the seemingly chronic medical inflation, private regulators such as insurance companies became every bit as intrusive on medical decisions as the most maligned government bureaucrats.

If we accept that the overall goal is to provide a system of universal access to health care for the entire population, two big questions sort out: (1) For universal coverage, who pays?; and (2) Should health insurance and health care be provided on a for-profit or not-for-profit basis?

In their book *The Crisis in Health Care: Costs, Choices and Strategies*, Dean Coddington and his colleagues made these predictions in 1990 for outcomes under our market-based system:[3]

- No solution to the uninsured problem (expect more than 40 million uninsured).
- Double-digit health plan rate increases.
- Smaller employers dropping health plans or cutting coverage.
- Continued gaps in safety net coverage.
- Shift toward managed care and away from indemnity coverage.
- Large rate increases for private insurers in shrinking market.
- Increased co-payments and deductibles for employees.
- Numerous failures of HMOs and withdrawal from market by larger insurance companies.
- Overall continued inflation of health care costs.
- Continued cost shifting in an increasingly fragmented market.

Fourteen years later, their predictions are precisely on target. In view of this accuracy, I will use their four basic categories of reform alternatives: (1) Incremental changes to the present system; (2) Building on the employer-based insurance system with public coverage of the unemployed; (3) Abandoning the employer-based system in favor of a consumer choice model; and (4) Single-payer universal coverage. We shall see that there is often overlap between these categories, but together they subsume all of the potential approaches to reform while providing a useful framework for discussion. As we go through these different options, it is instructive to pay attention to which groups will bear the major responsibility for leadership, management and payment of health care costs. As we have seen earlier, the main players are employers, insurers, consumers and government.

FOUR BASIC OPTIONS

Incrementalism

In earlier chapters, we have seen how our present patchwork non-system of health care has evolved to its near crisis point of uncontrolled escalating costs, limited access, and variable, often poor quality of care. This situation is non-sustainable. Incrementalism has been the prevailing policy in health care for more than 25 years. In view of its obvious failures, it is surprising that its proponents continue to support this concept. On closer scrutiny, however, it becomes less surprising, as the stakeholders go to every effort to continue the mostly for-profit market-based system which, increasingly, is leaving the public interest behind.

Following the demise of the flawed Clinton Health Plan in 1994, we have seen a flurry of legislative activity at the state level, largely in response to public opposition to for-profit managed care. Between 1990 and 1995, for example, about 90% of states adopted specific instruments intended to guarantee issue and renewal of insurance coverage, while another 60% attempted to limit premium increases. Each of these efforts to reform state insurance practices generated intense opposition from the insurance industry.[4] More recently, a 2001 national survey of Blue Cross and Blue Shield plans revealed a plethora of new state laws adopted around the country in response to wide-

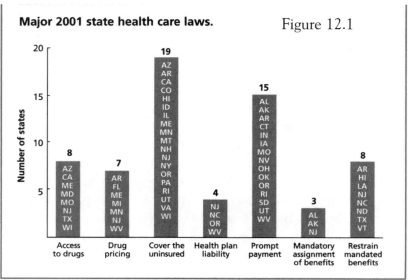

Major 2001 state health care laws.   Figure 12.1

SOURCE: BLUE CROSS AND BLUE SHIELD ASSOCIATION, DECEMBER 2001 (AVAILABLE FEBRUARY 14, 2002)

Reprinted with permission from Blue Cross and Blue Shield Association. State legislative health care and insurance issues, 2001 survey of plans. *Med Benefits* 2002; 19 (5): 11.

spread public concerns about health care (Figure 12.1).[5]

At the federal level, the major incremental strategies have been to expand coverage for the uninsured through Medicaid and the state Children's Health Insurance Program (CHIP) while attempting to modify the private health insurance market. National legislative attempts to increase access to care have run headlong into state budget deficits and the 1996 federal welfare reform law, which delinked Medicaid enrollment from welfare participation. Studies have shown decreasing Medicaid enrollments since welfare reform. For example, the probabilities of enrollment for children in families without income dropped from 81% to 68% between 1995 and 1998.[6] The federal Health Insurance Portability and Accountability Act of 1996 (HIPAA) set the first national standards for the availability and portability of individual and group health insurance coverage.[7] While well intended, however, this complex law has been ineffectual in important ways (e.g., it intentionally avoided any regulation of rating practices by insurers).[8]

The California Public Employees Retirement System (CalPERS) is second in size only to the Federal Employees Health Benefits Program (FEHBP). After a 25% increase in its HMO premiums for 2003, CalPERS dropped its PacifiCare and Health Net plans (which held out for a 30% increase), and announced that it will explore a self-funded single-risk pool.[9] In 2003, CalPERS was forced to raise its premiums for 2004 by another 16 to 18%, and called for major system reform.[10] Here is the view of Dr. Henry Simmons, President of the National Coalition on Health Care (which includes CalPERS as a member):[11]

> The message is that the problem is far more serious than anybody in the political process is acknowledging. The incremental strategy is bankrupt. We need a big debate on how to get a grip on this system.

Building on the Employer-Based Insurance System

As we saw in Chapter 1, a voluntary employer-based system of health insurance was hurriedly started early in World War II as the country mobilized for the war effort. As such, it is an "accidental system," hardly what one might design as the basis for our country's health care system if starting over from scratch. It has persisted for 60 years because of tax preferences for employers and employees established in the 1940s. It represents the status quo, and clearly serves the interests of the nation's $300 billion insurance industry.

The shortfall of health insurance coverage for American workers remains serious. One in six Americans lack health insurance (about 45 million). Of uninsured workers, three out of five work for an employer that doesn't sponsor health insurance, while one-fifth are not eligible for the employer's plan and another one-fifth cannot afford coverage if offered.[12]

Employers today find themselves burdened by the rising costs of health insurance, increased liability and regulatory exposure, and employee dissatisfaction with their health care benefits. The average annual cost to the employer for each employee is now over $6,000.[13] Many employers are looking for ways to relieve this burden.

Proponents for shoring up the employer-based system have proposed various incremental strategies, including employer mandates, tax credits to assist employees purchase of insurance, pooled purchasing alliances to help small employers offer health insurance, tax breaks for employers offering insurance, and a "defined contribution" approach whereby employers provide employees with a set amount of dollars each year to enable them to purchase their own insurance policies either individually or from a menu of group plans.

Many argue that the employer-based system of health insurance is too unreliable, and should be eliminated altogether. Current trends support this conclusion. Future rates of employer-based insurance coverage will continue to decline as the numbers of part-time workers grows and as the labor force becomes even more mobile.[14] Almost one-half of small employers with three to nine employees now offer no health benefits.[15] The three largest statewide health insurance alliances have failed to increase insurance coverage by small employers.[16] Retired workers less than 65 years of age, who once had generous retiree health benefits from large employers, are now being required to pay higher co-payments each year, and many large companies no longer provide retiree coverage for new hires.[17,18] It is now well established that many lower-income workers cannot afford health insurance even if offered by their employers.[19] All of these trends have led Dr. James Robinson of the School of Public Health at the University of California Berkeley to this summary observation:[20]

> The natural role of the employer is to manufacture automobiles, distribute newspapers, and sell coffee. Their central role in the financing and design of the health care system developed through a combination of historical accidents, tax loopholes, and the paternalism of a passing era of lifetime employment. No one today would design a health insurance system that places industrialists, entrepreneurs, and convenience store owners in charge of adjudicating health benefits on behalf of employees.

Expanding Consumer Choice

This is the currently popular approach to "reform" which is driven by a number of trends, including a backlash to managed care; retreat of employers, insurers, physician and hospital organizations from responsibilities of financing and managing care; distrust of big business and big government; the belief that more choice (and responsibility for payment) should rest with consumers; and the increasing use by consumers of the Internet as a source of health-related information.[21] The common denominator of all of the initiatives and proposals for the consumer choice model is the progressive transfer of risk and "control" to consumers with the hope that they will steward their money wisely and become more prudent buyers.

Proponents for this approach include legislators in both major political parties and stakeholders in the present market-based system. The insurance industry will profit enormously from this approach, and is an active supporter, both in terms of new products and behind-the-scenes lobbying. A vigorous debate continues in Congress as to the best ways to expand consumer choice. Many Republicans want to move away from employer-based insurance by giving individuals tax credits to buy their own insurance, while Democrats tend to favor building on the employer-based system with new tax incentives to employers.[22]

Here are some typical examples of consumer choice initiatives:

- For-profit Medicare+Choice HMOs as an option to traditional Medicare.
- Vouchers whereby seniors could buy their own health insurance.
- Tax credits to individuals for them to purchase their own insurance.
- Medical savings accounts (MSAs).
- Flexible savings accounts, which can be carried forward from one year to the next.
- Statewide pools to help high-risk patients gain health insurance.
- New insurance products offered to employers (Table 12.1).[23]

Advocates of these strategies argue that patients will be empowered to make their own decisions on their personal priorities, have more incentives to pursue more healthful lifestyles, and that costs can thereby be better controlled. As the Internal Revenue Service opened the door to MSA-type accounts, an editorial in the *Wall Street Journal* drew this wishful but misguided conclusion:[24]

> *This little-noticed ruling is a great leap forward for patient-directed health care. Over time it could signal the end of double-digit increases in employer health-care costs, and thus*

Table 12.1
THREE NEW TYPES OF INSURANCE POLICIES

High-deductible insurance plans with spending accounts

Employers pay into special spending accounts used by workers to pay for medical care. The amounts could fall short of a year's worth of medical care premiums or deductibles. The worker makes up the difference, with out-of-pocket costs ranging from $250 to $3,500 or more.

Defined contribution plans

Employers pay a set amount toward insurance and offer workers a selection of options, including HMOs and other types of managed care plans. Workers then pay the difference between what the employer pays and the actual cost of the plan they select. Monthly premiums paid by workers range from as little as $5 to more than $100. Deductibles range from very little to more than $3,500 a year.

After-tax savings accounts

This model couples a traditional insurance plan for major medical expenses with a savings account that the employee uses to pay for routine care. Because the money contributed by employers and workers to the savings account is paid after taxes are taken out, the employee can take any money left in the account when he or she leaves the firm.

Source: Appleby J. New insurance plans turn patients into shoppers. *USA Today*, January 8, 2002: B1-2.

---

the end of the era of stuffing employees into unpopular health-maintenance organizations.

The jury is in on some of the above strategies, which have already been demonstrated as failures. Medicare+Choice plans, for example, marketed their plans to healthy seniors, avoided the sick, pocketed profits and high administrative fees, then largely exited the market as they found the market less profitable than hoped. Expanded consumer choice actually *increased* costs. Elderly and disabled enrollees in these for-profit Medicare HMOs spent almost 50% more in out-of-pocket money in 2001 then they did in 1998.[25] At the same time, the heralded expansion of consumer choice did not occur, with seniors finding *decreased* choice as HMOs left the market.[26] Meanwhile, high-risk pools, as another example, have been found ineffective in 29 states, where only about 1% of patients with preexisting conditions gained coverage in the individual market through pooled risk.[27]

It doesn't take a rocket scientist to foresee what the outcomes of the other strategies toward "expanded consumer choice" will be. They will all end up segmenting risk pools even further by shrinking the risk pools for older and chronically ill patients (thereby increasing costs) and by displacing the group insurance market to the individual market. They will discriminate against the poor and sick and failing to contain costs. Take the idea of tax credits as an example. The plan offered by President Bush and Republicans in Congress would provide low-income individuals with $1,000 reimbursement and families with $3,000. Yet the cost of health insurance is much higher than that. A study by Families USA found that the coverage premium for a healthy, non-smoking 55 year-old woman would be almost $5,000 per year in 25 states (about $9,000 in Alaska), so that the tax credit would be "like throwing a 10-foot rope to an uninsured person in a 40-foot hole."[28] Jonathan Gruber, Professor of Economics at the Massachusetts Institute of Technology, has estimated that the numbers of uninsured might be reduced by only 5%.[29]

In a recent essay on the outcomes of the consumer choice model, Humphrey Taylor, chairman of the Harris Poll at Harris Interactive in New York City, observes that insurance only works if the many subsidize the few. He warns that the widespread use of consumer choice strategies, such as defined-contribution plans, will certainly lead to the erosion of the social contract upon which health insurance is based; he predicts a death spiral of adverse selection which ultimately will lead to the collapse of employer-based health insurance.[30]

Who will be the winners and losers as consumerism marches forward? The biggest winner, of course, is the insurance industry. Employers will win to the extent that they can relieve their burdens of covering health care of their employees. The biggest losers will be patients (bearing more costs for less benefits), the government and taxpayers (as the pool of patients unable to afford care grows and shifts to public programs). Victor Fuchs, Professor Emeritus of Economics at Stanford University, sums up the consumer choice model as follows:[31]

...the actuarial model applied to health care conflicts with

a sense of justice and collective responsibility: it attacks a core element of what it means to be a society. In the long run, the extreme actuarial approach will probably be rejected by the people of the United States as an unsatisfactory way of providing basic health care for all—National health insurance will probably come to the United States after a major change in the political climate—the kind of change that often accompanies a war, a depression, a large-scale civil unrest. Until then, the chief effect of the new plans will be to make young and healthy workers better off at the expense of their older, sicker colleagues.

Single-Payer Universal Coverage

Universal coverage through a not-for-profit single-payer system is becoming a more attractive option all the time as our health care non-system continues to deteriorate and becomes unaffordable for a growing part of the population. As we saw in Chapter 1, this concept is not new. It was first raised in 1912, while the fourth attempt to enact a national health insurance plan came close to enactment in the early 1970s. This approach represents a return to the original concept of health insurance as a social contract as established in the 1930s and 1940s by non-profit companies such as Blue Cross/Blue Shield and the Kaiser Permanente Health Plan.

In effect, single-payer universal coverage, whether nationally or state by state, would be like extending Medicare to the entire population. While Medicare is not perfect, is currently underfunded, and not comprehensive in coverage, it remains the most efficient and popular part of our health care system. It operates with an overhead of less than 3%, and extends coverage by law to everyone 65 years of age and older. Based on a single large risk pool and greater efficiencies of a not-for-profit approach, universal coverage can be achieved by converting the more than $280 billion now siphoned off each year by bureaucracy, administrative waste and corporate profiteering to full coverage of the population. A 2003 study estimated that these savings would amount to almost $7,000 for every American without health insurance.[32] Some proponents' arguments:

Quinton Young, MD, National Coordinator of Physicians for a

National Health Program (PNHP) and past president of the American Public Health Association:[33]

> We don't need any more piecemeal strategies that are, in effect, tactics by the drug and insurance industries to delay real reform. We need a system in which we have "everybody in, nobody out."

Marcia Angell, MD, former editor of *New England Journal of Medicine*:[34]

> We live in a country that tolerates enormous disparities in income, material possessions, and social privilege. That may be an inevitable consequence of a free market economy. But those disparities should not extend to denying some of our citizens certain essential services because of their income or social status. One of those services is health care. Others are education, clean water and air, equal justice, and protection from crime, all of which we already acknowledge are public responsibilities. We need to acknowledge the same thing for health care. Providing these essential services to all Americans, regardless of who they are, helps ensure that we remain a decent, cohesive, and optimistic country. It says that when it comes to vital needs, we are one community, not 280 million individuals competing with one another. In seeking to ensure adequate health care for all our citizens, we have an opportunity today to reassert that we are indeed a single nation.

Recent studies in California, Vermont, Massachusetts, Maryland and Georgia have documented that single-payer universal coverage can be achieved in those states and still save money.[35-38] In California, annual cost savings of about $7 billion have been projected, while other "reform" alternatives would *increase* costs and still fail to assure universal coverage.[39]

A persuasive case can be made that what we are already paying would be plenty to provide universal coverage of medically necessary care for the entire population. Despite the widespread belief that we have mainly a private system of health care, government expenditures, including tax subsidies for private insurance and payments for private health coverage of public employees, already account for

60% of total health expenditures each year in the U.S. As Woolhandler and Himmelstein observe:[40]

> *We pay the world's highest health care taxes. But much of the money is squandered. The wealthy get tax breaks. And HMOs and drug companies pocket billions in profits at the taxpayers' expense. But politicians claim we can't afford universal coverage. Every other developed nation has national health insurance. We already pay for it, but we don't get it.*

Numerous studies have shown what Americans want in their health care—guaranteed access, free choice of physician, affordable care of high quality, trust and respect. All of these expectations could be met through single-payer, not-for-profit universal coverage through a blend of federal and state governmental roles. This would not be socialized medicine (as Medicare is not!), but socialized insurance. The private practice of medicine would continue under negotiated compensation arrangements with a sharp reduction in administrative and regulatory burdens.

DEBATE OF THE OPTIONS

Since any resolution of reform alternatives depends largely on ideological and political factors, a broad historical perspective is useful before dealing with the politics of health care reform. Mark Peterson, a well-known policy analyst and scholar in government affairs, sees competing interests in terms of stakeholders (who benefit from the status quo) or stake challengers (who either do not benefit or are harmed by the status quo). From 1890 to 1950, health care was dominated by the major stakeholders (the American Medical Association, American Hospital Association, specialty organizations, the health insurance industry, and after World War II, business). Since 1950, the stake challengers have become increasingly vocal, including consumer, civil rights, and women's groups. By the mid-1990s, the traditional "iron triangle" of closely allied stakeholders (the medical profession, business and the insurance industry) was breaking down under increasing external pressures and starting to fight among themselves.[41] As an example, the interests of small business are increasingly different from big business.

The medical community has been splintered in recent decades by loss of autonomy and micromanagement by a bureaucratic insurance industry. Organized medicine is no longer a primary player in determining the structure and methods of financing of our health care system. Most physicians and their organizations support the concept of universal coverage. Consensus among physicians breaks down, however, on how to assure that coverage. For example, well-intended proposals developed by the American Academy of Family Physicians, as well as the American College of Physicians/American Society of Internal Medicine, both leave the private health insurance industry in place without requiring either community rating practices or non-profit status. We saw in the last chapter how an unfettered private insurance industry works against affordable health coverage of the whole population. As a result, we are seeing continued growth in membership of Physicians for a National Health Program as the only effective way to guarantee affordable universal coverage.

Another useful framework to better understand the health care debate is the matrix designed by Thomas Friedman in his interesting book on globalization, *The Lexus and the Olive Tree.* Four poles of

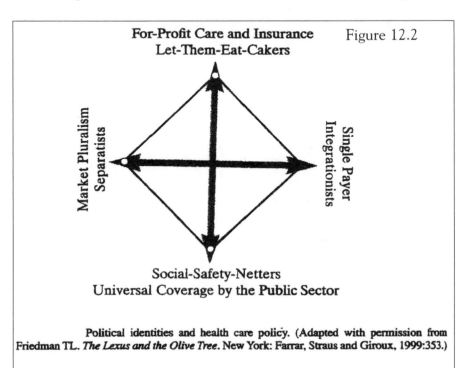

For-Profit Care and Insurance   Figure 12.2
Let-Them-Eat-Cakers

Market Pluralism Separatists

Single Payer Integrationists

Social-Safety-Netters
Universal Coverage by the Public Sector

Political identities and health care policy. (Adapted with permission from Friedman TL. *The Lexus and the Olive Tree.* **New York: Farrar, Straus and Giroux, 1999:353.)**

political identities permits us to locate the views of all competing interests somewhere along the horizontal axis from market pluralism to single-payer and along the vertical axis from for-profit care and insurance to universal coverage by the public sector (Figure 12.2).[42]

Commenting on the growing trend of physicians' refusing to accept Medicare patients, Paul Krugman, Professor of Economics and International Affairs at Princeton University, observes:[43]

> ...recent cuts in Medicare payments are inducing many doctors to avoid treating Medicare recipients at all. But this is just the beginning of a struggle that will soon dominate American politics. Think of it as the collision between an irresistible force (the growing cost of health care) and an immovable object (the determination of America's conservative movement to downsize government). Why don't we just leave medical care up to individuals? Basically, even in the United States there are limits to how much inequality the public is prepared to tolerate. It's one thing if the rich can afford bigger houses or fancier vacations than ordinary families; Americans accept such differences cheerfully. But a society in which rich people get their medical problems solved, while ordinary people die from them, is too harsh even for us.

Returning to our two most basic questions at the start of this chapter—for universal coverage, who pays? and should health insurance and health care be provided as a for-profit or not-for-profit basis?—these questions are still clearly not resolved. But they underpin the important debate heating up again. The consumer choice approach to health care "reform" holds sway, but all of the evidence points to its failure to contain costs or improve access or quality of health care. Of the four alternatives to health care reform presented here, the first three will continue to shift costs to consumers and undermine the public interest. Only the fourth option—single-payer universal coverage—can assure affordable comprehensive health care for our population. We are about to enter another intense national debate on this issue, and that leads us to the next chapter.

CHAPTER THIRTEEN

THE POLITICS OF HEALTH CARE REFORM

> *I know of no safe depository of the ultimate power of the society but the people themselves; and if we think them not enlightened enough to exercise their control with a wholesome discretion, the remedy is not to take it from them, but to inform their discretion.*
>
> —Thomas Jefferson[1]

The U.S. stands alone among all developed Western industrialized nations in not yet having a national health insurance program in one form or another. Its health care industry is enormous—accounting for about one-seventh of the U.S. economy, including more than 750,000 physicians and 5,200 hospitals. But, as we have seen, large size does not connote strength, stability, or sustainability.

Here is the health care landscape that confronts the nation as the political campaigns for the 2004 election year heat up:

- Runaway costs of health care, with 44% of Americans reporting problems affording health care.[2]
- Managed care discredited and health care "experts" without ready prescriptions for solutions to cost problem.
- After its nine-year study of 12 major U.S. health care markets, a 2004 report of the landmark Community Tracking Study found widespread and deep skepticism that markets can improve efficiency and quality in our health care system.[3]
- Lack of consumer confidence concerning their ability to obtain needed health care (Figure 13.1).[4]
- Erosion of public trust in corporations and other American institutions.[5]
- Evaporation of $5 trillion in "wealth" from the stock market, threatening retirement planning for many mil-

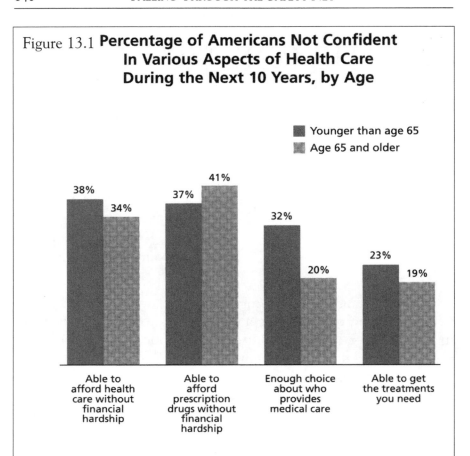

Figure 13.1 **Percentage of Americans Not Confident In Various Aspects of Health Care During the Next 10 Years, by Age**

SOURCE: *MEDICARE: AWARENESS, CONFIDENCE, SATISFACTION AND REFORM: RESULTS FROM THE 2001 HEALTH CONFIDENCE SURVEY*, EMPLOYEE BENEFIT RESEARCH INSTITUTE (7/01). TEXT OF A FACT SHEET PRESENTING PRELIMINARY FINDINGS OF THE 2001 SURVEY IS AVAILABLE ON THE INTERNET. WEB SITE: *WWW.EBRI.ORG/FACTS/0701FACT.PDF*

Reprinted with permission from Employee Benefit Research Institute: Results from the 2001 Health Confidence Survey, July 2001.

lions of Americans.[6]

- Political paralysis of both major parties in the midst of a jobless economic recovery and wartime economy.
- Federal and state budgets in deficit, with new tension nationally between guns and butter in the aftermath of September 11, the Iraq War, and the increasing needs of homeland security.

Since incremental patchwork changes seeking to prop up the employer-based insurance system and/or to expand consumer choice cannot be expected to produce lasting health care reform, this chapter will focus on the politics of structural reform through single-payer universal health insurance, whether state by state or nationally. We will consider four dimensions of the subject: (1) experience of other countries in establishing national health insurance; (2) what's different in the U.S.; (3) campaign politics for the 2002 and 2004 years; and (4) the building of public support and new alliances in this country toward reform.

POLITICAL EXPERIENCE ELSEWHERE

Before looking at the political experience of industrialized Western nations in enacting social health insurance, it is useful to take a broad macro view of evolving health care systems. Victor Rodwin, Professor of Health Policy and Management at New York University, has categorized five major types of health care systems as they have developed over the last 100 years (Table 13.1).[7] The U.S. is now alone as a Type 2 pluralistic system. The question is whether, and how, it can move to a Type 3 system in order to provide universal access while becoming more cost effective and improving quality.

In a fascinating paper exploring explanations for why the U.S. still has no form of universal health insurance, Vicente Navarro, Professor of Health Policy and Management at Johns Hopkins University and Editor of the *International Journal of Health Services*, offers a persuasive argument that the power and influence of the labor movement is the primary factor in establishing a national health program in any country. He notes the close timing in European countries between development of trade union federations and working-class political parties with enactment of social health insurance. He also notes the effectiveness of alliances in achieving a comprehensive, universal health program, such as an early alliance between Sweden's Social Democratic Party with the Farmers' Party.[8]

Australia has some important things in common with the U.S. Both countries have parallel public and private sectors, a shared heritage, and similar medical practice. After World War II, Australia had voluntary health insurance partly subsidized by the government. Compulsory health insurance was enacted in 1975. Many efforts have been made since then to increase the role of private insurance, but while they have made some gains, they have not achieved dom-

Table 13.1   **The Evolution of Health Systems**

Health System	Type 1: Private	Type 2: Pluralistic	Type 3: National health insurance	Type 4: National health service	Type 5: Socialized health service
General definition	Health care as item of personal consumption	Health care as predominantly a consumer good or service	Health care as an insured, guaranteed consumer good or service	Health care as a state-supported consumer good or service	Health care as a state-provided public service
Position of the physician	Solo entrepreneur	Solo entrepreneur and member of variety of groups, organizations	Solo entrepreneur and member of medical organizations	Solo entrepreneur and member of medical organizations	State employee and member of medical organizations
Role of professional associations	Powerful	Very strong	Strong	Fairly strong	Weak or nonexistent
Ownership of facilities	Private	Private and public	Private and public	Mostly public	Entirely public
Economic transfers	Direct	Direct and indirect	Mostly indirect	Indirect	Entirely indirect
Prototypes	U.S., Western Europe, Russia in the 19th century	U.S. in 20th century	Sweden, France, Canada, Japan in 20th century	Great Britain in 20th century	Soviet Union in 20th century

Sources: V. G. Rodwin, *The Health Planning Predicament: France, Quebec, England, and the United States.* Berkeley: University of California Press, 1984, p. 245. Adapted from M. G. Field, *Comparative Health Systems: Differentiation and Convergence,* Final Report under Grant No. HS-00272, Rockville, MD: National Center for Health Services Research, 1978.

Reprinted with permission from Rodwin VG. Comparative analysis of health systems: an international perspective. In: Kovner AR, Jonas S (eds). *Health Care Delivery in the United States.* New York: Springer Publishing, 1999; 122.

inance due to high premium costs and large, often unpredictable out-of-pocket expenses. Broad public support for universal coverage through its Medicare program carries the day in each instance.[9]

Canada also has much in common with the United States, including a border and many similarities in history, culture, and economics. While much maligned in some quarters for its currently underfunded national health program, its health care system performs much better than the U.S. by most quality of care measures while spending only about one-half of what the U.S. health care system spends per person.[10] There are some valuable lessons for us south of the border as to the political process that led to its enactment of a national health program in 1984. First, the process started in a single province, Saskatchewan, where the provincial government established a universal hospital insurance plan in 1947. Although Saskatchewan was then poor and in debt, there was a growing hospital admission rate and shortages of hospital beds, physicians, and nurses. A per capita tax or premium was levied, and no resident was refused hospital care. With government support of hospital costs, the program was successful, and the number of hospital beds and their utilization grew as well. Second, the national government established a set of five basic principles in 1957, encouraging the provinces to set up their own health plans. By 1971, all 10 provinces had established hospital and health insurance plans which met federal requirements for 50% matching funds.[11] The five basic principles—*public administration, comprehensiveness, universality, portability,* and *accessibility*—led to unanimous passage by Parliament of the Canada Health Act in 1984 which established its Medicare program for its population.[12] Of special interest is the way in which major reform was carried out through a short document based on essential principles (in contrast to the flawed Clinton Health Plan of 1,342 pages in 1994!).

Public funding accounts for about 70% of Canada's health care spending[13] compared to about 60% in the U.S.[14] But the federal share of funding for its Medicare program has declined in recent years from about 40% in the 1970s to about 30% in the 1990s. These cutbacks led to closure of 30% of Canadian hospitals, overcrowding of emergency rooms, longer waiting lists for some diagnostic imaging services and elective surgical procedures and other strains on the public system.[15] U.S. and Canadian corporate firms sought new opportunities to privatize parts of the system, and have successfully infiltrated such areas as expanded diagnostic imaging and cancer treatment facilities. Affluent groups lobbied for tax cuts and further privatization of the system, while some right-wing groups carried out misleading surveys exaggerating the waiting list problem. Since two-thirds of Canadian newspapers are owned by one person who is an advocate for privatization, the press has often given a sympathetic ear to opponents of Medicare.

The Commission on the Future of Medicare was established in 2001 to assess the strengths and problems of the Canadian health care system, to examine reform proposals, and to recommend its future directions. It was chaired by the former premier of Saskatchewan, Roy Romanow. The Romanow Commission issued its final report in November 2002 calling for recommitment to its five founding principles plus the addition of a sixth—*accountability.* Increased public financing was recommended to update and strengthen the public system, particularly to improve diagnostic services, expand home care services, and increase the use of tele-health in rural health care. Expanded coverage of prescription drugs was also recommended, together with a national formulary for these drugs.[16] In coming to these recommendations, Romanow summarized the work of the Commission in these words:[17]

> *Friends, early in my mandate, I challenged those advocating radical "private" solutions for reforming health care— user-fees, medical savings accounts, de-listing services, greater privatisation, a parallel private system—to come forward with evidence that these approaches would improve and strengthen our health care system. The evidence has not been forthcoming. I have also carefully explored the experiences of other jurisdictions with co-payment models and with public-private partnerships, and have found these lacking. These is no evidence these solutions will deliver better or cheaper care, or improve access (except, perhaps, for those who can afford to pay for care out of their own pockets). More to the point, the principles on which these solutions rest cannot be reconciled with the values at the heart of Medicare or with the tenets of the Canada Health Act that Canadians overwhelmingly support. It would*

be irresponsible of me to jeopardize what has been, and can remain, a world-class health care system and a proud national symbol, by accepting anecdote as fact, or on the dubious basis of "making a leap of faith." Tossing overboard the principles and values that govern our health care system would be betraying a public trust. Canadians will not accept this, and without their consent, these so-called "new" solutions are doomed to fail. Canadians want their health care system renovated; they don't want it demolished. Some have described it as a perversion of Canadian values that they cannot use their money to purchase faster treatment from a private provider for their loved ones. I believe it is a far greater perversion of Canadian values to accept a system where money rather than need, determines who gets access to care.

WHAT'S DIFFERENT IN THE U.S.?

Some will answer quickly that "everything is different in the U.S." That answer, however, would deny many similarities across borders in the political obstacle course toward achieving social health insurance. As is recounted in some detail in an interesting 1998 book by Pat and Hugh Armstrong, *Universal Healthcare: What the United States Can Learn From the Canadian Experience*, the medical profession, private insurers, and other opponents of a public system in Canada set up much the same arguments and roadblocks as we have seen in this country over the years.[18]

On the other hand, there are some important differences in the U.S. that suggest that coalition building toward universal health care coverage will have to be a uniquely American journey. These differences stand out between the U.S. and other Western industrialized nations with one or another form of universal health care coverage:

- The frontier ethic of rugged individualism still pervades our entrepreneurial capitalist system, with less emphasis on the collective good than is seen in other Western societies.
- The capitalist and management class is closely interwoven with government and has effectively thwarted populist movements of the working class.

- The labor movement in the U.S. is much weaker than in the other industrialized countries (only 13% of workforce unionized, down from 25% in the mid-1970s).[19]
- The labor movement has no closely aligned political party; over the last 40 years, the Democratic Party has largely retreated from the interests of labor, and has not endorsed social health insurance since President Truman's effort in 1948.
- The Congress remains closely divided between the two major political parties.
- There is an enormous and largely invisible corporate lobbying and public relations campaign for corporate self-interest in the status quo.
- Current policy trends continue to be strongly pro-market, even though our market-based system is failing.

Robert Kuttner sums up our times in these words:[20]

For the past quarter-century, America has been deregulating capitalism in expectation of a more dynamic and efficient economy. In fact, average economic growth since 1976 has slightly lagged that of the previous quarter-century, when capitalism was more highly regulated. But there has been a much more serious set of consequences—widening inequality, the dismantling of public remedy, and the neutering of the Democratic Party as a medium of progressive politics.

CAMPAIGN POLITICS FOR 2002 AND 2004 ELECTION YEARS

With the problem of escalating costs of health care, refractory to all policy strategies, as the overriding health care issue in 2003, the "blame game" best described health care politics during both the 2002 mid-term election cycle and the opening rounds of the 2004 election campaigns. Insurers blamed the drug industry, which in turn blamed HMOs and hospitals. Employers blamed the insurers. Physicians blamed insurance companies and attorneys. And then all the parties blamed patients, claiming that they want all the latest of treatments while having someone else pay for them. As Drew Altman of the Kaiser Family Foundation saw it:

> *We've had no meaningful and sustained way to control health care costs. There's no big new idea for controlling costs, so the result is a free-for-all. Working people will pay more, benefits will be cut back, and we're likely to see an increase in the ranks of the uninsured.*[21]

It is of interest to review the experience of the 2002 midterm elections for signs of how the 2004 election year will play out. The 2002 election campaign offered no surprises in terms of politics as usual. Republicans pushed the priority of the war on terrorism over domestic issues. Democrats argued for more domestic programs, warning about military deficit spending. The Administration pushed for further privatization of foundering Medicare HMOs, despite the retreat of many private Medicare HMOs from the market.[22] Meanwhile, corporate lobbyists remained true to form. The insurance industry lobbied legislators for more consumer-choice through private plans and against mental health parity (fear of increased utilization, prices, and governmental regulation). The drug industry lobbied hard against generic drugs, importation of prescription drugs, and any threat of price controls. Reports by Public Citizen exposed a seniors' group (United Seniors Association) as a hired gun conduit for the pharmaceutical lobby to promote Republican candidates and prescription drug benefits for seniors without any price controls through sham "issue ads," Internet and direct mail campaigns.[23,24] The Health Benefits Coalition (insurers and business executives) lobbied against patients' rights and mental health parity legislation.[25]

The process and outcome of Oregon's Initiative 23 is instructive in the aftermath of the 2002 cycle. The initiative put forward single-payer universal coverage on the November 2002 ballot, but its fate was determined even before the campaign started. The five-person Explanatory Committee for the Initiative was dominated by the private sector health care industry (two were registered lobbyists for the insurance industry and hospital association, one was until recently a CEO of Oregon's chapter of the National Kidney Foundation); two consumer representatives were out maneuvered in writing up the initiative. As a result, the final language of the initiative was skewed with disinformation which grossly exaggerated the impact on taxes, disregarded the strengths of the proposal, and otherwise misrepresented and denigrated the Initiative. The grass-roots campaign across the State which generated the Initiative was not even permitted to write the title of their own initiative, even after appealing all the way to the Oregon Supreme Court.[26] Supporters of the measure were outspent by more than 30 to 1 by a coalition of insurance companies that overwhelmed the airwaves with negative and distorted ads. Nationally, NBC's coverage of the issue also misrepresented the issue, showing obvious bias for the current pro-market system. There was no disclosure that NBC is owned by General Electric, which is heavily invested in the insurance and medical industries.[27]

The 2002 midterm elections can be viewed as a victory for corporate America, purchased through a record $900 million by candidates and special interest groups (almost double that spent in the midterm elections of 1998).[28] The drug industry poured over $16 million into its efforts to avoid price controls of its prescription drugs.[29] The media are pressured by corporate agendas and funding to pass along advocacy ads only as it suits their interests. A television ad developed by AARP is an interesting example of pressure politics. The AARP's television spot, a key part of a $10 million broadcast and print campaign, initially called upon consumers to substitute generics for brand-name drugs whenever possible and to resist the urge to buy heavily advertised drugs unless needed. Some networks refused to run the ad at all. Another network did run the ad, but only after it was changed to say "Remember, no matter what our ad says about a drug, it may not be right for you."[30]

Public Citizen has recently called attention to high re-election rates in the 2000 election (98% in the House and 80% in the Senate) as evidence of the need for free air time to make congressional races more competitive and reduce candidate dependence on special interest money. At the same time, it acknowledged that broadcast corporations themselves lobby Congress heavily in their own interest and will resist such legislation.[31] In view of the enormous revenues accruing each year to the broadcast media from ads sponsored by well-heeled special interest groups, there is clearly a conflict of interest which is largely below the radar screen of public awareness. The experience described above with Oregon's Initiative 23 and the AARP's television spot on generic drugs, suggests the magnitude of this conflict of interest in the absence of public disclosure.

The 2002 midterm elections revealed an electorate, nationally as well as in many states, almost evenly split down the middle. While the Republicans barely regained control of the Senate and increased slightly their majority in the House, the results can hardly be interpreted as a strong mandate to govern.

Since 2002, the Democrats have been reassessing their priorities and strategies, while the Republicans, riding a wave of popular support for the war in Iraq, have pressed forward with tax cuts and a limited domestic legislative agenda. Overshadowing any new legislation are the competing priorities of Homeland Security, confronting global terrorism, and growing budget deficits.

Aside from budget deficits, there was a wide ideological chasm between the two major parties throughout government. Health care issues are being played out against more fundamental issues. Republicans favor personal responsibility, a limited role for government, devolution to the states, corporate freedom and free enterprise within a market-based system. Democrats favor a larger role for government with higher priority for domestic policies responsible to the needs of the disadvantaged. However, the policy differences between the two parties have become muted in recent decades as corporate power brokers hedge their bets in lobbying both parties. In the 1996 presidential campaign, only Ralph Nader and the Green Party took a strong stand for health care reform through single-payer universal coverage. In 2003, among a field of nine Democratic presidential candidates, only two called for single-payer universal coverage. Republicans and many Democrats tend to view the role of health insurance as protection against catastrophic health care costs, not as social insurance assuring a basic right of access to health care.

Most of the Democratic presidential candidates put forth incremental proposals involving various kinds of subsidies and tax credits while leaving the current flawed system largely intact. However, as Kuttner reminds us "If we leave intact the present system, with its wasteful fragmentation, billing, underwriting, and insurance company profits, there is only one big place to reap savings—by withholding more care as nonessential and by avoiding the sick."[32]

PUBLIC SUPPORT AND NEW ALLIANCES FAVORING HEALTH CARE REFORM

Many national polls over the last 50 years in the U.S. have shown considerable support for single-payer NHI, generally in the range of at least 40%.[33] It is likely that responses to national polls assessing public support for universal coverage through a national health insurance program would be even higher if different wording was used in the surveys. The question is usually asked whether respondents favor "a national health plan, financed by taxpayers in which all Americans get their insurance from a single government plan." This wording implies that taxes may be higher than what people are already paying for health care and may also imply a larger role for government in actual health care. Yet, even in the conservative state of Texas, a 2002 poll by the University of Houston Center for Public Policy found that 52% of respondents answered "yes" to that question.[34] Instead, we can be quite sure that responses would be more favorable if the question were asked this way: "would you support a program that would increase your benefits, give you free choice of providers, provide coverage for everyone, and control health care costs?" A 2003 poll by the *San Francisco Chronicle* of more than 1,100 respondents found that 77% support a single-payer system.[35]

If the American public were to understand that the benefits of national health insurance could be had with less costs than are now being paid (e.g., the California Health Care Options Project, chapter 12, page 135), support for NHI would probably become overwhelming. The experience of Kip Sullivan, well-known health policy expert and activist, is telling in this regard. He participated as a debate participant in two "citizen juries" during the 1990s. The first, sponsored by the Jefferson Center in 1993, was a 24-person jury of average Americans convened to address the question whether the Clinton Health Plan was the way to go. After five days of listening to experts debate a range of private and public options, the Clinton plan was voted down, 19 to 5, while informal support (17 of 24) was given to Senator Wellstone's single-payer universal coverage proposal. In 1996, Sullivan was one of three experts to speak to another citizen jury of 14 Minnesotans selected by the *Minneapolis Star*

Tribune and KTCA TV. The options debated included managed competition, medical savings accounts (MSAs), and single payer. Single payer received eight votes, with managed competition taking only three votes, the rest even less.[36]

In spite of the 2002 midterm election results and the vigorous efforts by stakeholders in the present system to protect and advance their interests, there is mounting evidence that public awareness and reaction against rising health care costs are building towards broader support for national health insurance (NHI) than we have seen in past decades. A 1999 study of more than 2,100 medical students, residents, faculty, and deans in U.S. medical schools found that 57% of respondents (80% response rate) favor single-payer NHI.[37] Sixty-two percent of Massachusetts' physicians now favor single-payer NHI.[38] Harris Interactive (originally, Louis Harris & Associates) has been conducting national polls in the U.S. for over 20 years, surveying American perceptions toward its health care system. In an August 2002 national survey of the public, physicians, employers, hospital managers, and health plan managers, they found that one-half of respondents now believe that "fundamental changes are needed." Only 19% of physicians and even smaller percentages of the other four groups felt that "on the whole the health care system works pretty well and only minor changes are necessary."[39] In 2003, about 12,000 U.S. physicians representing many specialties endorsed a proposal for NHI submitted to Congress.[40]

In the early 1990s, Mark Peterson observed that the long-entrenched "iron triangle" of closely allied stakeholders in the present health care system (business, the insurance industry, and the medical profession) was facing stronger opposition and breaking down into internecine competition.[41] Consider these examples of how much further this breakdown has proceeded in just the last 10 years, as new alliances take shape:

- The interests of small and mid-size employers are increasingly at odds with the interests of large employers; however, those employers that do offer health benefits to their employees are angered by health plan premium increases and want to limit their costs by shifting more costs to workers or getting out of the coverage business altogether; 40% of small business owners now favor single-payer NHI.[42]

- Business is now supporting state regulation over health insurance premiums, similar to state-approval systems for automobile and commercial insurance.[43]
- More businesses are moving out of the country as health care consumes a larger and uncontrolled part of labor costs; thus, Kraft Foods, Inc. closed its U.S. plant and moved to Canada where workers will be paid $3.00 less per hour and the Canadian government will pick up its annual $6.5 million cost of health benefits.[44]
- Some business leaders have joined the new National Coalition on Health Care (NCHC) which endorses these principles—health insurance for all, improved quality of care, cost containment, equitable financing, and simplified administration; these principles are no longer a utopian concept from the left but are becoming a mainstream reform initiative.[45]
- Faced by soaring health insurance premium increases, many large pension plans are also joining the National Coalition on Health Care as they seek cost containment and assured coverage; these include one of the country's largest purchasers of health care, the California Public Employees Retirement System (1.2 million members), the Commonwealth of Massachusetts Group Insurance Commission, and the New York State Teachers Retirement System.[46]
- Labor is increasingly energized around health care coverage, often trading wages for health care benefits; despite lower rates of unionization than in past years, labor will be increasingly influential in the health care debate; for example, with the steel industry in collapse in the U.S. heartland, the United Steelworkers of America recently called on its 600,000 steel retirees to push for universal health care.[47]
- The American Medical Association, which used to represent most of the nation's physicians and has consistently opposed social health insurance over the years, now includes only about one-third of U.S. physicians in its membership and has lost much of its past influence over national health policy.
- The powerful AARP, lobbying for many millions of Americans over age 50, has confronted the pharmaceutical industry over prescription drug prices with a $10 million

advertising campaign against the inaccuracies and false claims of direct-to-consumer drug ads;[48] unfortunately, AARP recently lost some of its credibility as an advocacy organization in its promotion of the flawed 2003 Medicare prescription drug bill, angering many of its members and consumer rights organizations; according to Public Citizen, AARP derives about 60% of its revenue from insurance-related ventures, including the sale of Medigap policies and its membership lists to corporations, and is under attack by many critics and members who feel that the public interest has been sold out through conflicts of interest.[49-51]

Within government, some developing trends are moving in the direction of containment of health care costs:

- The Medicare program is beginning to impose some cost restrictions, vehemently opposed by the drug industry, on coverage of drugs used in hospitals.[52]
- In Congress, rising anger among legislators and their constituents over soaring costs of prescription drugs have led to strong bipartisan support for legislation enabling greater use of less expensive generic drugs and importation of drugs from Canada and other countries.[53,54] This legislation has become embroiled in the larger legislative battle over the Medicare prescription drug benefit, with the underlying issue being the threat of price controls on prescription drugs.
- A new single-payer bill (HR 676) was introduced in Congress in February 2003 by Reps. John Conyers (D-MI) Dennis Kucinich (D-Ohio), Jim McDermott (D-WA) and Donna Christensen (D-Virgin Islands) (See Appendix 5); the bill is based on the Physicians' Proposal for National Health Insurance.[55]
- At the state level, many states are attempting to rein in drug costs in their Medicaid budgets by developing preferred drug lists and encouraging use of generic drugs over more expensive brand-name drugs; for their efforts, they are now being sued by the pharmaceutical industry's trade group, PhRMA.[56]

Recent decisions by the judiciary have also lent momentum to reform initiatives in some areas, as illustrated by these examples:

- A June 2003 ruling by the U.S. Supreme Court rejected an injunction by the drug industry, thereby supporting the efforts by Maine and other states to use their purchasing clout to secure discounted drug prices for their Medicaid beneficiaries.[57]
- A unanimous ruling by the U.S. Supreme Court in April 2003 provides that states can force HMOs to open their networks to physicians who agree to the network's terms.[58]
- A 2002 decision by the Missouri Supreme Court ruled that utilization review decisions by HMOs do constitute the practice of medicine, thereby holding medical directors of HMOs accountable for their coverage decisions.[59]
- The legal standing of external review mechanisms for review of HMO coverage decisions was upheld by the U.S. Supreme Court in 2000 in the *Rush Prudential HMO Inc v Moran* case.[60]
- In the 2000 *Pegram v Herdich* case, the U.S. Supreme Court held that some coverage decisions involve both interpretation of an insurance contract and the exercise of a medical judgment about medical diagnosis and treatment.[61]

As we have seen, there is a "new politics" beginning to emerge in support of health care reform beyond failed, incremental measures. The dominance of traditional stakeholders in the market-based system is under assault and starting to break apart as a large and growing part of the population finds health care increasingly unaffordable and inaccessible. For-profit, private health care corporations are robbing us of 25% of the health care dollar for administrative costs and profits (estimated to total $387 billion each year, even more than our entire defense budget).[62] Some new challengers are now promoting more comprehensive reform. The middle class is starting to join lower-income people in anger over the unaffordability of health care, and public resentment of recent exposure of corporate fraud is likely to add fuel to reform efforts. There is now a new opportunity for Progressives and the Democratic Party to pull together a broader constituency for serious health care reform. Health care reform has been an important domestic issue throughout the 2004 political campaigns. In the immediate aftermath of the passage of the flawed legislation for a Medicare prescription drug benefit in November 2003, including the threatened long-term dismantling of Medicare itself, there have been efforts made in Congress to repeal some of the bill's most contentious provisions. Before Congress adjourned in the summer of 2004, 183 House members from 40 states signed a petition demanding a vote in 2004 to make two big changes in the 2003 law: (1) to require Medicare to manage the prescription drug benefit itself, instead of for-profit insurers, HMOs and middlemen; and (2) to allow Medicare to use its purchasing clout to obtain discounted prices on drugs.[63]

Health care reform should not be a partisan issue. As Don McCanne observes:

> *Democrats are interested in ensuring access to affordable, comprehensive health care for everyone, or at least they should be. Republicans are interested in sound business principles which reduce administrative waste and contain costs, or at least they should be. It is true that rhetorical disputes over abstract ideology continue to defeat rational proposals. But when we have an opportunity to adopt reform that provides a meeting ground for those advocating for a sound business approach to reform and for those advocating for health care justice, isn't it time to set aside the superficiality of rhetorical debate, especially when so many lives are at stake?*[64]

Broad-based grassroots support will be needed to push politicians toward real health care reform against the powerful opposition of corporate stakeholders and their allies of the status quo. Campaign finance reform and "free media" legislation would go a long way in advancing the democratic process in restructuring health care in the public interest. The electorate is still held hostage by corporate stakeholders through lack of disclosure and disinformation concerning reform alternatives. Education and increased awareness of the middle class will be key to serious health care reform. The words of Thomas Jefferson, which opened this chapter, are timeless in their relevance today some two centuries later.

In our next and last chapter, we will examine what a single-payer health insurance program would be like, whether developed nationally or initially on a state-by-state basis.

CHAPTER FOURTEEN

THERE IS A FIX: NATIONAL HEALTH INSURANCE

In the aftermath of September's tragedy, a window of opportunity has opened for a sort of civic renewal that occurs only once or twice a century. And yet, though the crisis revealed and replenished the wells of solidarity in American communities, those wells so far remain untapped. At least, this is what that gap between attitudes and behavior suggests. Civic solidarity is what Albert Hirschman called a "moral resource"—distinctive in that, unlike a material resource, it increases with use and diminishes with disuse. Changes in attitude alone, no matter how promising, do not constitute civic renewal.

Americans today, our surveys suggest, are more open than ever to the idea that people of all backgrounds should be full members of our national community. Progressives should work to translate that national mood into concrete policy initiatives that bridge the ethnic and class cleavages in our increasingly multicultural society.

Robert D. Putnam, Professor of Public Policy at Harvard
University and author of *Bowling Alone*.[1]

It is now time to recap what we have seen in earlier chapters, and to reconsider how our failing health care system can be fixed. We saw in Parts I and II that our supposed safety net for those without health insurance is in tatters. Given our economic uncertainties, widespread deficits in federal and state coffers, and the market-based, consumer choice directions in health policy further advanced since the 2002 midterm elections, we can expect that the safety net will become even more porous in the next few years. We saw in Chapter 11 that for-profit investor-owned health care corporations are beholden to their investors more than to the public interest, and in Chapter 13 that these stakeholders represent a powerful obstacle to structural system reform. We reviewed the four major alternatives

for reform in Chapter 12. Although highly contentious and polarized as the debate continues among these four alternatives, we exam-
ined solid evidence that the first three alternatives—incrementalism, strengthened employer-based health insurance, and increased
consumer choice—cannot effectively reform a flawed system.
Although many still cling to hopes that pluralistic "reforms" which
retain a for-profit health insurance industry can be successful if given
more time or tweaks, a growing body of evidence-based opinion
holds that universal coverage through a publicly administered single-payer system will be required. As long as a private insurance
industry accountable only to its investors cherry picks the well from
the sick, the system will remain fragmented, inefficient, wasteful and
unfair. As is well stated by Dr. Bob LeBow, Idaho family physician
and past President of Physicians for a National Health Program:[2]

> The question remains, can we make the situation "better"
> without a "single-risk pool" or without universal coverage?
> Even a state-by-state strategy or the expansion of Medicare to
> an entire age group, such as every child or everyone 55-64
> years old, could serve as a starting point. But without a single-
> payer approach, we will just be playing the poke-the-balloon
> game, where pushing a finger in one spot just creates a blip on
> the other side.

The goals of this chapter are to: (1) summarize the rationale for
single-payer universal coverage, whether national or state-by-state;
(2) summarize the essential features of such a system; and (3) briefly
discuss 10 common questions and concerns about national health
insurance (NHI).

RATIONALE FOR SINGLE-PAYER UNIVERSAL COVERAGE

Here again, are some of the major points supporting NHI as the
only alternative which can be expected to provide lasting reform of
our deteriorating health care system.

* Administrative bureaucracy and profits of the 1,200 plus private insurers take at least 25% of the health care dollar from
  direct patient care.[3]

- Risk pools are fragmented by opportunistic insurers avoiding higher risk enrollees, shifting the care of sick people onto the public sector, and perpetuating inefficiency and inequity in the market-based system.

- Despite a booming economy through the 1990s, 45 million Americans remain uninsured, with many more underinsured, including those on Medicare and Medicaid (e.g., limited prescription drug coverage).

- The uninsured and underinsured delay or avoid needed care and treatments, thereby experiencing higher death rates and worse clinical outcomes than their insured counterparts.

- The for-profit sector has been shown to have poorer clinical outcomes than the not-for-profit sector.[4]

- Costs of U.S. health care are out of control, we already have by far the most expensive health care system in the world, and the health insurance industry continues to pass along double-digit increases in premiums to employees and consumers.[5]

- Almost one-half of Americans report difficulty in affording health care, and a "medical divide" exists disadvantaging those who earn less than $50,000 per year.[6]

- Our affluent nation is confronting significant economic problems, budget surpluses have disappeared and support for essential safety net programs has eroded as government at all levels faces growing fiscal deficits.

- Low reimbursement to providers in underfunded public programs (Medicaid, S-CHIP, Medicare) is resulting in decreased access to health care for many enrollees in these programs.

- The physician-patient relationship has been damaged by the volatility of the present system and the intrusion of corporate health care bureaucrats who are neither trained, responsible nor accountable for direct patient care.

- The present system has become far too complex, the average U.S. physician spends eight hours a week on burdensome paperwork,[7] and both patients and providers are frustrated and dissatisfied with the increasing bureaucracy of health care.

- The employer-based insurance system, an accident of history, provides less coverage at more cost and less value to only two-thirds of the U.S. workforce.[8]

- Present trends and underfunding of essential health care

services (e.g.s, medical education, trauma centers, burn units) threaten the future availability and quality of critical services for all Americans, whether affluent and well insured or not.

- U.S. business, with employers faced with escalating costs of employee health benefits, is becoming less competitive in a global economy while competitors in other countries are spared responsibility for employees' health care due to their availability of public universal coverage.[9]

- All incremental strategies to resolve access and cost problems in U.S. health care over the last 35 years have failed in those goals, leaving us with a costly and wasteful system returning decreasing value to patients as for-profit corporations siphon off profits for themselves and their shareholders.

- Access, cost and quality problems can be largely resolved by enacting a publicly administered single-payer system which provides universal access for all Americans for medically-necessary services by exchanging the wasted dollars now directed to the private insurance industry for the lower overhead of a simplified public system.

- Independent estimates by government agencies and private sector analysts indicate that NHI can cover all the uninsured and eliminate copayments and deductibles for the insured without increasing total health care costs and even saving money; administrative and billing costs would drop from their current 25% of health care spending to under 15%.[10-16]

While a change to a single-payer system would greatly simplify the present system, its implementation would be both complex and challenging. The transition to NHI would require an extended phase-in period plus a solid commitment to the values and principles propelling needed reform. Dennis Kucinich's "Medicare for All" proposal called for a ten-year transition period before the entire population would be covered.[17] In view of the pervasive problems of access, unaffordability, quality and equity in today's health care system, however, enactment of guaranteed universal coverage to health care should be viewed as a medical, economic and moral imperative.

In May 2001, a physician working group for single-payer NHI made a comprehensive proposal to a Congressional hearing before three caucuses representing about 120 Democratic members of Congress. The working group included presidents of the National

Medical Association, the American Medical Women's Association, and the American Medical Student Association, as well as past presidents of the American Academy of Pediatrics and the American College of Physicians—American Society of Internal Medicine. These are the principles advanced by this group, which have been incorporated into the single-payer bill, HR 676 introduced in Congress in 2003 (Appendix 4):[18]

It is time to change fundamentally the trajectory of America's health care—to develop a comprehensive National Health Insurance (NHI) program for the United States.

Four principles shape our vision of reform.

1. Access to comprehensive health care is a human right. It is the responsibility of society, through its government, to assure this right. Coverage should not be tied to employment. Private insurance firms' past record disqualifies them from a central role in managing health care.

2. The right to choose and change one's physician is fundamental to patient autonomy. Patients should be free to seek care from any licensed health care professional.

3. Pursuit of corporate profit and personal fortune have no place in caregiving and they create enormous waste. The U.S. already spends enough to provide comprehensive health care to all Americans with no increase in total costs. However, the vast health care resources now squandered on bureaucracy (mostly due to efforts to divert costs to other payers or onto patients themselves), profits, marketing, and useless or even harmful interventions must be shifted to needed care.

4. In a democracy, the public should set overall health policies. Personal medical decisions must be made by patients with their caregivers, not by corporate or government bureaucrats.

ESSENTIAL FEATURES OF SINGLE-PAYER UNIVERSAL COVERAGE

NHI would build on the present strengths of the Medicare program. As envisioned by the Physicians' Working Group for Single-

Payer National Health Insurance, coverage would be extended to all age groups, and expanded to include prescription medications and long term care. Payment mechanisms would be structured to improve efficiency and assure prompt reimbursement, while reducing bureaucracy and cost shifting. Health planning would be enhanced to improve the availability of resources and minimize wasteful duplication. Investor-owned facilities would be phased out.

Table 14.1 lists the key features of single-payer NHI.[18]

Table 14.1
Key Features of Single-Payer National Health Insurance

1. Universal, comprehensive coverage: Only such coverage ensures access, avoids a "2-class" system, and minimizes administrative expense.

2. No out-of-pocket payments: Copayments and deductibles are barriers to access, administratively unwieldy, and unnecessary for cost containment.

3. A single insurance plan in each region, administered by a public or quasi-public agency. A fragmentary payment system that entrusts private firms with administration ensures the waste of billions of dollars on useless paper pushing and profits. Private insurance duplicating public coverage fosters 2-class care and drives up costs; such duplication should be prohibited.

4. Global operating budgets for hospitals, nursing homes, HMOs, and other providers, with separate allocation of capital funds: billing on a per-patient basis creates unnecessary administrative complexity and expense. Allowing diversion of operating funds for capital investments or profits undermines health planning and intensifies incentives for unnecessary care (under fee for service) or undertreatment (in HMOs).

5. Free choice of providers: Patients should be free to seek care from any licensed health care provider, without financial incentives or penalties.

6. Public accountability, not corporate dictates: The public has an absolute right to democratically set overall health policies and priorities, but medical decisions must be made by patients and providers rather than dictated from afar. Market mechanisms principally empower employers and insurance bureaucrats pursuing narrow financial interests.

7. Ban on for-profit health care providers: Profit seeking inevitably distorts care and diverts resources from patients to investors.

8. Protection of the rights of health care and insurance workers: A single-payer reform would eliminate the jobs of hundreds of thousands of people who currently perform billing, advertising, eligibility determination, and other superfluous tasks. These workers must be guaranteed retraining and placement in meaningful jobs.

Source: Himmelstein DU, Woolhandler S. National Health Insurance or Incremental Reform: Aim High, or at our Feet? *American Journal of Public Health*, January, 2003, 93(1): 31.

The following essential features are excerpted directly from the Working Group's written proposal to Congress.[19]

Coverage

A single public plan would cover every American for all medically-necessary services including: acute, rehabilitative, long term and home care, mental health, dental services, occupational health care, prescription drugs and supplies, and preventive and public health measures. Boards of expert and community representatives would assess which services are unnecessary or ineffective, and exclude them from coverage. As in the Medicare program, private insurance duplicating the public coverage would be proscribed. Patient co-payments and deductibles would also be eliminated.

Payment for Hospital Services

The NHI would pay each hospital a monthly lump sum to cover all operating expenses—that is, a global budget. The hospital and the NHI would negotiate the amount of this payment annually, based on past expenditures, previous financial and clinical performance, projected changes in levels of services, wages and input costs, and proposed new and innovative programs. Hospitals would not bill for services covered by the NHI. Hospitals could not use any of their operating budgets for expansion, profit, excessive executives' incomes, marketing, or major capital purchases or leases. Major capital expenditures would come from the NHI fund, but would be appropriated separately based upon community needs. Investor-owned hospitals would be converted to not-for-profit status, and their owners compensated for past investment.

Payment for Physicians and Outpatient Care

The NHI would include three payment options for physicians and other practitioners: fee-for-service; salaried positions in institutions receiving global budgets; and salaried positions within group practices or HMOs receiving capitation payments. Investor-owned HMOs and group practices would be converted to not-for-profit status. Only institutions that actually deliver care could receive NHI payments, excluding most current HMOs and some practice management firms that contract for services but don't own or operate any clinical facilities.

1. Fee-for-service: The NHI and representatives of the fee-for-service practitioners (perhaps state medical societies) would negotiate a simplified, binding fee schedule. Physicians would submit bills to the NHI on a simple form, or via computer, and would receive extra payment for any bill not paid within 30 days. Physician payment would cover only the work of physicians and their support staff, and would exclude reimbursement for costly office-based capital expenditures for such items as MRI scanners. Physicians accepting payment from the NHI could bill patients directly only for uncovered services (e.g., for cosmetic surgery).

2. Salaries within institutions receiving global budgets: Institutions such as hospitals, health centers, group practices, migrant clinics, and home care agencies could elect to be paid a global budget for the delivery of care as well as for education and prevention programs. The negotiation process and regulations regarding capital payment and profits would be similar to those for inpatient hospital services. Physicians employed in such institutions would be salaried.

3. Salaries within capitated groups: HMOs, group practices, and other institutions could elect to be paid capitation premiums to cover all outpatient, physician, and medical home care. Regulation of payment for capital and profits would be similar to that for hospitals. The capitation premium would not cover inpatient services (except physician care) which would be included in hospital global budgets. Selective enrollment policies would be prohibited and patients would be permitted to disenroll with appropriate notice. HMOs would pay physicians a salary, and financial incentives based on the utilization or expense of care would be prohibited.

Long-Term Care

The NHI would cover disabled Americans of all ages for all necessary home and nursing home care. Anyone unable to perform activities of daily living (ADLs or IADLs*) would be eligible for services. A local public agency in each community would determine eligibility and coordinate care. Each agency would receive a single budgetary allotment to cover the full array of long-term care services in its district. The agency would contract with long-term care providers for the full range of needed services, eliminating the perverse incentives in the current system that often pays for expensive institutional care but not the home-based services that most patients would prefer.

NHI would pay long-term care facilities and home care agencies a global (lump sum) budget to cover all operating expenses. For-profit nursing homes and home care agencies would be transformed to not-for-profit status. Doctors, nurses, therapists, and other individual long-term care providers would be paid on either a fee-for-service or salaried basis.

Since most disabled and elderly people would prefer to remain in their homes, the program would encourage home and community based services. The seven million unpaid care-givers such as family and friends who currently provide 70% of all long-term care would be assisted through training, respite services, and in some cases financial support. Nurses and social workers, as well as an expanded cadre of trained geriatric physicians, would assume leadership of the system.

Capital Allocation, Health Planning, and Profit

Funds for the construction or renovation of health facilities, and for major equipment purchases would be appropriated from the NHI budget. Regional health planning boards of both experts and community representatives would allocate these capital funds. Major capital projects funded from private donations would require approval by the health planning board if they entailed an increase in future operating expenses.

NHI would pay owners of for-profit hospitals, nursing homes and clinics a reasonable fixed rate of return on existing equity. Since

---

*Activities of daily living (ADLs) include: bathing, dressing, going to the toilet, getting outside, walking, transferring from bed to chair, and eating. Instrumental activities of daily living (IADLs) include: cooking, cleaning, shopping, taking medications, doing laundry, making phone calls and managing money.

most new capital investment would be funded by the NHI, it would not be included in calculating return on equity. For-profit HMOs would receive similar compensation for their clinical facilities and for computers and other administrative facilities needed to manage NHI. They would not be reimbursed for loss of business opportunities or for administrative capacity not used by the NHI.

Prescription Drugs and Supplies

NHI would pay for all medically necessary prescription drugs and medical supplies, based on a national formulary. An expert panel would establish and regularly update the formulary. The NHI would negotiate drug and equipment prices with manufacturers, based on their costs (excluding marketing or lobbying). Where therapeutically equivalent drugs are available, the formulary would specify use of the lowest cost medication, with exceptions available in case of medical necessity. Suppliers would bill the NHI directly (for the negotiated wholesale price plus a reasonable dispensing fee) for any item in the formulary that is prescribed by a licensed practitioner.

Financing

NHI would disburse virtually all payments for health services. Total expenditures would be set at approximately the same proportion of the Gross National Product as in the year preceding the establishment of NHI.

Funds for NHI could be raised through a variety of mechanisms. In the long run, funding based on an income or other progressive tax is the fairest and most efficient solution, since tax-based funding is the least cumbersome and least expensive mechanism for collecting money. The following illustration of a possible financing mechanism, prepared by Physicians for a National Health Program, projects the likely impact of NHI on taxpayers:

> Employers would pay a 7.0 percent payroll tax and employees would pay 2.0 percent, essentially converting current premium payments to health care payroll tax, but covering everybody. For over 60 percent of households, a 2 percent income tax increase would add less than $1,000 to their annu-

al tax bill; for another 20 percent of households the increase would average $1,600. However, many households would experience an overall decrease in their health spending as the modest increase in taxes would be offset by a substantial reduction in out-of-pocket spending on health care since the items such as medications, medical treatment, co-payments, deductibles, etc. are now fully financed. In addition, households no longer carry the financial risk of an expensive illness in parent, senior or child.[20]

SOME COMMON QUESTIONS
AND CONCERNS

1. Wouldn't NHI bring on socialized medicine?

This is a widely held concern, fueled by opponents of NHI, but a misperception on any account. NHI would be a system of publicly funded and administered social insurance, but providers would not work for the government. Physicians would be in private or salaried group practice, and bill the government for services provided, as they now do for their Medicare patients.

2. Why must investor-owned for-profit industries be phased out under a program of NHI?

As has been well documented in earlier sections of this book (e.g., Chapter 11), investor-owned for-profit health care corporations pursue a mission of profits for themselves and their shareholders as their primary mission. Compared to non-profit providers and facilities, investor ownership has been shown to lower quality of care in hospitals,[21-23] nursing homes,[24] HMOs[25] and dialysis centers.[26] The market ethic holds that health care is merely a commodity, to be bought and sold at a profit. This ethic has put necessary health care beyond the reach of tens of millions of American families while corrupting the healing mission of medicine. With its traditional emphasis on civil liberties, it is ironic that the U.S. is still alone in not considering health care a basic right, as is the case in all other industrialized Western nations.

3. Under NHI, why must duplicative
private insurance coverage be proscribed?

This important question has been well answered by the Physicians' Working Group for NHI in this way:[27] "Private insurance that duplicates the NHI coverage would undermine the public system in several ways. (1) The market for private coverage would disappear if the public coverage were fully adequate. Hence, private insurers would continually lobby for underfunding of the public system. (2) If the wealthy could turn to private coverage, their support for adequate funding of NHI would also wane. Why pay taxes for coverage they don't use? (3) Private coverage would encourage doctors and hospitals to provide two classes of care. (4) A fractured payment system, preserving the chaos of multiple claims databases, would subvert quality improvement efforts, e.g., the monitoring of surgical death rates and other patterns of care. (5) Eliminating multiple payers is essential to cost containment. Only a true single payer system would realize large administrative savings. Perpetuating multiple payers—even two—would force hospitals to maintain expensive cost accounting systems to attribute costs and charges to individual patients and payers."

4. Won't NHI involve unacceptable rationing?

This question implies that we don't already ration care, which we do extensively by income and class, as is well documented in this book. As Robert Kuttner points out:[28]

> ...one form or another of rationing exists everywhere in the world. The real issue is whether it is rationing based on private purse or on medical need. A system that coddles wealthy patients with minor ailments but cannot find money for universal vaccinations is, of course, rationing. A system that spends millions keeping alive twenty-week premature babies, and subsidizing in vitro fertilizations, but has forty million people without basic health coverage, is also rationing.

The other side of the rationing question is whether the affluent will still be able to purchase additional services not covered by NHI. The answer to that, of course, is yes, by purchasing supplemental insurance or paying out-of-pocket for uncovered services such as cosmetic surgery. At the same time, universal coverage for all medically necessary services, as defined by evidence-based clinical science, will be achievable through a single-risk pool based on need, not ability to pay.

5. How can NHI provide universal access to comprehensive health care and still save money?

Single-payer coverage would provide enormous cost savings, estimated to be at least $280 billion a year, by eliminating excess administrative costs, profits, unnecessary duplication, and cost-shifting within our present system. An additional annual savings of $50 billion is projected as a result of bulk purchasing of prescription drugs.[29] Administrative simplicity under NHI is the major reason for cost savings. As we saw in Chapter 12 (page 135), large cost savings have already been demonstrated by the Lewin group in some states through micro-simulation models.[30-31] Universal coverage systems spend more on primary prevention and less on wasteful overhead (e.g., the overhead of health insurance in the U.S. is 10 times higher than in Canada).[32] Under NHI, public funds now directed to private insurers would be used to fund public coverage. Since very few Americans have coverage for the high costs of long-term care, the inclusion of long-term care benefits by NHI would require a modest increase in taxes, preferably on an equitable, progressive basis. In the end, however, most people would spend no more, and perhaps less than they are already spending on health care ($6,167 per capita in 2004)[33] while trading our wasteful and inefficient health care system for a more cost effective and efficient one with universal coverage in a single-risk pool.

6. Why would American business want to support NHI?

Although many U.S. employers have been expected to provide health benefits to their employees since the advent of the voluntary employer-based system in the 1940s, many are now seeking refuge from the increasing cost burden of such coverage. Health insurance which is financed by tax mechanisms and which helps to assure a healthy workforce, is clearly in the self-interest of business. In today's global economy, foreign companies such as Nokia and

Volkswagen get full medical benefits at much less cost, an advantage worth billions over their U.S. competitors, Motorola and Ford. Dr. Donald Light, a Fellow at the University of Pennsylvania's Center for Bioethics, observes that conservatives in every other industrialized country support universal access to needed health care. Noting that this has not yet been the case in the U.S., he argues that universal coverage is essential to achieve these four traditional conservative moral principles: anti-free-riding, personal integrity, equal opportunity, and just sharing. He offers these guidelines for conservatives to remain true to these principles:[34]

1. Everyone is covered, and everyone contributes in proportion to his or her income.
2. Decisions about all matters are open and publicly debated. Accountability for costs, quality, and value of providers, suppliers, and administrators is public.
3. Contributions do not discriminate by type of illness or ability to pay.
4. Coverage does not discriminate by type of illness or ability to pay.
5. Coverage responds first to medical need and suffering.
6. Nonfinancial barriers by class, language, education, and geography are to be minimized.
7. Providers are paid fairly and equitably, taking into account their local circumstances.
8. Clinical waste is minimized through public health, self-care, prevention, strong primary care, and identification of unnecessary procedures.
9. Financial waste is minimized through simplified administrative arrangements and strong bargaining for good value.
10. Choice is maximized in a common playing field where 90-95 percent of payments go toward necessary and efficient health services and only 5-10 percent to administration.

7. Who wins, who loses with NHI?

As with any major policy change, there will be winners and losers, just as there are with the status quo. Most parties win with NHI. Patients would have a right to comprehensive health care, gaining access to a better system with an NHI card without deductibles or copayments. They would have free choice of provider and could expect more continuity with their physicians with less administrative complexity. Taxes would increase, preferably based on ability to pay, but would be more than offset by elimination of insurance premiums and out-of-pocket health care costs. Physicians would be freed from many of today's bureaucratic hassles and could spend more of their time on direct patient care, with more continuity and with less overhead. Billing would be greatly simplified. The patient's NHI card would be reprinted, the complexity of the encounter would be checked, and a bill would be sent by mail or electronically to the physician payment board.

The administrative workload of other health care workers would be lightened. Some jobs, especially related to billing, would disappear, so that job retraining and placement would be necessary. Nurses could spend more time on nursing, thus relieving the current acute nursing shortage.

Hospitals would join the winners' circle as well with simplification of billing and administration. Their revenues would become more stable and predictable. For-profit hospitals would be required to convert to not-for-profit status, and benchmarks for future planning would be based on community need, quality of care, efficiency and innovation.

Business would win by becoming more competitive. Many employers would see cost savings, as their new taxes are more than offset by no longer needing to cover the high costs of private insurance coverage.

The main losers under NHI would be for-profit health care corporations which can no longer divide and conquer in a segmented, largely unregulated health care marketplace. Many administrative and marketing jobs in today's private health sector would disappear. Within a single risk pool, insurers could perform contracted services under NHI or offer supplemental coverage for services not covered.

8. In view of the current problems in the Medicare and Medicaid programs, how can we expect that a larger government program will be successful?

Despite its critics, Medicare is by far the most efficient and popular part of our entire health care system. It operates with an administrative overhead of less than 3%, a small fraction of that in the private sector.[35] It has been shown in an October 2002 report to outperform private sector plans in terms of satisfaction with insurance, access to care, and overall insurance ratings, despite widespread anger over its limited prescription drug coverage.[36] Its main weaknesses have been its lack of a reasonable prescription drug benefit (which would be resolved under NHI) and underfunding which has reduced access to patients due to unacceptably low reimbursement to providers. As a program, it has nevertheless been a great success since 1965, and no politician could face the consequences of any attempt to curtail it. The Medicaid program is even more seriously underfunded, while being hobbled by wide variations from state to state in eligibility and administrative procedures. The fundamental problem with both Medicare and Medicaid, of course, is that they end up with the highest and most expensive risk pools in the country—Medicare, with its elderly population at high risk for chronic disease and long-term disability, and Medicaid, with its population of low-income people at high risk for disease and disability. Both of these programs would be folded in under NHI, simplifying administration and efficiency with improved and more predictable funding.

9. Since we are now hearing so much about Canada's problems, how can we expect NHI to succeed in the U.S.?

The Canadian health care system, involving NHI in all provinces since 1984, has been structurally successful, remains politically popular, but has been seriously underfunded since the early 1990s. Successive governments have been pressed by more healthy and affluent voters into funding cutbacks with the intent to avoid cross-subsidizing care for the sick and poor. Increasing pressure has been brought by for-profit interests wanting to divide the system into privatized and public sectors. Canada directs only about one-half the annual per capita spending on health care than does the U.S. While it is presently plagued (due to underfunding) by prolonged and increasing waits for some elective surgical procedures as well as some screening tests (e.g., mammography), the health outcomes for its population remain much better than in the U.S. by almost any measure.[37-38] Most health policy experts agree that these problems would evaporate if Canada spent anywhere near as much on health care per person as we do south of the border. The problem is not the structure of the Canadian system, but its grossly under-funded status with its opponents exaggerating its problems in their own self-interests. There is no question but that the Canadian system requires a more adequate and stable funding base, yet its strengths are frequently underestimated and its problems overstated. On the plus side, Canadians have free choice of physician, have full access to emergency and urgent care (not true in many U.S. emergency rooms), maintain high standards in medical education, and operate their health care system with an overhead of only 1%.[39] Myths abound on the negative side, such as an alleged high number of Canadians seeking care south of the border. Most of these myths are groundless. A recent example is a study reported in *Health Affairs* showing only a very small number of Canadians seeking care in the U.S., and most of that number for urgent or emergency care while already traveling in this country.[40]

10. What if states move ahead with single-payer universal coverage before NHI?

As Thomas Bodenheimer observed 10 years ago, some states may develop single-payer systems of universal coverage as demonstration projects before NHI is initiated.[41] That may well occur, since considerable momentum in that direction has been developing in California, Oregon, Vermont, Massachusetts, Maine, and some other states. A state enacting single-payer universal coverage would likely establish a new non-profit foundation, funded by the state, to pay for all medically necessary services, including emergency care, dental, vision, mental health, long-term care, and alternative medicine. Such a plan would be financed with federal funds already allocated to the state's public programs (Medicare, Medicaid, S-CHIP, current government expenditures for employee health benefits), as well as by additional income and payroll taxes. Universal coverage would be provided to the state's population without any exclusions for pre-existing conditions. In the longer term, all payments would be through an NHI trust fund, with a shift to funding by a progressive, income tax and employer payroll taxes.[42]

CONCLUSION

As we have seen from the family stories and personal vignettes earlier in this book, as well as from the fully documented trends in our failing health care system, the "safety net" is a cruel illusion for a large and growing part of the U.S. population. How can this affluent, otherwise advanced country tolerate the disparities and inequities of the market-based system? Where is our sense of outrage? The social injustice embedded in our present system, where health care is bought and sold as a commodity, is not fitting for a society which avows its commitment to civil rights and equal opportunity for all.

Would NHI give the U.S. a perfect health care system? By no means; any country's system is less than perfect and a work in progress. Would NHI be our best alternative to effectively reform our collapsing system? Emphatically yes, for all the reasons and evidence advanced in this book. Given the political will to confront the powerful defensive maneuvers of opposing special interest groups, the U.S. has the potential to develop the best health care system in the world. It already has these assets to build on—well-trained health professionals, excellent hospitals and facilities, strong biomedical research, more than 15% of its GDP already committed to health care, and a popular (though underfunded) existing Medicare program. NHI won't solve all of our health care problems, but will provide a framework to resolve other problems once the system is restructured and stabilized.

There are many, including some who believe that NHI is a good idea, who believe that it is still politically unrealistic. The events of September 11 certainly shifted priorities away from domestic social needs. The nation is grappling with economic problems and deficits as it mounts a military response to global terrorism. Yet history tells us that war and its aftermath have often coincided with major social advances. Examples include desegregation of the U.S. military and Saskatchewan's hospital insurance program soon after World War II, and the Great Society programs (including Medicare and Medicaid) during the Vietnam War in the 1960s.[43]

Health care reform in the U.S. has become urgent, and gets more so every day. An intense national debate is again underway as to reform alternatives. As public opinion is shaped during this debate, a critical public needs to value facts over ideology and trans-parency over obfuscation. It is fitting to close with this observation by Avedis Donabedian, international expert in quality assessment of health care, during an interview a month before his death in November 2000:[44]

> One positive aspect of the current chaos is that it is gener-ating dissatisfaction on all sides. Sooner rather than later we are going to have to develop a national health plan. The design and implementation of such a plan will be an exciting task of the fairly near future, I believe. This country has tremendous wis-dom and tremendous goodness. Eventually they will triumph in health care.

Appendix 1

Suggested Reading and Other Resources

Articles

1   Himmelstein DU, Woolhandler S. A national health program for the United States: A physician's proposal. *N Engl J Med* 1989; 320:102-8.

2   Grumbach K, Bodenheimer T. Reins or fences: a physician's view of cost containment. *Health Aff* (Millwood) 1990; 9(4): 120-6.

3   Bodenheimeer T. Underinsurance in America. *N Engl J Med* 1992; 327(4): 274-8.

4   Navarro V. Why Congress did not enact health care reform. *J Health Polit Policy Law* 1995; 20:455-62.

5   Kuttner R. Must good HMOs go bad? First of two parts: the commercialism of prepaid group health care. *N Engl J Med* 1998; 338:1558-63.

6   Himmelstein DU, Woolhandler S, Hellander I, Wolfe SM. Quality of care in investor-owned versus not-for-profit HMOs. *JAMA* 1999; 282:159-63.

7   Kuttner R. The American health care system—employer-sponsored health coverage. *N Engl J Med* 1999; 340:248-52.

8   Pellegrino ED. The commodification of medical and health care: the moral consequences of a paradigm shift from a professional to a market ethic. *J Med Philos* 1999; 24(3): 243-66.

9   Simon SR, Pan RJ, Sullivan AM, et al. Views of managed care—a survey of medical students, residents, faculty, and deans at medical schools in the United States. *N Engl J Med* 1999; 340:928-36.

10 Woolhandler S, Himmelstein DU. When money is the mission—the high costs of investor-owned care. *N Engl J Med* 1999; 341:444-6.

11 Bell H. Life without insurance: true stories of unnecessary sickness, death and humiliation. *The New Physician* (AMSA). September 2000.

12 Grumbach K. Insuring the uninsured. Time to end the aura of invisibility. *JAMA* 2000; 284(16): 2114-16.

13 Pellegrino ED. Medical professionalism: can it, should it sur-

vive? *J Am Board Fam Pract* 2000; 13:147-9.

14 Ferrer RL. A piece of my mind: within the system of no-system. JAMA 2001; 286:2513-4.

15 Miller JE. A Perfect Storm: The Confluence of Forces Affecting Health Care Coverage. National Coalition on Health Care. November 2001.

16 Himmelstein DU, Woolhandler S. National health insurance. Liberal benefits, conservative spending. *Arch Intern Med* 2002; 162:973-975.

17 Fuchs R. What's ahead for health insurance in the United States. *N Engl J Med* 2002; 346(23): 1822-24.

18 The Unraveling of Health Insurance. *Consumer Reports*, (July 2002):48-53.

19 Himmelstein DU, Woolhandler S. National health insurance or incremental reform: aim high or at our feet? *Am J Public Health* 2003; 93(1):31-4.

20 Proposal of the Physicians Working Group for single-payer national health insurance. JAMA 2003; 290:798-805.

21 Geyman JP. The corporate transformation of medicine and its impact on costs and access to care. *J Am Board Fam Pract* 2003; 16(5):443-54.

22 Woolhandler S, Campbell T, Himmelstein DU. Costs of health care administration in the United States and Canada. *N Engl J Med* 2003; 349:768-75.

23 Himmelstein DU, Woolhandler S, Wolk SM. The cost (of Health Care Administration) to the Nation, the States and the District of Columbia, with state-specific estimates of potential savings. Public Citizen, The Health Research Group, August 20, 2003.

Books

1 Eddy DM. *Clinical decision making from theory to practice: a collection of essays from the Journal of the American Medical Association.* Boston: Jones & Bartlett Publishers, 1996.

2 Kuttner R. *Everything for sale: the virtues & limits of markets.* Chicago: University of Chicago Press, 1999.

3 Himmelstein DU, Woolhandler S, Hellander I. *Bleeding the patient: the consequences of corporate health care.* Monroe, Me: Common Courage Press, 2001.

4 Mueller R. *As Sick as It Gets.* Dunkirk, NY: Olin Frederick, Inc.,

2001.

5   Bodenheimer TS, Grumbach K. *Understanding health policy: a clinical approach.* New York: Lange Medical Books/McGraw-Hill, 2002.

6   Geyman JP. *Health care in America: can our ailing system be healed?* Woburn, Mass: Butterworth-Heinemann, 2002.

7   LeBow B. *Health care meltdown: confronting the myths and fixing our failing system.* Boise, Idaho: JRI Press, 2002.

8   Geyman, JP. *The Corporate Transformation of Health Care: Can the Public Interest Still Be Served?* New York: Springer Publishing Company, 2004.

Newsletters

1   PNHP (Physicians for a National Health Program) quarterly newsletter, 29 E. Madison, Suite 602, Chicago, IL 60602.

2   Health letter. Public Citizen Health Research Group, 1600 20th Street, NW, Washington, DC 20009 (www.citizen.org/hrg).

Other

1   Quote of Day. (QoD). Available daily from Don McCanne, MD, retired family physician in Orange County, Calif, and past president, Physicians for a National Health Program (don@mccanne.org).

2   www.pnhp.org The newly revised PNHP web site contains a bibliography with many full articles on-line, a section for PNHP press releases and other breaking news ("news and updates"), and links to many state-based campaigns for single payer health care reform.

3   www.everybodyinnobodyout.org This web site has information about many state efforts for non-incremental health care reform.

4   Kaiser Family Foundation website: www.kff.org.

5   The Commonwealth Fund website: www.cmwf.org.

6   *Damaged Care*, starring Laura Dern. This Showtime film is based on the struggle of Dr. Linda Peeno with Humana. Call the PNHP office to borrow a copy (312) 782-6006.

Appendix 2

Distribution of Uninsured Population Under Age 65 and
Uninsured Rates, by State of Residence, 2001

	No. in Population (<65 years) (millions)	Distribution in Population (%)	No. of Uninsured (est.) (millions)	Distribution of Uninsured (%)	Uninsured Rate (%)
Totals	247.5	100	40.9	100	16.5
Alabama	3.8	2	0.6	1	15.0
Alaska	0.6	0	0.1	0	17.0
Arizona	4.7	2	0.9	2	20.1
Arkansas	2.3	1	0.4	1	18.9
California	31.1	13	6.7	16	21.4
Colorado	4.0	2	0.7	2	17.3
Connecticut	2.9	1	0.3	1	11.8
Delaware	0.7	0	0.1	0	10.6
District of Columbia	0.5	0	0.1	0	14.2
Florida	13.6	6	2.8	7	20.7
Georgia	7.5	3	1.4	3	18.2
Hawaii	1.0	0	0.1	0	11.0
Idaho	1.2	0	0.2	1	18.0
Illinois	10.9	4	1.7	4	15.3
Indiana	5.2	2	0.7	2	13.6
Iowa	2.5	1	0.2	1	8.7
Kansas	2.2	1	0.3	1	13.6
Kentucky	3.5	1	0.5	1	14.2
Louisiana	3.8	2	0.8	2	21.9
Maine	1.1	0	0.1	0	12.4
Maryland	4.7	2	0.6	2	13.8
Massachusetts	5.5	2	0.5	1	9.4
Michigan	8.7	4	1.0	2	11.7
Minnesota	4.5	2	0.4	1	8.8
Mississippi	2.5	1	0.5	1	18.5
Missouri	4.9	2	0.6	1	11.6
Montana	0.8	0	0.1	0	16.0
Nebraska	1.5	1	0.2	0	10.8
Nevada	1.9	1	0.3	1	17.9
New Hampshire	1.1	0	0.1	0	11.0
New Jersey	7.2	3	1.1	3	15.2
New Mexico	1.6	1	0.4	1	23.9
New York	16.4	7	2.9	7	17.7
North Carolina	7.1	3	1.2	3	16.5
North Dakota	0.5	0	0.1	0	11.3
Ohio	9.7	4	1.2	3	12.8
Oklahoma	2.9	1	0.6	2	21.0
Oregon	3.1	1	0.4	1	14.2
Pennsylvania	10.5	4	1.1	3	10.6
Rhode Island	0.9	0	0.1	0	9.0
South Carolina	3.5	1	0.5	1	14.2
South Dakota	0.6	0	0.1	0	10.9
Tennessee	5.0	2	0.6	2	12.7
Texas	19.0	8	4.9	12	26.0
Utah	2.1	1	0.3	1	16.0
Vermont	0.5	0	0.1	0	10.8
Virginia	6.2	2	0.8	2	12.4
Washington	5.2	2	0.8	2	14.8
West Virginia	1.5	1	0.2	1	15.8
Wisconsin	4.6	2	0.4	1	8.8
Wyoming	0.4	0	0.1	0	18.2

SOURCE: Fronstin, 2002, estimates from March 2001 Current Population Survey.

Appendix 3

Federal Poverty Guidelines, 2002 and 2003

Family Size in 48 Contiguous States	FPL for 2002			FPL for 2003		
	100% FPL	200% FPL	300% FPL	100% FPL	200% FPL	300% FPL
1 person	$8,860	$17,720	$26,580	$8,980	$17,960	$26,940
2 persons	$11,940	$23,880	$35,820	$12,120	$24,240	$36,360
3 persons	$15,020	$30,040	$45,060	$15,260	$30,520	$45,780
4 persons	$18,100	$36,200	$54,300	$18,400	$36,800	$55,200

Federal Poverty Level (FPL)

SOURCE: DHHS, 2003.

Appendix 4

The "United States National Health Insurance Act," H.R. 676

("Expanded & Improved Medicare For All Bill")
*Introduced by Cong. John Conyers, Jim McDermott, Dennis Kucinich, and Donna Christensen

Brief Summary of Legislation

The United States National Health Insurance Act establishes a new American program by creating a single-payer health care system. The bill would create a publically financed, privately delivered health care program that uses the already existing Medicare program by expanding and improving it to all U.S. residents, and all residents living in U.S. territories. The goal of the legislation is to ensure that all Americans, guaranteed by law, will have access to the highest quality and cost effective health care services regardless of one's employment, income, or health care status.

With over 75 million uninsured Americans, and another 50 million who are under insured, the time has come to change our inefficient and costly fragmented health care system.

The USNHI would reduce health spending in 2005 from $1,918 billion to 1,861.3 billion. Over-all government spending would be reduced by 56 billion while covering all of the uninsured. In 2005, without reform, the average employer that offers coverage will contribute $2,600 to health care per employee (for much skimpier benefits). Under this proposal, the average costs to employers for an employee making $30,000 per year will be reduced to $1,155 per year, less than $100 per month. Previous Medicare For All studies concluded that an average family of three would pay a total of $739.00 annually in total health care costs.

Who is Eligible

Every person living in the United States and the U.S. Territories would receive a United States National Health Insurance Card and I.D. number once they enroll at the appropriate location. Social Security numbers may not be used when assigning I.D. cards. No co-pays or deductibles are permissible under this act.

Benefits/Portability

- This program will cover all medically necessary services, including primary care, inpatient care, outpatient care, emergency care, prescription drugs, durable medical equipment, long term care, mental health services, dentistry, eye care, chiropractic, and substance abuse treatment. Patients have their choice of physicians, providers, hospitals, clinics, and practices.

Conversion to a Non-Profit Health Care System

- Private health insurers shall be prohibited under this act from selling coverage that duplicates the benefits of the USNHI program. They shall not be prohibited from selling coverage for any additional benefits not covered by this Act; examples include cosmetic surgery, and other medically unnecessary treatments.
- The National USNHI program will annually set reimbursement rates for physicians, health care providers, and negotiate prescription drug prices. The national office will provide an annual lump sum allotment to each existing Medicare region, which will then administer the program. Payment to health care providers include fee for service, and global budgets.
- The conversion to a not-for-profit health care system will take place over a 15-year period, through the sale of U.S. treasury bonds; payment will not be made for loss of business profits, but only for real estate, buildings, and equipment.

Funding & Administration

- The United States Congress will establish annual funding

outlays for the USNHI Program through an annual entitlement. The USNHI program will operate under the auspices of the Dept of Health & Human Services, and be administered in the former Medicare offices. All current expenditures for public health insurance programs such as S-CHIP, Medicaid, and Medicare will be placed into the USNHI program.

- A National USNHI Advisory Board will be established, comprised primarily of health care professionals and representatives of health advocacy groups.

Proposed Funding For USNHI Program:

- Maintaining current federal and state funding of existing health care programs. A modest payroll tax on all employers of 3.3%. A 5% health tax on the top 5% of income earners. A small tax on stock and bond transfers. Closing corporate tax shelters. Charitable contributions. For more details, see Physicians For A National Health Program *Financing National Health Insurance.*

*For more information, contact Joel Segal, legislative assistant, Rep. John Conyers, at 202-225-5126, or e-mail at Joel.Segal@mail.house.gov.

END NOTES

Preface

1   Mabin C. Funds to treat breast, cervical cancer lacking, *Dallas Morning News*, March 26, 2002.

Chapter One
Everyone Gets Health Care Anyhow,
So What's the Problem?

1   Tumulty K. Health care has a relapse. *Time* March 11, 2002, 42.
2   Somers AR, Somers HM. *Health and Health Care: Policies in Perspective.* Germantown, MD: Aspen Systems Corp, 1977:179-180.
3   Starr P. *The Social Transformation of American Medicine.* New York: Basic Books, 1982.
4   Ibid #2.
5   Burrow JG. AMA: *Voice of American Medicine.* Baltimore: Johns Hopkins Press, 1963:144.
6   Ibid #3.
7   Karson M. *American Labor Unions and Politics, 1900-1918.* Carbondale, IL: Southern Illinois University Press, 1958.
8   Rothman DJ. A century of failure: Health care reform in America. *J Health Polit Policy Law.* 1993;18(2):271-286.
9   Ibid #8.
10 A National Health Program: Message from the president. Soc Secur Bulletin. 1945;8(12).
11 Thai KV, Qiao Y, McManus SM. National health care reform failure: The political economy perspective. *J Health Hum Serv Adm.* Fall 1998;21(2):236-259.
12 Kuttner R. *Everything for Sale: The Virtues and Limits of Markets.* Chicago: University of Chicago Press, 1997:114.
13 Ibid #3.
14 Andrews C. *Profit Fever: The Drive to Corporatize Health Care and How to Stop It.* Monroe, Me: Common Courage Press, 1995:33.

15 Ibid #8.

16 Toner R, Stolberg SG. Decade after health care crisis, soaring costs bring new strains. *New York Times* on the Web. August 11, 2002.

17 Burton TM. Cardiac-device sales to surge further. *Wall Street Journal*, September 24, 2002, D3.

18 Pennachio DL. Full-body scans-or scams? *Med Econ* August 9, 2002, 62-71.

19 2003 Health Care Cost Survey: Report of Key Findings. Towers Perrin, December 2002.

20 Heffler, S., et al. Health spending projections through 2013. *Health Aff* Web-Exclusive Abstract, February 11, 2004.

21 Institute for the Future. Health and Health Care 2010: The Forecast, the Challenges. San Francisco: Jossey-Bass, 2000;123-137.

22 Ibid #21, p 130.

23 Relman AS. Book Reviews. The Institute of Medicine. Report on the Quality of Health Care. Crossing the Quality Chasm: A New Health System For the 21st Century. *N Engl J Med* 2001;345 (9):702.

24 Miller, W., Vigdor, ER, Manning, WG. Covering the uninsured: what is it worth? Web Exclsuive Abstracts *Health Affairs* 23(3): 290-1, 2004.

25 U.S. Census Bureau. Income, Poverty and Health Insurance Coverage in the United States: 2003. August 26, 2004.

26 Committee on the Consequences of Uninsurance. Health Insurance Is a Family Matter. Institute of Medicine. Washington, DC: National Academies Press, 2002:4.

27 Ibid. #26, p 49.

28 May, J.H. & Cunningham, P.J., Issue Brief #85. Washington, D.C. Center for Studying Health System Change, 2004.

29 According to a report by *Families USA* as cited in America's uninsured include middle-class, minorities. *Physicians Financial News* 22 (8) August 15, 2004, p.5.

30 Swartz K. Who owns the problems of the uninsured? *Inquiry* Summer 1996; 33(2):103-5.

31 Data Update. *PNHP Newsletter*. January 2002:4-5.

32 Ibid #31.

33 Ibid #25.

34 Committee on the Consequences of Uninsurance. Institute of Medicine. *Insuring America's Health: Principles and Recommendations.* National Academy Press, Washington, DC, 2004: 162, 166-7.

35 Ibid. Ref. 26, 213-223.

36 Duchon L, et al. Findings from the Commonwealth Fund 2001 Health Insurance Survey. *Med Benefits* 19(2), January 30 2002; 10.

37 Wyn R, Solis B, Ojeda VD, Pourat N. Falling through the cracks: Health insurance coverage of low-income women. Kaiser Family Foundation, February 2001.

38 Commonwealth Fund press release. June 12, 2001.

39 Garrett B, Holahan J. Health insurance coverage after welfare. *Health Aff* (Millwood) 2000;19(1):175-84.

40 Kaiser Commission on Medicaid and the Uninsured. The Uninsured: A Primer. March 2002:4.

41 Case BG, Himmelstein DU, Woolhandler S. No care for the caregivers: declining health insurance coverage for health care 1988-1998. *Am J Public Health* 2002; 92(3):404-8.

42 Norton's Bankruptcy Advisor, May 2000.

43 Billings J, Minanoviteh T, Blank A. Barriers to Care for Patients with Preventable Hospital Admissions. New York: United Hospital Fund, 1997.

44 Ibid Ref 24, 133.

45 Cantor JC, Long SH, Marquis S. Challenges of state reform: variations in ten states. *Health Aff* (Millwood) 1998; 17(1): 191-200.

46 Baker DW, Sudano JJ, Albert JM, Borawski EA, Dor A. Lack of health insurance and decline in overall health in late middle age. *N Engl J Med* 2001;345:1106-12.

47 Finger AL. Caring for the uninsured: Will the problem ever be solved? *Med Econ.* December 20, 1999:132-141.

48 Ibid #36.

49 *The New York Times*, Reuters June 11, 2001, as summarized in *PNHP Newsletter*, January 2002, 6-7.

50 Lagnado, L. Medical Seizures: Hospitals Try Extreme Measures to Collect Their Overdue Debts, *Wall Street Journal*, October 30, 2003, A1.

51 Hadley J. Sicker and poorer: The consequences of being uninsured. Kaiser Commission on Medicaid and the Uninsured. Kaiser Family Foundation. May 2002.

52 Committee on the Consequences of Uninsurance, Hidden Costs, Value Lost: Uninsurance in America. Washington, D.C., Institute of Medicine 2003:4-5.

53 Lagnado L. Hospitals urged to end harsh tactics for billing uninsured. *Wall Street Journal* July 7, 2003:A9.

54 Friedrich MJ. Medically underserved children need more than insurance card. *JAMA* 2000;283:3056-7.

55 The Kaiser Commission on Medicaid and the Uninsured News Release. July 23, 2004.

56 Washington DC: Center on Budget and Policy Priorities. May 10,2001 www.cbpp.org/pubs/recent-2001.htm.

57 Ibid #19.

58 Findley S. Research Brief. National Institute for Health Care Management Research and Educational Foundation (September 2000). *Med Benefits* 2000; 17(2): 5-6.

59 Andrews, E.L., Budget Office forecasts record deficit in '04 and sketches a pessimistic future. *New York Times*, January 27, 2004: A19.

Chapter Two
Is There a Safety Net?

1 Ferrer RL. A piece of my mind: within the system of no-system. *JAMA* 2001;286:2513-4.

2 Altman S, Reinhardt U, Shields A (eds). *The Future of the U.S. Healthcare System: Who Will Care for the Poor and Uninsured?* Chicago: Health Administration Press, 1998.

3 Toner R, Pear R. Cutbacks imperil health coverage for states' poor. *New York Times* April 28, 2003:A1.

4 Friedman E. The little engine that could: Medicaid at the millennium. *Front Health Serv Manage.* Summer 1998;14(4):3-24.

5 Ibid #3.

6 Spillman BC. Adults without health insurance: Do state policies matter? *Health Aff* (Millwood) 2000;19(4):178-187.

7 Halfon N, Inkeles M, DuPlessis H, Newacheck PW. Challenges in securing access to care for children. *Health Aff* (Millwood)1999;18(2):48-63.

8 Friedrich MJ. Medically underserved children need more than insurance card. *JAMA* 2000;283:3056-7.

9 Special report. Families USA. Children losing health coverage. September 14, 2002.

10 Institute of Medicine. In: Lewin ME, Altman S (eds). *America's Health Care Safety Net: Intact but Endangered.* Washington, DC: National Academy Press, 2000:47-80.

11 Lambe S, Washington DL, Fink A, et al. Trends in the use and capacity of California's emergency departments, 1990-1999. *Ann Emerg Med* 2002;39(4):430-2.

12 Weber T, Ornstein C. County USC doctors say delays fatal. *Los Angeles Times.* latimes.com April 23, 2003.

13 Data Update. *PNHP Newsletter*, May 2001, 9.

14 Hospital emergency rooms and "patient dumping." Public Citizen's Health Research Groups. *Health Letter* August 2001; 6, 7,11.

15 Light DW. Price discrimination. Quote of Day. don@mccanne. org May 5, 2002.

16 Ornstein C. Bill could aid uninsured patients. *Los Angeles Times* April 3, 2002, B1,5.

17 Lagnado L. Full price: A young woman, an appendectomy, and $19,000 debt. *Wall Street Journal* March 17, 2003:A1.

18 Mullan F. Tin-cup medicine. *Health Aff* (Millwood) 2001;20(6):216-18.

19 McAlearney JS. The financial performance of community health centers, 1996- *Health Aff* (Millwood) 2002;21:219-25.

20 Gusmano MK, Fairbrother G, Park H. Exploring the limits of the safety net: community health centers and care for the uninsured. *Health Aff* (Millwood) 2002;21(6):188-94.

21 Practice Briefs. Doctors offer less time to charity care: study. *Physician Financial News* 2001; (November 15):38.

22 Iglehart JK. The dilemma of Medicaid. *N Engl J Med* 2003;348:2140-8.

23 Simon S. Medicaid ax is falling as recession saps states. *Los Angeles Times*. Available from. latimes.com March 5, 2002.

24 Pear R. Many on Medicaid lack drugs, study says. *New York Times*, April 9, 2002. (based on study by Cunningham PJ, Center for Studying Health System Change).

25 Smith V, Gifford K, Ramesh R, Wachino V. Medicaid spending growth: a 50-state update for fiscal year 2003. Menlo Park, Calif: Henry J. Kaiser Family Foundation, January 2003.

26 Ibid #23.

27 Ibid #23.

28 Ornstein C. States cut back coverage for poor. *Los Angeles Times*, February 25, 2002.

29 California Healthline. California Healthcare Foundation Around California. Nearly half of California doctors do not treat Medi-Cal beneficiaries, survey says (University of California, San Francisco study). February 12,2002.

30 Practice Beat. Our Web Poll. How doctors react to Medicaid's low payment rates. *Med Econ* March 8, 2002:19.

31 Gollin G. Health care meltdown. *Los Angeles Times* November 26, 2001.

32 Pear R. U.S. nears clash with governors on Medicaid cost. *New York Times*, February 16, 2004: A1.

33 Pear, R. Governors say Medicaid needs more federal help to control rising costs. *New York Times*, February 25, 2002.

34 Ibid #25.

35 Holahan J, Spillman B. Health care access for uninsured adults: A strong safety net is not the same as insurance. Washington, DC: Urban Institute. Available from http://newfederalism.urban.org/html/series_b/b42/b42.html.

Chapter Three
I Work, But My Employer
Doesn't Provide Insurance

1 Abstracted from Kaiser Commission on Medicaid and the Uninsured. In Their Own Words: The uninsured talk about living without health insurance. Kaiser Family Foundation. September 2000;2-7.
2 Wessel, D. Health care costs blamed for hiring gap. *Wall Street Journal*, March 11, 2004: A2.
3 Mills RJ. U.S. Census Bureau, Health insurance coverage: 2000. *Med Benefits* October 30, 2001;18(2): 10.
4 Ibid. #1, p 43.
5 Bell H. Life without insurance: True stories of unnecessary sickness, death and humiliation. *The New Physician*. September 2000;19-28.
6 Ibid #5.
7 Ibid #5.
8 Callahan P. Delivering the news. Children injured on paper routes often go uninsured. *Wall Street Journal* July 19, 2002:A1, A6.
9 Himmelstein D, Woolhandler S, Hellander I. *Bleeding the Patient: The Consequences of Corporate Health Care*. Monroe, ME, Common Courage Press, 2001; 33.
10 Kaiser Family Foundation Survey. May 5, 2002, as reported in *PNHP Newsletter*, Chicago, IL, Fall, 2002:5.
11 Finger AL. Caring for the uninsured: will the problem ever be solved? *Med Econ* December 20, 1999:132-41.
12 Ibid #5.
13 Ibid #5.
14 Federal poverty levels, DSHS, 2002.
15 Kaiser Commission on Medicaid and the Uninsured. The Uninsured and Their Access to Health Care. Fact Sheet. December 2003.
16 Ibid #5.
17 Ibid #14, p. 4.
18 Kaiser Commission on Medicaid and the Uninsured. Health Insurance in America: 2000 Data Update. February 2000; 1.
19 Ibid #5, p 28.

Chapter Four
My Employer Offers Insurance,
But I Can't Afford It

1 Abstracted from Kaiser Commission on Medicaid and the Uninsured. In Their Own Words: The uninsured talk about living without health insurance. Kaiser Family Foundation. September 2000;38-42.

2 Ibid #1.

3 Preliminary results of survey by Mercer Human Resource Consulting as cited in Fuhrmans, VO, Employers say they can slow rate of health-care cost gains. *Wall Street Journal*, August 27, 2004: A2.

4 Lee D. Health costs irk public employees. *Los Angeles Times* April 20, 2002: C1-2.

5 Terhune C. Side effect. Insurer's tactic: If you get sick, the premium rises. *Wall Street Journal* April 9, 2002.

6 Appleby J. Many health workers uninsured. *USA Today*. Available at www,usatoday.com/money/health/2002-03-28-no-insurance.htm.

7 Ibid #1: 8-10.

8 Kaiser Family Foundation Survey June 5, 2002; reported in *PNHP Newsletter*. Fall, 2002:5.

9 Kaiser Commission on Medicaid and the Uninsured. Health Insurance Coverage in America: 2000 Data Update. February 2002:9.

10 U.S. Census Bureau, as cited in Egan, T., Economic squeeze plaguing middle-class families. *New York Times*, August 28, 2004: A11.

11 Economic Policy Institute. *Los Angeles Times* May 18, 2002.

12 Schiff GD, Young QD. You can't leap a chasm in two jumps. The Institute of Medicine Health Care Quality Report. *Public Health Reports*, September/October 2001;116:54.

13 Hilsenrath JE. Income gap narrowed at end of 90s. *Wall Street Journal* April 24, 2002:A2.

14 Consumers Union. The Health Care Divide October 2000, as reported in *PNHP Newsletter*, May 2001:4.

15 Gabel J, Levitt L, Holve E, Pickreign J, Whitmore H et al. Job-based health benefits in 2002: some important trends. *Health Aff* (Millwood) 2002;21(5):145.

16 Wolff EN. Top Heavy: *The Increasing Inequality of Wealth in America And What Can Be Done About It*. New York: The New Press, 2002.

17 Gabel JR, Pickreign JD, Whitmore HH, Schoen C. Embraceable you: how employers influence health plan enrollments. *Health Aff* (Millwood) 2001;20(4);205.

18 Committee on the Consequences of Uninsurance. Institute of Medicine. Care Without Coverage: Too Little, Too Late. Washington, DC: National Academy Press, 2002:1-2.

19 Blumberg LJ, Nichols LM. The health status of workers who decline employer-sponsored insurance. *Health Aff* (Millwood) 2001;20(6):180-7.

20 Hanson, K.W., et al. Uncovering the health challenges facing people with disabilities: the role of health insurance. *Health Aff* Web Exclusive. November 19, 2003: W3-553.

21 McCanne D. E-mail Quote of the Day commenting on report of Institute of Medicine (reference 14 above); May 21, 2002.

Chapter Five
Once You Lose Your Insurance, Just Try to Get It Back

1 Abstracted from Kaiser Commission on Medicaid and the Uninsured. In Their Own Words: The uninsured talk about living without health insurance. Kaiser Family Foundation. September 2000:14-19.

2 Ibid #1.

3 Report by Families USA, February 12, 2002.

4 Institute for Health Care Research and Policy for the Kaiser Family Foundation. Georgetown University Health Policy. How accessible is individual health insurance for consumers in less-than-perfect health? *Med Benefits* 2001; 18(14):10.

5 *Orange County Register*. September 2, 2001, as reported in *PNHP Newsletter*. January 2002:5.

6 Terhune C. Health insurers' premium practices add to profit surge, roil customers. *Wall Street Journal* on line. April 9, 2002. Accessed April 13, 2002 at http://online.wsj.com/article_print/0,4287.SB10183057004602491160,00.html.

7 Ibid #1, p 28.

8 Rowland, D. Uninsured in America. Kaiser Commission on Medicaid and the Uninsured. Testimony for U.S. House of Representatives, Committee on Ways and Means, Subcommittee on Health, March 9, 2004.

9 Kaiser Commission on Medicaid and the Uninsured. Kaiser Family Foundation, 1999.

10 Commonwealth Fund. Press release. Only one-fourth of workers would keep health coverage through COBRA if they lost their jobs. August 29, 2002.

11 Cohn J. The next big health care crisis is now. Health scare. *The New Republic* online. December 24, 2001:3.

12 Atchinson BK, Fox DM. The politics of the Health Insurance Portability and Accountability Act. *Health Aff* (Millwood) 1997;16(3):146-50.

13 Pollitz K, Tapay N, Hadley E, Specht J. Early experience with "new federalism" in health insurance regulation. *Health Aff* (Millwood) 2000;19(4):7-22.

14 Achman L, Chollat D. Insuring the uninsurable: an overview of state high-risk health insurance pools. Mathematics Policy Research Inc. for The Commonwealth Fund. August 2001; as summarized in *Med Benefits* 2001;18(17):10.

15 Policy and Practice. Ineffective insurance pools. *Fam Pract News*, September 15, 2001:29.

16 Data Update, *PNHP Newsletter* January 2002:5.

17 Monheit AC, Vistnes JP, Eisenberg JM. Moving to Medicare: trends in the health insurance status of non-elderly workers, 1987-1996. *Health Aff* (Millwood) 2001;20(2):204-13.

18 Simantov E, Schoen C, Bruegman S. Market failure? Individual insurance markets for older Americans. *Health Aff* (Millwood) 2001;20(4):139-49.

19 Fishman E. Aging out of coverage: young adults with special health needs. *Health Aff* (Millwood) 2001;20(6):245-66.

20 Ibid #19.

21 Committee on the Consequences of Uninsurance. Institute of Medicine. Care Without Coverage: Too Little, Too Late, Washington, DC: National Academy of Sciences. 2002:68-71.

22 Sturm R, Wells. Health insurance may be improving- but not for individuals with mental illness. *Health Serv Res*, 2000.

23 Frank RG, Koyanagi C, McGuire TG. The politics and economics of mental health "parity" laws. *Health Aff* (Millwood) 1997;16(4):108-119.

24 Ibid #21.

25 Data Update, *PNHP Newsletter*, May 2001:4.

26 Little Hoover Commission Report and *Los Angeles Times* November 21, 2000, as reported in *PNHP Newsletter*, May 2001; 3.

27 Pear, R. Many youths reported held waiting for help. *New York Times*, July 8, 2004: A18.

28 Frommer, F.J., Health insurance firms block parity bills. Associated Press. June 10, 2004.

29 Gitterman DP, Sturm R, Schaffer RM. Toward full mental health parity and beyond. *Health Aff* (Millwood):2001;20(4):68-76.

30 Reinhardt U. On our dishonest health system. E-mail message to Dr. Don McCanne, President, Physicians for a National Health program. Quote of the Day; don@mccanne.org August 2, 2002.

Chapter Six
I Had Medicaid, But I Lost It

1   Abstracted from Kaiser Commission on Medicaid and the Uninsured. In Their Own Words: The uninsured talk about living without health insurance. Kaiser Family Foundation, September 2000: 26-31.

2   Himmelstein D, Woolhandler S, Hellander I. *Bleeding the Patient. The Consequences of Corporate Health Care*. Monroe, Me, Common Courage Press, 2001:24.

3   Kaiser Commission on Medicaid and the Uninsured. Women who left welfare: health care coverage, access, and use of health services. June 2002:1.

4   Ibid. #2, pp 17-18.

5   Center on Budget and Policy Priorities. May 10, 2001, www.cbpp.org.

6   Families USA. Press Release, November 20, 2000.

7   Uchitelle L. Red ink in states beginning to hurt economic recovery. *New York Times* July 28, 2003:A1.

8   Simon S. The nation. Medicaid ax is falling as recession saps states. *Los Angeles Times* latimes.com March 5, 2002.

9   Rosenbaum DE. White House sees a $455 billion gap in '03 budget. *New York Times* July 16, 2003, A1.

10 Toner R, Stolberg SG. Decade after health care crisis, soaring costs bring new strains. *New York Times* on the web, August 11, 2002.

11 Ibid #8.

12 Smith V, Ellis E, Gifford K, Ramesh R, Wachino V. Medicaid spending growth: Results from a 2002 survey. Kaiser Commission on Medicaid and the uninsured. October 2002.

13 American Healthline April 3, 2002. CMS approves Tenn-Care waiver application, as reported in *PNHP Newsletter*, Fall 2002:3.

14 Ryan J. Third-world quality of care. *San Francisco Chronicle*, June 11, 2002.

15 Ornstein C, Kay LF. Critics decry medical cuts. *Los Angeles Times*, May 16, 2002.

16 Nelson AA, Reeder CE, Dickson M. The effect of a Medicaid drug copayment program on the utilization and cost of prescription services. *Med Care* 1994;22:724-36.

17 Bloom BS, Jacobs J. Cost effects of restricting cost effective therapy. *Med Care* 1985;23:872-79.

18 Reeder CE, Nelson AA. The differential impact of copayment drug use in a Medicaid population. *Inquiry* 1986; 22:396-403.

19 Lurie N, Ward NB, Shapiro MF, Gallego C, Vaghaiwalla R, Brook RH. Termination of medical benefits: a follow-up study one-year later. *N Engl J Med* 1986;314:1266-68.

20 Soumerai SB, Avom J, Ross-Degnan D, Gortmaker S. Payment restrictions for prescription drugs under Medicaid: effects on therapy, cost and equity. *N Engl J Med* 1987;317:550-56.

21 Soumerai SB, Ross-Degnan D, Avorn J, McLaughlin TJ, Choodnovskkiy I. Effects of Medicaid drug-payment limits on admission to hospitals and nursing homes. *N Engl J Med* 1991;325:1072-77.

22 Soumerai SB, McLaughlin TJ, Ross-Degnan D, Casteris CS, Bollini P. Effects of limiting Medicaid drug-reimbursement benefits on the use of psychotropic agents and acute mental health services by patients with schizophrenia. *N Engl J Med* 1994; 331:650-5.

23 Tamblyn R, Laprise R, Hanley JA, Abrahamowitz M, Scott S. Adverse events associated with prescription drug cost-sharing among poor and elderly persons. *JAMA* 2001;285:421-9.

24 Carroll J. Cuts in Medicaid limit medication available to poor. *Wall Street Journal*, April 9, 2002:D2.

25 Joyce GF, Escarce JJ, Solomon MD, Goldman DP. Employer drug benefit plans and spending on prescription drugs. *JAMA* 2002:288(14):1733-39.

26 Goldman, D.P., Joyce, G.F., Escarce, J.J., et al. Pharmacy benefits and the use of drugs by the chronically ill, *JAMA* 2004; 291:2344-50.

27 Light DW. Cost sharing. e-mail communication with don@mccanne.org (president, Physicians for a National Health Program), September 16, 2002.

28 *Wall Street Journal*, October 29, 2002:A1.

29 Janofsky M. Deep cuts have not closed deficit in many states, report says. *New York Times* April 26, 2003:A30.

Chapter Seven
I'm Not Poor Enough for Medicaid, But I Can't Afford Care

1 Abstracted from Kaiser Commission on Medicaid and the Uninsured. In Their Own Words: The uninsured talk about living without health insurance. Kaiser Family Foundation, September 2000:20-25.

2 Kaiser Commission on Medicaid and the Uninsured. Low-income parents' access to Medicaid five years after welfare reform. June 2002.

3 Families USA Press Release, November 20, 2000, as reported in *PNHP Newsletter* May 2001:4.

4 Ibid #2, p 5.

5 Tumulty K. Health care has a relapse. *Time* March 11, 2002:44-5.

6 *Rochester Democrat and Chronicle*. January 16, 2001, as reported in *PNHP Newsletter*, May 2001:3.

7 Foster H. Kids, poor will feel pain of health care crisis. *Seattle Post Intelligencer*, March 15, 2001:A1, A8.

8 Committee on the Consequences of Uninsurance. Institute of Medicine. Washington, DC: National Academies Press, 2002:69.

9 Marlis M. Family out-of-pocket spending for health services: A continuing source of financial insecurity. Commonwealth Fund. June 2002:IX.

10 Himmelstein D, Woolhandler S, Hellander I. *Bleeding the Patient: The Consequences of Corporate Health Care.* Monroe, ME, Common Courage Press, 2001:34.

11 Blendon R J, Schoen C, DesRoches, et al. Inequities in health care: A five-country survey. *Health Aff* (Millwood) 2002;21(3):186.

12 March of Dimes Press Release, as reported in *PNHP Newsletter* January 2002:4.

13 Bell H. Life without insurance: true stories of unnecessary sickness, death and humiliation. *The New Physician.* September 2000:25.

14 Donohue TJ, Sweeney JJ. Let's insure America. *Washington Post* February 12, 2002:A25.

15 Smith S. Study finds more infants going hungry. *Boston Globe* On Line. May 8, 2002.

Chapter Eight
I Can't Afford My Prescriptions

1 Study by NDC Health, a health information company, as reported by Peterson M. *New York Times* On the Web. March 8, 2002.

2   Barry P. Ads, promotions drive up costs. *AARP Bulletin* March 2002, 43(3): 1, 17.
3   Harris G. Drug firms 'bad year' wasn't so bad. *Wall Street Journal* February 21, 2003:B4.
4   Frank R. Prescription drug prices: why do some pay more than others do? *Health Aff* (Millwood) 2001;20(2):115-28.
5   Ibid #4.
6   Publications and Reports. Prescription drugs. Hard to swallow rising prices for America's seniors. *Health Aff* (Millwood) 2000;19(1):254.
7   Brock F. A health care revolt remembered. *New York Times* April 7, 2002,3.15.
8   Laschober MA, Kitchman M, Neuman P, Strabic AA. Trends in Medicare supplemental insurance and prescription drug coverage, 1996-1999. *Health Aff* (Millwood) 2002;21(2):11.
9   Freudenheim M. Companies trim health benefits for many retirees as costs surge. *New York Times* On the Web. May 10, 2002.
10 Appleby J. Patients drop treatment due to costs. Copayments too steep for some Medicare HMO clients. USA Today. com January 28, 2002.
11 Greene K. More disabled say care falls short. *Wall Street Journal* April 29, 2003:D4.
12 Prescription drug access: not just a Medicare problem. HSC Issue Brief, April 2002.
13 LeBow B. *Health Care Meltdown: Confronting the Myths and Fixing Our Failing System*, Boise, Idaho, JRI Press, 2002, 97.
14 Kaiser Commission on Medicaid and the Uninsured. In Their Own Words: The uninsured talk about living without health insurance. Kaiser Family Foundation, September 2000;31.
15 Ibid #14, p 46.
16 Taylor H, Leitman R, editors. Out-of-pocket costs are a substantial barrier to prescription drug compliance. Harris Interactive, *Health Care News*, November 20, 2001; 1(32).
17 Shearer G. "Medicare Prescription Drugs: Conference Committee Agreement asks Beneficiaries to Pay Too High a Price for a Modest Benefit," Consumers Union, Washington, DC, November 25, 2003.
18 McGinley L., Lueck S., Rogers D. "Senate Democrats Wage Fight to Block Medicare Legislation," *Wall Street Journal*, November 24, 2003.
19 Stolberg S., Freudenheim M. "Sweeping Medicare Change Wins Approval in Congress; President Claims a Victory," *New York Times*, November 26, 2003: A1.
20 Lueck S. "The New Medicare: How It Works," *Wall Street Journal*, November 25, 2003: D1.

21 Abboud L., Hensley S. "Drug-Discount Cards to Have 'Ifs'," *Wall Street Journal*, November 26, 2003: D2.

22 Pear R. Medicare actuary gives wanted data to Congress. *New York Times*, March 20, 2004: A8.

23 Bodenheimer T. "The Dismal Failure of Medicare Privatization," Senior Action Network, San Francisco, June 1, 2003.

24 Rogers D. Medicare actuary reveals e-mail warning. *Wall Street Journal*, March 18, 2004: A4.

25 Sherman S. Seniors to face increasing costs for drugs. Associated Press, *Seattle Post Intelligencer*, November 26, 2003, p.A3.

26 Greenberger RS. A prescription for change. Maine drug plan, awaiting high court review, may sway U.S. *Wall Street Journal* January 15, 2003:B2.

27 Lueck S, Greenberger RS. Justices lift big barrier in effort by Maine to rein in drug costs. *Wall Street Journal* May 20, 2003:A3.

28 Pear R. The Supreme Court: drug pricing decision and its impact, ruling may embolden other states to act. *New York Times* May 20,2003:A21.

29 *Washington Post* March 25, 2002, as reported in *PNHP Newsletter*, Fall 2002:9.

30 Parker-Pope T. Health Journal. The latest craze in coupon-clipping: free trial offers for prescription drugs. *Wall Street Journal* April 16, 2002:D1.

31 Waldholz M. Prescriptions: new drug cards for seniors: PR ploy or great bargain? *Wall Street Journal* April 18, 2002;D5.

32 Carroll J. Prescription drug spending jumps 17%. *Wall Street Journal* March 29, 2002;A3.

33 Petersen A. How to buy cheap drugs online. *Wall Street Journal* August 13, 2002;D1, D2.

34 Lueck S. Upstart Texas firm makes stir with cheap drugs from Canada. *Wall Street Journal*, October 21, 2002, A1.

Chapter Nine
My Doctor Won't See Me Now

1 Managed Care Report. *Physicians Financial News*, Quarterly Supplement; June 30, 2002;5.

2 DeVoe J, Fryer Jr. GE, Hargraves JL, Phillips RL, Green LA. Does career dissatisfaction affect the ability of family physicians to deliver high-quality patient care? *J Fam Pract* 2002;51(3):223-28.

3 Practice Beat. Doctor's misery index continues to worsen. *Medical Economics* June 7, 2002;22.

4 Rosenberg J. Studies point to doctor dissatisfaction. *Physicians Financial News* 19(4): October 15, 2001;1,22.

5 AAFP, family physicians turn up heat, tell lawmakers about liability crisis. F P Report 2002;8(8):7.

6 Paige L. The blame game. *Modern Physician* 2002;6(8):1.

7 Collins K, Hughes DL, Doty MM, Ives BL, Edwards JN, et al. Diverse communities, common concerns: assessing health care quality for minority Americans. Commonwealth Fund. New York: March 2002:P41.

8 Brennan TA. Luxury primary care—market innovation or threat to access? *N Engl J Med* 2002;346:1165-8.

9 Himmelstein DU, Woolhandler S, Hellander I. Bleeding the Patient: The Consequences of Corporate Health Care. Monroe, Me: Common Courage Press, 2001;77.

10 Shane A. Physician supply: from glut to shortage. *Physicians Financial News* 2002; 20(6):1, 14.

11 Silverman J. Medicare fee fix means 1.6% raise for fiscal 2003. *Fam Pract News* 2003; 33(5):1.

12 Szabo, J. Sweetening the pot. *Physicians Financial News*, 22(2): S11, 2004.

13 Iglehart JK. Medicare's declining payments to physicians. *N Engl J Med* 2002; 346:1924-30.

14 Guglielmo WJ. Will the states cook up a health care fix? *Med Econ* July 12, 2002:38-43.

15 Thomas R. State may cut health care for poor. *Seattle Times* August 18, 2002:B1-2.

16 Ibid #2.

17 Wagner L. Citing national losses of $2.2 billion, physicians closing doors to seniors. *Physicians Financial News* May 15, 2002, 20(7):1,24.

18 American Academy of Family Physicians FP Report, 2002, Leawood, Kan: AAFP, September, 8(9).

19 No new patients. Policy and Practice. *Family Practice News*, October 1, 2002:32(19):53.

20 Ostrom CM. Seattle is losing Medicare doctors. *Seattle Times*, September 6,2002:B1.

21 Ibid #17.

22 Ibid #17.

23 Ibid #17.

24 California Healthline, California Healthcare Foundation. Nearly half of California doctors do not treat Medi-Cal beneficiaries. February 12, 2002.

25 Pear R. Many doctors shun patients with Medicare. *New York Times* March 17, 2002:A29.

26 Abstracted from Kaiser Commission on Medicaid and the Uninsured. In Their Own Words: The uninsured talk about living without health insurance. Kaiser Family Foundation, September 2000; 41, 48.

27 Ibid #9, p 23.

28 *Los Angeles Times*, December 29, 2001, as reported in *PNHP Newsletter*, Fall 2002, 8.

29 Skaggs DL, Clemens SM, Vitale MG, Femino JD, Kay RM. Access to orthopedic care for children with Medicaid versus private insurance in California. Pediatrics 2001;107:1405-8.

30 Health Insurance Report. Second-class medicine. *Consumer Reports*, September 2000;50.

Chapter Ten
Is Basic Health Care a Right?

1 Light DW. Health care for all: A conservative case. *Commonwealth Magazine* February 22, 2002.

2 Marwick C. Report: Health care reform must affirm "right." JAMA 1993;270: 1284-5.

3 Mariner WK. Medical care for prisoners: The evolution of a civil right. Medicoleg News. 1981;9(2):4-8.

4 Halfon N, Inkeles M, DuPlessis H, Newacheck PW. Challenges in securing access to care for children. *Health Aff* (Millwood):1999;18(2):48-63.

5 Giesen D. A right to health care? A comparative perspective. *Health Matrix* 1994;4(2):277-95.

6 Curran WJ. The constitutional right to health care. Denial in the court. *N Engl J Med* 1989;320:788-9.

7 Annas GJ. A national Bill of Patients' Rights. *N Engl J Med* 1998;338:695-9.

8 Churchill LR. Rationing Health Care in America: Perceptions and Principles of Justice. Notre Dame, Ind: University of Notre Dame, 1987; 70-71, 90, 91.

9 Ivins M. Health care sky is indeed falling. *Star Telegram* March 28, 2002. (http://www.dfw.com/mld/startelegram/news/columnists-/molly_ivins/2950472.htm).

10 Adopted by the General Assembly on December 10, 1948. Printed in: von Munch I, Buske A (eds). International Law the Essential Treaties and Other Relevant Documents. 1985:435ff.

11 Carmi A. On patients' rights. *Med Law* 1991;10(1):77-82.

12 Hayes JA. Health care as a natural right. *Med Law* 1991;11(5-6):405-16.

13 Roemer R. The right to health care—gains and gaps. *Am J Public Health* 1988;78(3):241-47.

14 Ibid #12.

15 Kaye NS. The right to health care, letter. *N Engl J Med* 1989; 321:693.

16 Ibid #2.

17 Ruddick W. Why not a general right to health care? *Mt Sinai J Med* 1989; 56(3):161-3.

18 News Release. Kaiser Family Foundation. New national survey finds significant minority of women report delaying or going without care due to costs. May 7, 2000.

19 Wrich J. Audit findings submitted to Congressional Budget Office. March 1998.

20 Sade R. Medical care as a right: A refutation. *N Engl J Med* 1971;285:1288.

21 Ibid #20.

22 Beauchamp DE. Public health as social justice. *Inquiry* 1976;13(1):4-6.

23 Ibid. #8;76-8.

24 Smith HL, Churchill LR. Professional ethics and primary care medicine. Durham, NC: Duke University Press, 1986;93-6.

25 Bulger RJ, McGovern JP, editors. Physician and Philosopher—The Philosophical Foundation of Medicine: Essays by Dr. Edmund Pellegrino. Charlottesville, Va, Carden Jennings Publishing, 2001.

26 Enthoven AC. The history and principles of managed competition. *Health Aff* (Millwood) 1993;12(suppl) 24.

27 Thorpe KE. Health care cost containment: reflections and future directions. In: Kovner AR, Jones S (eds). Health Care Delivery in the United States. New York: Springer Publishing Company, 1999;439-73.

28 Himmelstein DU, et al. Administrative Waste in the U.S. Health Care System in 2003: The cost to the Nation, the States and the District of Columbia, with State-Specific Estimates of Potential Savings. Washington, DC: The Public Citizen Health Research Group, August 20, 2003.

29 Himmelstein DU, Woolhandler S. National health insurance or incremental reform: aim high, or at our feet? *Am J Public Health* 2003;93(1):102-5.

30 www.pnhp.org.don@mccanne.org. Quote of the Day. Feb 9, 2002.

31 Smith RF. Universal health insurance makes business sense. *Rutland Herald* Nov. 2, 2001.

32 Schuster M, McGlynn EA, Brook RH. How good is the quality of health care in the United States? Milbank Q 1998;76(4):517-63.

33 Nozick R. Anarchy, State and Utopia. New York: Basic Books, 1974;149,233-5.

34 Ibid. #8; 87-8.

35 Veatch RM. Voluntary risks to health: the ethical issues. *JAMA* 1980;243:50-5.

36 Ibid #22.

37 Denby D. The Current Cinema. Calculating Rhythm. John Q and Crossroads. *The New Yorker* March 4, 2002;90.

38 Ibid. #8; 94-6.

39 Rosenbaum S, Frankford DM, Moore B, Borgi P. Who should determine when health care is medically necessary? *N Engl J Med* 1999;340:229-32.

40 Ibid. #17, 163.

41 Moynihan DP. Quoting Judge Edwin Torres of the New York Supreme Court, Twelfth Judicial District in defining deviancy down. *The American Scholar* (Winter) 1993;26.

42 Ibid. #8; 103.

Chapter Eleven
Corporate Health Care and the Public Interest

1 Jacobson PD, Pomfret SD. ERISA litigation and physician autonomy. *JAMA* 2000;283:921-6.

2 Mariner WK. State regulation of managed care and the Employee Retirement Income Security Act. *N Engl J Med* 1996;335:1986-90.

3 Court J, Smith F. Making a Killing: HMOs and the Threat to Your Health. Monroe, Me, Common Courage Press, 1999, 130-1.

4 Kuttner R. Must good HMOs go bad? First of two parts: the commercialism of prepaid group health care. *N Engl J Med* 1998;338:1558-63.

5 Kuttner R. The American health care system: Wall Street and health care. *N Engl J Med* 1999;340:664-8.

6 Peeno L. A physician answers questions about denial of care in managed care corporations. (Citizen Action, 1996).

7 Hellander I. Executive Director of Physicians for a National Health Program (PNHP), Chicago, Ill. Personal communication, January 19, 2001.

8   Woolhandler S, Himmelstein, DU, When Money is the Mission—The High Costs of Investor-Owned Care. *New England Journal of Medicine*, 1999; 341: 444-6.
9   McCormick D, Himmelstein DU, Woolhandler S, Wolfe S, Bor DH. Relationship between low quality-of-care scores and HMOs' subsequent public disclosure of quality-of-care scores. JAMA 2002;288(12):1484-1490.
10 Data Update. PNHP Newsletter, January 2002, p 10.
11 Brubaker B. Confronting health care 'demons'. *Washington Post* May 27,2002.
12 Munoz R. How health care insurers avoid treating mental illness. *San Diego Union Tribune*, May 22, 2002.
13 Lee D. A bright spot in health insurance. *Los Angeles Times*, April 25, 2002, C1.
14 Medicare Minus Choice. *Fam Pract News* 32(2): January 15, 2002.
15 CMS Medicare Fact Sheet, Centers for Medicare and Medicaid Services, September 2002.
16 Barry P. More HMOs leave Medicare. *AARP Bulletin*, November 2002:43(10):1.
17 Lee D. Rising costs put pressure on Kaiser. *Los Angeles Times*, September 29, 2002.
18 VHA 1998 Environmental Assessment: Setting foundations for the Millennium. Irving, Tex.: VHA Inc., 1998.
19 Ibid #10, p.7.
20 Ibid #18.
21 Needleman J, Chollet DJ, Lamphere JA. Hospital conversion trends. *Health Aff* (Millwood) 1997;16(2):187-95.
22 Coye MJ. The sale of Good Samaritan: A view from the trenches. *Health Aff* (Millwood) 1997;16(2):107.
23 Martinez B. After an era of dominant HMOs, hospitals are turning the tables. *Wall Street Journal* Online, April 12, 2002.
24 Ibid #10, p.7.
25 Pasztor A. *Wall Street Journal*, April 3, 2002, B10.
26 Data Update, *PNHP Newsletter*, Spring 2003, p.10.
27 Ibid #10, pp.7-8.
28 Ibid #23.
29 White RD. Tenet continuing resurgence. *Los Angeles Times*, January 5, 2002.
30 Rundle, R.L. Tenet healthcare to sell hospitals and take charge of $1.4 billion. *Wall Street Journal*, January 28, 2004: A3.
31 Ibid #23.

32 Walsh MW. A mission to save money, a record of otherwise. *New York Times* on the Web, June 7, 2002.

33 Ibid #10, p 6.

34 Public Citizen report. April 18, 2002. Full report available at h t t p : / / w w w . c i t i z e n . o r g / - congress/reform/drug_industry/profits/articles.ctm?ID= (416).

35 Mintz M. Still hard to swallow. *Washington Post* Outlook Section. February 2001.

36 Light, D.W., Lexchin, J. Will lower drug prices jeopardize drug research? A policy fact sheet. *American Journal of Bioethics*, 4(1): W3-W6, 2004.

37 Lueck S. Drug industry exaggerates R & D costs to justify pricing, consumer group says. *Wall Street Journal* July 24, 2001, B6.

38 Public Citizen report, July, 2001.

39 Baker D. Patent medicine. *The American Prospect*, January 29, 2001:34-5.

40 Ibid #10, p 9.

41 Public Citizen Report, November 9, 2001.

42 Editorial. Gaming the patent drug system. *Los Angeles Times*, June 10, 2002.

43 Angell M, Relman AE. Prescription for profit. www.washingtonpost.com.

44 Hensley S. How generics can cut your drug bills. *Wall Street Journal*, June 6, 2002, D1.

45 Ivins M. Drug companies can really make you sick. Public Citizen's Health Research Group. Health Letter, July 2001:4.

46 Ibid #10, p. 9.

47 CBS. 60 Minutes. December 19, 1999.

48 Psaty BM, Heckbert SR, Kopesell TD, et al. The risk of incident myocardial infarction associated with anti-hypertensive drug therapies. *Circulation* 1995;91:925.

49 Deyo RA, Psaty BM, Simon G, et al. The messenger under attack—Intimidation of researchers by special interest groups. *N Engl J Med* 1997;336:1176-80.

50 Burton TM. Reining in drug advertising. *Wall Street Journal* March 13, 2002, B1.

51 Wolfe SM. Direct-to-consumer (DTC) ads: illegal, unethical or both. Public Citizen's Health Research Group. Health Letter. September 2001:3.

52 Zimmerman A, Armstrong D. Swallow this: How drug makers use pharmacies to push pricey pills. *Wall Street Journal*, May 1, 2002:A1.

53 Armstrong D, Zimmerman A. Drug makers find new way to push pills. *Wall Street Journal* June 14, 2002:B1.

54 Ibid #10, p.10.

55 Data Update. *PNHP Newsletter*. May 2001:8.

56 Grembowski DE, Diehr P, Novak LC, et al. Measuring the "managed-ness" and covered benefits of health plans. *Health Serv Res* 2000;35(3):707-34.

57 News release. FTCR calls for health care rate regulation. Santa Monica, CA: The Foundation for Taxpayer and Consumer Rights, October 4, 2002.

58 Appleby, J. Health insurance premiums crash down on middle class. *USA Today*, March 17, 2004: B1.

59 Ibid #10, p. 8.

60 Vital signs. *Fam Pract News*. February 1, 2002; 32(3):1.

61 Kuttner R. Everything for Sale: The Virtues and Limits of Markets: Chicago: University of Chicago Press, 1999.

62 Freudenheim, M. Acquisition Would Create Nation's Largest Health Insurer. *New York Times*, October 28, 2003: C1.

63 Terhune C. Side effect. Insurer's tactic: If you get sick, the premium rises. *Wall Street Journal*, April 9, 2002.

64 Ibid # 61.

65 Morrison AB, Wolfe SM. Outrage of the month. None of your business. Public Citizen's Health Research Group. Health Letter, February 2001:11.

66 Terhune C. Insurers avoid state regulations by selling via groups else-where. *Wall Street Journal*, April 9, 2002:A20.

67 Chaker AM. A pinch hit on health coverage. *Wall Street Journal*, May 7, 2002:D6.

68 Court J. Insurance: you pay, they bait and switch. *Los Angeles Times*, May 8, 2002.

69 Frishauf P. Book review. *Medscape*. February 26, 2002.

70 Kleinke JD. Oxymorons: The Myth of a U.S, Health Care System. San Francisco: Jossey-Bass, 2001.

71 McGinley L. General American to pay $76 million in Medicare case. *Wall Street Journal*, June 26, 2002:A2.

72 Wysockie B. Bogus insurers leave patients with big bills. *Wall Street Journal*, October 2, 2002:D1.

73 Ibid #62.

74 Geyman JP. The corporate transformation of medicine and its impact on costs and access to care. *J Am Board Fam Pract* 2003;16(5) 443-54.

75 Silverman EM, Skinner, J.S., Fisher, E.S., "The Association Between For-Profit Hospital Ownership and Increased Medicare Spending," *New England Journal of Medicine*, 1999; 341: 420-6.
76 Yuan Z, Cooper GS, Einstadter D, Cebul RD, Rimm AA. The Association Between Hospital Type and Mortality and Length of Stay: A Study of 16.9 Million Hospitalized Medicare Benificiaries. *Med Care* 2000, 38: 231-45.
77 Woolhandler S, Himmelstein DU. Costs of Care and Administration at For-Profit and Other Hospitals in the United States, *New England Journal of Medicine*, 1997; 366: 769-74.
78 Hartz AJ, Krakauer H, Kuhn EM, et al.,Hospital Characteristics and Mortality Rates. *New England Journal of Medicine*, 1989; 321: 1720-5.
79 Chen J, Radford MJ, Wang Y, et al. Do 'America's Best Hospitals' Perform Better for Acute Myocardial Infarction? *New England Journal of Medicine*, 1999; 340: 286-92.
80 Kovner C, Gergen PJ, Nurse Staffing Levels and Adverse Events Following Surgery in U.S. Hospitals, *Image J Nurs Sch* 1998; 30: 315-21.
81 Himmelstien DU, Woolhandler S, Hellander I, Wolfe SM, Quality of Care in Investor-Owned vs. Not-for-Profit HMOs. JAMA, 1999; 282(2): 159-63.
82 The HMO Honor Roll. *U.S. News and World Report*, 1997 Oct 23: 62.
83 Harrington C, Woolhandler S, Mullen J, Carrillo H, Himmelstein DU, Does Investor-Ownership of Nursing Homes Compromise the Quality of Care? *Am J Public Health* 2001; 91(9):1.
84 Garg PP, Frick KD, Diener-West M, Powe NR, Effect of Ownership of Dialysis Facilities on Patients' Survival and Referral for Transplantation. *New England Journal of Medicine*, 1999; 341: 653-60.
85 Devereaux PJ, Schunemann HJ, Ravindran N, et al. Comparison of Mortality Between Private For-Profit and Private Not-For Profit Hemodialysis Centers: A Systematic Review and Meta-Analysis. JAMA, 2002; 288: 2449-57.
86 Munoz R. How health care insurers avoid treating mental illness. *San Diego Union Tribune*, May 22, 2002.
87 Ibid #81.
88 Tu HT, Reschovsky JD. Assessments of medical care by enrollees in for-profit and non-profit health maintenance organizations. *N Engl J Med* 2002;346(17):1288-93.
89 Ibid #55, p 9.
90 *New York Times* February 6, 2002, as reported in *PNHP Newsletter*, Fall 2002, p.9.
91 Ibid #55, p 8.
92 Ibid #48.

93 GAO report backs link between drug user fees and higher rate of drug withdrawals. Public Citizen Health Research Group, Health Letter 2002 (November): 18 (11): 11-12.

94 Barry P. Drug industry spends huge sums guarding prices. AARP Bulletin. May 2002;43(5):3-15.

95 Ibid #10, p 10.

96 Ibid #8.

Chapter Twelve
How, and Can, Our Failing System Be Fixed?

1 Sidel V. E-mail message to Don McCanne MD, president of Physicians for a National Health Program, March 17, 2002.

2 Kuttner R. Everything for Sale: The Virtues and Limits of Markets. Chicago: University of Chicago Press, 1999;112-3.

3 Coddington DC, Keen DJ, Moore KD, et al. The Crisis in Health Care: Costs, Choices, and Strategies. San Francisco: Jossey-Bass, 1990.

4 Oliver TR. The dilemmas of incrementalism: Logical and political constraints in the design of health insurance reforms. J Policy Anal Manage 1999;18(4):652-83.

5 Blue Cross and Blue Shield Association. State legislative health care and insurance issues: 2001 survey of plans. Med Benefits 2002;19(5):11.

6 Kronebusch K. Medicaid for children: Federal mandates, welfare reform and policy backsliding. Health Aff (Millwood) 2001;20(1):97-111.

7 Atchison BK, Fox DM. The politics of the Health Insurance Portability and Accountability Act. Health Aff (Millwood) 1997;16(3):146-50.

8 Pollitz K, Tapay N, Hadley E, Specht J. Early experience with "new federalism" in health insurance regulation. Health Aff (Millwood) 2000;19(4):7-22.

9 Colliver V. CalPERS to increase '03 health care rates. San Francisco Chronicle, April 18, 2002.

10 Krolicki K. CalPERS approves HMO fee hikes, says reform needed. Reuters. June 18, 2003.

11 Broder D. Health care in a 'death cycle.' The Washington Post, April 17, 2002;A.15.

12 Garrett B, et al. The Urban Institute for the W.K. Kellogg Foundation. August 29, 2001. In: Med Benefits October 15, 2001;18(19): 10.

13 Wessel, D. Health care costs blamed for hiring gap. Wall Street Journal, March 11, 2004: A2.

14 Acs G, Blumberg LJ. How a changing workforce affects employer-sponsored health insurance. Health Aff (Millwood) 2001;20(1):178-83.

15 Freudenheim M. Small employers severely reduce health benefits. *New York Times*, September 6, 2002.

16 Long SH, Marquis MS. Have small-group health insurance purchasing alliances increased coverage? *Health Aff* (Millwood) 2001;20(1):154-63.

17 Freudenheim M. Companies trim health benefits for many retirees as costs surge. *The New York Times*, May 10, 2002;A.1.

18 Tejada C. Work week. Declining health. *Wall Street Journal* July 24, 2002:B2.

19 Gabel JR, Pickreign JD, Whitmore HH, Schoen C. Embraceable you: how employers influence health plan enrollment. *Health Aff* (Millwood) 2001;20(4):205.

20 Robinson JC. The end of managed care. JAMA 2001;285(20): 2622-8

21 Ibid #18.

22 Gleckman H. Health coverage: who should get the bill? *BusinessWeek*, March 4, 2002:64-5.

23 Appleby J. New insurance plans turn patients into shoppers. *USA Today*, January 8, 2002;B1-2.

24 Editorial. Three cheers for the IRS. *Wall Street Journal*, July 2, 2002;A18.

25 Freudenheim M. Personal costs for Medicare H.M.O.'s. rise. *New York Times*, February 14, 2002.

26 Gold M. Medicare+Choice: An interim report card. *Health Aff* (Millwood) 2001;20(4):120-38.

27 Report of Commonwealth Fund. Summarized in Policy and Practice. Ineffective insurance pools. *Fam Pract News* 2001;September 15:29.

28 Families USA. Abstracted in Med Benefits November 15, 2001:10-11.

29 Gruber J. Written testimony at Hearing on Health Insurance Credits before the House Ways and Means Subcommittee on Health. February 13, 2002.

30 Taylor H. How and why the health insurance system will collapse. *Health Aff* (Millwood) 2002;21(6):195-7.

31 Fuchs VR. What's ahead for health insurance in the United States? *N Engl J Med* 2002;346:1823-4.

32 Himmelstein, DU, et al. Administrative Waste in the U.S. Health Care System in 2003: The cost to the Nation, the States and the District of Columbia, with State-Specific Estimates of Potential Savings. Washington, DC: The Public Citizen Health Research Group, August 20, 2003.

33 Young Q. Press Release, Physicians for a National Health Program, Chicago, May 1, 2001.

34 Angell M. Testimony to the Congressional Black Caucus, Hispanic Caucus and Progressive Caucus, May 1, 2001.

35 Smith RF. Universal health insurance makes business sense. *Rutland Herald*, November 2, 2001.

36 Brand R, Ford D, Sager A, Socolar D. Universal comprehensive coverage: a report to the Massachusetts Medical Society. Waltham, MA: The Massachusetts Medical Society, 1998.

37 Sheils JF, Haught RA. Analysis of the costs and impact of universal health care models for the state of Maryland: the single-payer and multi-payer models. Fairfax, VA: The Lewin Group, 2000.

38 Miller, A. 'Single-payer' Georgia health plan pushed. *Atlanta Journal-Constitution*, June 22, 2004.

39 California Health Care Options project; preliminary- full drafts of each proposal are available at http://www.healthcareoptions.ca.gov/doclib.asp.

40 Woolhandler S, Himmelstein DU. Paying for national health insurance—and not getting it. *Health Aff* (Millwood) 2002;21(4):88-98.

41 Peterson MA. Political influence in the 1990s: From iron triangles to policy networks. *J Health Polit Policy Law* 1991;18(2):395-438.

42 Friedman TL. The Lexus and the Olive Tree. New York: Farrar. Strauss and Giroux, 1999;353.

43 Krugman P. Bad medicine. *The New York Times*, March 19, 2002.

Chapter Thirteen
The Politics of Health Care Reform

1 Thomas Jefferson. Writings. New York: Library of America, 1984:493.

2 National poll by National Public Radio (NPR), the Kaiser Family Foundation, and the Harvard Kennedy School of Government, June 2002.

3 Nichols, L.M., et al. Are market forces strong enough to deliver efficient health care systems? Confidence is waning. *Health Aff.* (Millwood). 23(2): 8-21, 2004.

4 Medical Benefits. M B Stat, September 15, 2001:11.

5 Harwood J. Americans distrust institutions in poll. *Wall Street Journal* June 13, 2002:A4.

6 Bigler R. Wall Street meltdown worsening pension crisis facing American workers. LRA online. Labor Research Association, July 9, 2002.

7   Rodwin VG. Comparative analysis of health systems: An international perspective. In: Kovner AR, Jonas S (eds). Health Care Delivery in the United States. New York: Springer Publishing Company, 1999:116-51.

8   Navarro V. Why some countries have national health insurance, others have national health services, and the United States has neither. *Int J Health Serv* 1989;19(3):383-404.

9   Hall J. Incremental change in the Australian health care system. *Health Aff* (Millwood) 1999;18(3): 95-103.

10 World Health Report 2000. Available at http://www.who.int/whr/2000en-/report.htm.

11 Naylor CD. Private Practice, Public Payment: Canadian Medicine and the Politics of Health Insurance, 1911-1966. Kingston, Ontario: McGill—Queen's University Press, 1986.

12 Armstrong P, Armstrong H. *Universal Health Care. What the United States Can Learn from the Canadian Experience.* New York: The New Press, 1998:6-32.

13 Sullivan T, Baranek PM. First Do No Harm: Making Sense of Canadian Health Reform. Vancouver, BC: UBC Press, 2002:23-5.

14 Woolhandler S, Himmelstein DU. Paying for national health insurance and not getting it. *Health Aff* (Millwood) 2002;21:88-98.

15 Ibid #13.

16 Commission on the Future of Health Care in Canada. Final Report. November 2002. Available at www.healthcarecommission.ca/.

17 Romanow R. Creating a national health care system for Canadians. Speech at the Canadian Club of Winnipeg. November 20, 2002.

18 Ibid #12.

19 Snider K. Unions fight cuts in health benefits. *Seattle Times* June 23, 2002.

20 Kuttner R. The road to Enron. *The American Prospect* March 25, 2002:2.

21 Appleby J. Finger pointers can't settle on who's to blame for health costs. *USA Today* August 21, 2002.

22 Lueck S. Medicare patients to be offered private plans. *Wall Street Journal* August 28, 2002:D4.

23 New report unmasks United Seniors Association as hired gun for drug industry. Public Citizen Press Report, July 16, 2002.

24 Seniors group continues to do bidding of drug industry. Public Citizen Press Report. October 21, 2002.

25 Health Benefits Coalition asks Congress not to pass patients' rights, mental health parity legislation. California Healthline, California Healthcare Foundation, May 16, 2002.

26 PNHP release, Chicago, IL, November 14, 2002.

27 Action Alert. FAIR Fairness & Accuracy in Reporting, New York City. NBC slams universal health care. November 12, 2002.

28 Dreazen YJ. TV election ads cost a record $900 million. *Wall Street Journal*, November 5, 2002:A6.

29 Hitt G. Drug makers pour ad money into final days of campaign. *Wall Street Journal*, November 4, 2002:22D.

30 Green K, McGinley L. AARP to alter TV ad that touts more scrutiny of drug purchases. *Wall Street Journal* May 14, 2002:B6.

31 Claybrook J. Free air time needed to break special interest stranglehold. Public Citizen Press Release. June 19, 2002.

32 Kuttner R. Democrats must offer bolder health plans. *Boston Globe* May 21, 2003.

33 Blendon RJ, Benson JM. Americans' views on health policy: a 50 year Historical perspective. *Health Aff* (Millwood) 2001;20(2):33-46.

34 Texans want guaranteed health care. Statewide Survey on Health Care. University of Houston, Center for Public Policy. Texas Public Policy Survey, June 20-29,2002.

35 *San Francisco Chronicle* single-payer poll. May 1, 2003.

36 E-mail communication between Kip Sullivan and Don McCanne, president of Physicians for a National Health Program, July 19, 2002.

37 Simon SR, Pan RJ, Sullivan AM, et al. Views of managed care—a survey of medical students, residents, faculty and deans at medical schools in the United States. *N Engl J Med* 1999;340:928-36.

38 McCormick D, Woolhandler S, Himmelstein DU, Bor DH. View of single payer national health insurance: a survey of Massachusetts physicians. *J Gen Intern Med* 2002;17(suppl):204.

39 Attitudes toward the United States health care system; long-term trends. Views of the public, employers, physicians, health plan managers are closer now than at any time in the past. Harris Interactive August 21, 2002; 2(17).

40 Woolhandler S, Himmelstein DU, Angell M, et al. Proposal of the Physicians' Working Group for Single-Payer National Health Insurance. JAMA 2003; 290:798-805.

41 Peterson MA. Political influence in the 1990s: from iron triangles to policy networks. *J Health Polit Policy Law* 1993;18(2):395-438.

42 National Survey of Small Businesses. Menlo Park, Calif: Kaiser Family Foundation, 2000.

43 Court J, Smith F. State must take lead on health care. *San Diego Union Tribune*, August 20, 2002.

44 Frammolino R. Workers feel like suckers. *Los Angeles Times*, March 20, 2002.

45 Simmons H. Controlling health spending in the private sector. Presentation to Council on Health Care Economics and Policy. Ninth Princeton Conference. The Robert Wood Johnson Foundation. June 6-8, 2002.

46 Freudenheim M. Next big health debate: how to help uninsured. *New York Times*, August 27, 2002.

47 Edwards DW. USWA calls for national health care. *People's Weekly World*, April 20, 2002.

48 Greene K. Advertising. AARP is targeting big drug firms. *Wall Street Journal*, April 17, 2002:B2.

49 Himmelstein DU, Woolhandler S, AARP's conflict of interest in the Medicare drug bill. Press Release, Harvard Medical School and Physicians for a National Health Program, November 19, 2003.

50 Press Release. AARP has financial conflict of interest in Medicare drug bill. Public Citizen, Washington, DC, November 21, 2003.

51 Drinkard J, AARP Accused of Conflict of Interest. *USA Today*, November 21, 2003: 11A.

52 Editorial. A first step on drug costs. *Los Angeles Times* May 9, 2000.

53 Pear R, Toner R. Senate votes to give consumers faster access to generic drugs, amending Medicare bill. *New York Times* June 20, 2003:A19.

54 Lueck S, McGinley L. Drug-import bill unlikely to be law. *Wall Street Journal* July 28, 2003:B4.

55 Ibid #40.

56 Connoly C. States sued for pushing cheaper drugs via Medicaid. *Washington Post*, August 21, 2002:A1.

57 Lueck S, Greenberger R, Rundle R. Court backs patient appeals in battle over HMO coverage. *Wall Street Journal* June 25, 2002.

58 Anderson M. States can force HMOs to open networks to doctors. Justices rule. *New York Times* April 3, 2003:A2.

59 Rice B. When an HMO denial is practicing medicine. *Med Economics* June 7, 2002:100.

60 Rush Prudential HMO Inc v Moran, No. 00-1021 (SCT 2002).

61 Pegram v Herdrich, 530 US 211 (2000).

62 Health care administration costs are greater than defense budget Quote of Day October 27, 2002. don@mccanne.org.

63 UHCAN Health-e-Action #4. Sound the alarm on health care. This year's FINAL EXAM on Medicare—Can Congress get the Rx laws right? Universal Health Care Action Network, Cleveland, Ohio. Accessed August 23, 2004 at uhcanlist@uhcan.org.

64 McCanne D. Quote of Day. Should partisan debate trump reform? May 22, 2003;mccanne.org.

Chapter 14: There Is a Fix: National Health Insurance

1 Putnam RD. Bowling together. *The American Prospect* 2002; 13(3).
2 LeBow B. *Health Care Meltdown: Confronting the Myths and Fixing Our Failing System*. Boise, Idaho: JRI Press, 2002:219.
3 Himmelstein DU, Lewontin JP, Woolhandler S. Who administers? Who cares? Medical administrative and clinical employment in the United States and Canada. *Am J Public Health* 1996;86:172-8.
4 Himmelstein DU, Woolhandler S, Hellander I, Wolfe SM. Quality of care in investor-owned vs not-for-profit HMOs. JAMA 1999; 282(2): 159-63.
5 News release. FTCR calls for health care rate regulation. Santa Monica, Calif: The Foundation for Taxpayer and Consumer Rights, October 4, 2002.
6 Marlis M. Family out-of-pocket spending for health services. A continuing source of financial insecurity. Commonwealth Fund. June 2002: IX.
7 Remler DK, Gray BM, Newhouse JP. Does managed care mean more hassles for physicians? Inquiry 2000; 37: 304-16.
8 Institute for the Future. *Health and Health Care 2010: The Forecast, the Challenges*. San Francisco: Jossey-Bass, 2000; 123-37.
9 Light DW. A conservative call for universal access to health care. *Penn Bioethics* 2002; 9(4): 4-6.
10 U.S. Government Accounting Office. Canadian health insurance: lessons for the United States. Washington, DC: U.S. Government Accounting Offiice (GAO/HRD-91-90), 1991.
11 Congressional Budget Office. Single-payer and all-payer health insurance systems using Medicare's payment rates. Washington, DC: Congressional Budget Office, April, 1993.
12 Grumbach K, Bodenheimer T, Woolhandler S, Himmelstein DU. Liberal benefits conservative spending: the Physicians for a National Health Program proposal. *JAMA* 1991; 265:2549-54.
13 Brand R, Ford D, Sager A, Socolar D. Universal comprehensive coverage: a report to the Massachusetts Medical Society. Waltham, Mass: The Massachusetts Medical Society, 1998.
14 Sheils JF, Haught RA. Analysis of the costs and impact of universal health care models for the state of Maryland: the single-payer and multi-payer models. Fairfax, VA: The Lewin Group, 2000.
15 California Health Care Options Project http://www.healthcareoptions-.ca.gov/doclib.asp.

16 Smith RF. Universal health insurance makes business sense. *Rutland Herald*, November 2, 2001.

17 Eilperin J. Kucinich's "Medicare for All" offers no role for private insurers. *Washington Post*, May 11, 2003: A7.

18 Himmelstein DU, Woolhandler S. National health insurance or incremental reform: aim high, or at our feet? *Am J Public Health* 2003; 93(1):31.

19 Woolhandler S, Himmelstein DU, Angell M, et el. Proposal of the Physician's Working Group for Single-Payer National Health Insurance. *JAMA* 2003;290:798-805.

20 Single-Payer Fact Sheet, Physicians for a National Health Program. Chicago, IL, 2003. www.pnhp.org.

21 Hartz AJ, Krakauer H, Kuhn EM, et al. Hospital characteristics and mortality. *N Engl J Med* 1989; 321: 1720-5.

22 Kovner C, Gergen P. Nurse staffing levels and adverse events following surgery in U.S. hospitals. Image J Nursing Scholarship 1998; 30: 315-21.

23 Taylor DH, Whellan DJ, Sloan FA. Effects of admission to a teaching hospital on the costs and quality of care for Medicare beneficiaries. *N Engl J Med* 1999; 340: 293-9.

24 Harrington C, Woolhandler S, Mullan J, Carrillo H, Himmelstein DU. Does investor-ownership of nursing homes compromise the quality of care? In press, *Am J Pub Health* 2001, 91:1.

25 Ibid #4.

26 Garg PP, Frick KD, Diener-West M, Powe NR. Effect of the ownership status of dialysis facilities on patients' survival and referral for transplantation. *N Engl J Med* 1999; 341: 1653-60.

27 Ibid #19.

28 Kuttner R. *Everything for Sale: The Virtues and Limits of Markets.* Chicago: University of Chicago Press, 1999: 157.

29 Woolhandler S, Campbell T, Himmelstein DU. Costs of health care administration in the United States and Canada. *N Engl J Med* 2003;349:768-75.

30 Ibid #15.

31 Ibid #16.

32 Ibid #28, p. 155.

33 Heffler S, Smith S, Keehan S, et al. Health spending projections through 2013. Health Aff Web-Exclusive Abstract February 11, 2004.

34 Ibid #9.

35 Sherlock Company, *PULSE* (Newsletter) September 2001): III.

36 Davis K, et al. Medicare versus private insurance: rhetoric and reality. Web exclusive. Health Affairs October 9, 2002.

37 Organization for Economic Cooperation and Development, OECD Health Data 2001 (computer database) Paris, France: Organization for Economic Cooperation and Development; 2001.

38 Starfield B. *Primary Care. Balancing Health Needs, Services and Technology*. New York: Oxford University Press, 1998.

39 Woolhandler S, Himmelstein DU. The deteriorating administrative efficiency of U.S. health care. N Engl J Med 1991; 324: 1253-8.

40 Katz SJ, Cardiff K, Pascali M, Barer ML, Evans RG. Phantoms in the snow: Canadians' use of health care services in the United States. 2002; 21(3): 19-31.

41 Bodenheimer T. Single-payer—fifty players? Alternative payers for universal health insurance. *Health/PAC Bulletin*. Fall 1992:24-8.

42 Woolhandler S, Himmelstein DU. National health insurance: liberal benefits, conservative spending. Arch Intern Med 2002; 162(9): 973-75.

43 Woolhandler S, Himmelstein DU. Opportunities for health reform. Unpublished paper. Chicago, Ill: Physicians for a National Health Program, October 19, 2001.

44 Donabedian, A. A founder of quality assessment encounters a troubled system firsthand. Interview by Fitzhugh Mullan. Health Aff (Millwood) 2001; 20(1): 141.

Index

About the Author

John Geyman, MD is Professor Emeritus of Family Medicine at the University of Washington School of Medicine in Seattle, where he served as Chairman of the Department of Family Medicine from 1976 to 1990. As a family physician with over 25 years in academic medicine, he has also practiced in rural communities for 13 years. He was the founding editor of *The Journal of Family Practice* (1973 to 1990) and the editor of *The Journal of the American Board of Family Practice* from 1990 to 2003. His most recent books are *Health Care in America: Can Our Ailing System Be Healed?* (Butterworth-Heinemann, 2002) and *The Corporate Transformation of Health Care: Can the Public Interest Still Be Served?* (Springer Publishing Company, 2004). Dr. Geyman is a member of the Institute of Medicine.